❝I think my interest in climbing came from the freedom I sensed in the mountains that you don't have in town. If you want to scream and yell, you can scream and yell. ❞
— *Pete Schoening*

❝It's asinine to think that you conquer the mountain. You climb it and enjoy it. It's your friend, not your enemy. ❞
— *Jim Whittaker*

❝I think that some people go into medicine with the perspective of a mountaineer. I know I did. Everything I have done has been colored by the mountains, not the other way around. ❞
— *Tom Hornbein*

▲

CASCADE VOICES

▲

CONVERSATIONS WITH WASHINGTON MOUNTAINEERS

▲

MALCOLM S. BATES

CLOUDCAP

Published in the United States by
CLOUDCAP
P.O. Box 27344, Seattle, WA 98125

Distributed by Alpenbooks, P.O. Box 761,
Snohomish, WA 98291-0761

ISBN 0-938567-34-9

Printed in the U.S.A.

Front cover photo: by Cliff Leight — Climber halfway up Roman Wall on Mount Baker.

Back cover photo: by Cliff Leight — Nooksack Tower

Photo of Author: by Darrin Schreder

Portrait photo credits: All portraits were shot by Cliff Leight except those of Kenneth and Priscilla Chapman and Jim Martin which were taken by Liz Gemmato; those of Gene Prater, Fred Stanley and John Roskelley, by the author; and that of Ray Clough, furnished by the interviewee. Credits for the scenic photos and snapshots in each of the five sections are listed under their respective photos.

CONTENTS

▲

FOREWORD

Cascade Voices tells the story of Cascade climbers of this century, and does it in a pleasantly informal way through interviews. Great stories, often famous ones, appear in these interviews.

Nearly fifty climbers show how attitudes toward climbing have changed from the alpenstock days of Professor Meany to the present time when Cascade climbers are in global demand to take part in expeditions to the highest peaks in the Karakoram, China and Nepal.

Interviews with early mountaineers like Wolf Bauer and Lloyd Anderson are followed, among others, by ones with Fred Beckey, Pete Schoening, Tom Hornbein, Jim Whittaker and Jim Wickwire, and finally by Chris Kopczynski, John Roskelley and members of the Vertical Club. Obviously the Cascades have been a grand training area for different kinds of climbers and ways of climbing.

Malcolm Bates (no relative) has put together fresh, first-hand accounts, a history that will be read and re-read for many years to come.

— Robert H. Bates

(Robert H. "Bob" Bates has climbed extensively in Alaska and the Yukon, made the third ascent of Mount McKinley and has gone high on K-2, in 1938 and 1953. His last expedition was in 1985 to the Ulugh Muztagh, a peak on the Xinjiang-Tibet border. His books include **Five Miles High** *and* **K-2, the Savage Mountain,** *co-authored with Charles Houston, and* **Mountain Man: the Story of Belmore Browne.** *He is honorary president of the American Alpine Club. Except for five years in World War II and a leave of absence to set up and direct the first Peace Corps program in Nepal, Dr. Bates has been a teacher, retiring from Phillips Exeter Academy in 1976.)*

▲

ACKNOWLEDGEMENTS

I am forever grateful to those kind people who graciously invited Cliff and me into their homes for an hour or two of conversation, and those to whom I spoke via phone. Special thanks to a few people who went out of their way to be helpful: Dee Molenaar, Pete Schoening, Alex Bertulis, Tom Hornbein, Norval Grigg, Tom and Nancy Miller, Carla Firey, Harold Engles, and Wolf Bauer. Thanks also to the many people who lent us photos and memorabilia for the book.

My editor, John Grassy, helped me to see that many of my "little darlings" would have to die, and did so with kindness, sensitivity and the occasional smart-ass remark. I also used a sentence of his. It will remain our secret. John Horton, at Helena Black and White, did yeoman work in the darkroom to make sure we got top quality prints. Jim Hays, who designed the book, seemed, at times, to understand better than I what this book was all about. It shows in his design and exquisite artwork. My father, William Bates, juggled all the loose ends of this project, and seemed to make everything fit. He continues to be my favorite partner in the mountains. Many years ago, somewhere on the Devil's Dome Trail, my mother took the pack from my ten-year-old shoulders and carried it the last miles into camp. I might have hated hiking, except for that simple act. My mother hated carrying a pack. And thanks to all the people I have shared mountain adventures and misadventures with: Stu, Andy, Liz, Jim, Brad, Martha, Janet, Dick, Ruth, Chris, Ron, Scott, Craig, Cliff, ROIF members everywhere, and my wife, Carol, who wondered where the hell we were going on Tonga Ridge on a sunny day in June, the day I asked her to marry me.

I would also like to thank two people no longer living. Many years ago Brad, Andy and I met Willi Unsoeld in Batchelor Meadows. We were heading off to climb Spire Point and were ill-prepared to tackle such a peak. Willi most likely saw that, but he didn't patronize or chastise. He gave us advice as mountaineering peers, understanding intuitively that this was our adventure, our lesson to learn. We struggled to the summit, and were scared spitless in the process, but those moments on the tiny summit were unforgettable. I regret that I never got the chance to thank him.

While a student at the University of Washington, I signed up for a rock climbing class. My instructor was Al Givler. Although only a few years my senior, he was my first and last climbing hero. I was awed by his skill on rock and ice, but in a sport, that too often breeds macho breast-beating, Al showed me that it was all right to be afraid, okay to back down.

Finally I must apologize to the many people who are not in this book and should be, people like Lou Whittaker, Phillip Dickert, Julie Bruegger, Phil Erschler, Steve Marts, Agnes Dickert, Otto Trott, Larry Penberthy, Carlos Buhler, Jolene Unsoeld, Louis Ulrich, Dave Page, et al; certainly another volume's worth of conversations. It is my hope, though, that I have been able to capture the variety of experience that characterizes Washington mountaineering in the 20th century.

▲

This book is lovingly dedicated to
CAROL AND ROSALIE

INTRODUCTION

Dad threw open the rain fly and poked his whiskered face in the tent. "Mac," he said, "You've got to come out and see this." Barely awake, half in my cotton sleeping bag, I peered around the tent and saw first the meadow, redolent of hellebore and lupine and wet with dew. Fog had hidden it the night before as my father and I huddled next to a sputtering campfire, watching Earl Clark doctor his blistered, bony feet; feet that would never find a comfortable shoe.

The lush meadow fell gently away from our campsite and disappeared into the clouds that eddied down the Suiattle River Valley and spilled out to cover the rest of the world. Above, cloudless blue sky and across the valley, Glacier Peak, an honest-to-god volcano. Sunlight warmed its cracked glaciers, which fanned out from the summit in ever-widening ribbony esses and slid beneath the soft clouds. I quickly laced up my soggy leather boots, tripped out of the tent and stood shivering next to my father. Not yet comfortable with silence, I babbled on about that massive, glaciered mountain, the clouds below us and the sun above. The day before there had only been mist. Now, in every direction, there were mountains, ridges, snowfields. I wanted to know all their names. And I wanted to get back on the trail.

We hiked 25 miles that day—or so it seemed—through Douglas fir forests to Miner's Creek. Up to Miner's Ridge, where we left our packs and almost jogged to Suiattle and Cloudy passes. I looked north into the broad Agnes Creek Valley, east to Lyman Lake and Bonanza Peak, south to Flower Dome and Buck Creek Pass, and west to the edge of civilization shrouded in clouds. That night we watched the sun set on Glacier Peak from our camp at the Image Lake shelter—when camping there was still permitted. As the alpenglow faded from the high peaks, I lay in the heather and savored every exquisite ache and throbbing in my body. For one day I had shed the awkward skin of a shy high school freshman with one of the last crewcuts on earth, and I had stood above the clouds.

The next morning we reluctantly switchbacked down into the Suiattle Valley. I returned to school and nobody noticed my transformation. Couldn't they see I was stronger, wiser and had been places no letter-jacketed upperclassman would ever visit? I had a story to tell, but nobody wanted to hear it. Soon the details began to fade from memory, but there wasn't a day after the trip that I didn't think of the Cascades. Trips, peaks and trails inhabited the corner of my daydreams not occupied by girls.

Shortly after our hike to Middle Ridge, I came across an old photo album in our attic. As a teenager in the summer of 1941, my father had taken a three-week backpack into the Olympic Mountains with three friends. The black-and-white photos and typed daily journals were his record of that trip. Under the heading August 15, he wrote:

> "Clint, Jack and I finally took a trip that promises to be an outstanding one, one that we will doubtlessly remember for a long time. We went through two miles of the Press Valley Canyon, a trip that had been enjoyed by very few.
>
> "We fished many pools that were flanked by walls at least 100 feet high. Most of them were covered by dripping moss upon which grew countless dainty maiden hair ferns.
>
> "We found the mouth of the Goldie, a sight which supposedly had never been seen by more than two or three persons . . . We finished the canyon at about 5:00 and started back. Len, who had done "just a little fishing around camp," had caught three fish: one 17 inches . . . Cruel fate! However, I wouldn't have missed the canyon trip for a 20-incher."

I reread my father's teenage prose until his story became my own. Change river canyon to meadowed ridge, and it was. In the 25-year gulf that separated our mountain experiences, there was a common thread of discovery, seeing the world for the first time and knowing somehow we'd never be the same. Over the years I came to understand that every person who has ever spent time in the Cascades has had his morning on Middle Ridge. We are bound by those stories, stories that make us smile when we meet as strangers on an alpine trail. *Cascade Voices* is about mountains and the stories that mountains make: funny, sad, profound, silly. From these stories emerge lives indelibly marked by mountains.

My daughter Rosalie is not yet two, but I am already planning trips with her—as my father must have with me—into Batchelor Meadows, Goat Flats, Hidden Lakes and Crater Mountain. Rosalie may never take to the mountains—she may carry with her only a handful of Cascade stories. I won't push her, but I think someday we will hike to Middle Ridge.

—Malcolm S. Bates

A Few Words About the Conversations

Throughout the book, my questions and, in some cases, the names of the interviewees appear in italics, the subject of the conversation in plain type. Cliff Leight, the photographer for the project, accompanied me on almost every interview. When he asks a question, he is identified and his question appears in italics. In the case of Fred Beckey, Cliff conducted the interview.

In some cases there were three, four, and in one case, eight, people talking about Cascade experiences. In those cases we initially identify the speaker using the full name. Thereafter we use the first name.

▲

About the Photographer

Most of the evocative black-and-white portraits, as well as the cover photography, were shot by Cliff Leight, one of the more prolific climbers in Washington and my climbing partner for the past 20 years.

Cliff's work has appeared in numerous guides, calendars and coffee table books, including *More Reflections on the Meaning of Life,* published by Time-Life and *America on My Mind,* published by Falcon Press.

Cliff was with me on almost every interview. He got lost with me, sat in freeway gridlock with me, drank too much coffee and ate too many cookies with me. It was probably the best trip of all.

— Dan Waters Photo

S epia-toned photos of favorite Cascade peaks, taken at the turn of the century, reveal few startling changes over the intervening 90+ years. Glaciers were most likely retreating, perhaps even advancing. Logger's roads and saws had not yet invaded the interior forests of the range. Only game trails criss-crossed alpine meadows. Most of the mountains had neither names nor first ascents.

In the foreground of those old photos, climbers pose stiffly for the photographer. Nobody smiles. All seem dressed for church. The men wear high-topped boots, wool suit jackets and pants or knickers, broadbrimmed felt hats, and even straw boaters. The women wear ankle-length dresses, knitted button-down sweaters, scarves, and Easter bonnets with mosquito netting. Most of the men smoke pipes and have bushy mustaches. All climbers carry long wooden alpenstocks. The captions identify no Freds, Petes, Jims, or even Harveys. Instead there is Asahel, Hazard, Philamen, Montelius, Lulie, Cora and Winona. They are members of Washington's first organized climbing club, The Mountaineers.

These oddly-named, neatly-dressed men and women did not come to the mountains desperately seeking El Dorado or intent on placing boundaries on the land. They climbed for recreation, companionship, and the physical rewards of putting one foot in front of the other along forested trails and up meadowed mountain slopes. There was, to be sure, a bit of the explorer, and perhaps even miner in them, but climbing, or "valley pounding," was their play.

Asahel was Asahel Curtis, one of the first guides on Mount Rainier and a noted photographer. Montelius was W. Montelius Price, a Seattle businessman. On a Mazama climb of Mount Baker in 1906, Curtis and Price fleshed out the outline for a Seattle club, which they

1

originally called The Seattle Mountaineer's Club auxiliary to the Mazamas. The club adopted a constitution in 1907 calling itself the Seattle Mountaineers. The 151 charter members included educators and the educated: physicians, attorneys, bankers, businessmen, even Will G. Steel, who had founded the Mazamas in 1894. A few years later chapters were formed in Everett and Tacoma.

The object of the Mountaineers was stated in one paragraph. It has changed little in 85 years:

> The object of this organization shall be to explore the mountains, forests and water-courses of the Pacific Northwest, and to gather into permanent form the history and traditions of this region; to preserve, by protective legislation or otherwise, the natural beauty of the Northwest Coast of America; to make frequent or periodical expeditions into these regions in fulfillment of the above purposes. Finally, and above all, to encourage and promote the spirit of good fellowship and comradry among the lovers of outdoor life in the West.

In the first years of its existence, the Mountaineers more often than not explored areas close to home. In 1910 there was no Bellevue, Kirkland, or Burien surrounding Seattle, only forest. A wilderness experience was a trolley ride away. A Mountaineer bulletin from 1914 described one such walk:

> Local Walk No. 239. E.W. Harrison, Leader. Houghton to Juanita, following ridge between Lake Sammamish and Lake Washington; fine view of Cascades; six miles road and six miles trail. Take Anderson S.S. Co. boat leaving Madison Park 9:15 a.m. Distance 12 miles. Expense, 25 cents. Bring lunch, cup and spoon.

Even nearby mountains—short day hikes today—were overnight adventures. A 1911 Mountaineer bulletin advertised a three-day "Special Outing to Mount Pilchuck:"

> . . . Leave Dr. Hinman's office Friday, May 26th, 5 p.m., by auto, which will take us to within 4 1/2 miles of base of mountain. Walk to camp at Hansen's Lake that night. Make climb and return to lake Saturday. Walk to Granite Falls Sunday, returning thence Sunday afternoon by auto. Total expense not to exceed $4.00.

Mountaineers did attempt the highest peaks in the range and theirs were often the first footsteps on many important summits. A Mountaineers outing made the first ascent of Mount Olympus in 1907, Mount Shuksan in the same year, many of the peaks near Snoqualmie Pass, and the first ascent of Whitehorse in 1913. The Whitehorse climb was made despite a warning in the bulletin that stated, "No attempt will be made to scale the peak, which has never been climbed and is dangerous on account of loose rock."

In 1914 the Mountaineers built the Snoqualmie Lodge. Until it burned down in the early 1940s, it served as the base camp for exploration of the peaks in the area. The club initiated the pin peaks program which awarded special pins to members after they had climbed ten designated peaks in the Snoqualmie Pass area: Chair, Denny, Guye, Kaleetan, Kendall, Red, Silver, Snoqualmie, Thompson and the Tooth. A second ten were added shortly thereafter. Everett and Tacoma had their own pin peaks. There were also the most coveted pin peaks, the six majors: Olympus, St. Helens, Adams, Glacier, Baker, and Rainier.

Mountaineers climbs, especially on the glaciered peaks, were massed assaults, 100 people or more. In the early years small climbing groups of three and four were frowned upon—there was safety in numbers. The second generation of Mountaineers in the 1920s would open the club's eyes to the wisdom of smaller, roped climbing parties.

The most popular of the Mountaineers trips was the annual summer outing, usually three weeks long; 50-100 mountaineers, with pack train and hired cook—and on the first outing

in 1907 a live steer. Some members would make climbs, most would be content to hike. Early trips included a circumnavigation of Mount Rainier, a trip into the Glacier Peak wilderness and the trip into Olympus; on that outing, the Mountaineers pioneered the first trail into the heart of the Olympics. These huge outings were to remain a feature of the Mountaineers for another fifty years.

From 1908 until his death in 1935, Professor Edmund Meany was president of the Mountaineers and a leader of many summer outings. It was Meany, perhaps, more than any other, who set the tone for the Mountaineers during its first 30 years of existence. Tall and slender with Van Dyke beard, the University of Washington science professor and author brought a sense of decorum to the organization, whether at meetings or around campfires. Scholarly and philosophical, Meany appreciated time alone to write and meditate in the midst of the huge summer outings. And he loved a good cigar. At the same time, Meany could be counted on to regale a rapt campfire audience with stories and poems. He would even conduct Sunday church services on the trail.

The Meany years saw Mountaineer membership grow steadily; there were almost 600 in 1930. Another, independent, club would form east of the mountains, the Cascadians in Yakima.

Climbing became only one of many Mountaineer activities. Skiing, coolly received by snowshoers in the early years of the Mountaineers, became a popular club activity. In 1927, on land donated by Edmund Meany just east of Snoqualmie Pass, the Meany Ski Hut was built. Mountaineer plays became an annual event at the Kitsap Cabin. There also emerged a new generation of climbers, far more ambitious than most of the original members, athletically daring men like Art Winder, Forest Farr, Bill Degenhardt, and Herb Strandberg. They set their sights on the imposing unclimbed summits of Dome, Chimney Rocks, Big Four, Bonanza and Goode.

Lloyd Anderson, who would become one of the most prolific and adventurous climbers in the Northwest, remembers his second climb, up Mount Elinor in the Olympics in 1929. On the descent he chased after group leader, Art Winder, who took a shortcut. "I had to run through the woods to keep up with him. He went right straight down the mountain, through trees and everything else."

Farther up the mountain, Edmund Meany, the Mountaineers' revered president, made his way slowly down the mountain, hobbled by a pulled tendon. A sympathetic group of five climbers feigned exhaustion and stayed with him. He recognized the charade, but appreciated the kindness. It was Meany's last climb. Five years later Edmund Meany died. The Mountaineers would never again reflect so strongly the personality of one man.

E mily Harris apologizes, but she is going to have to cut our conversation short. She has an engagement this evening. Harris's schedule is fairly hectic. I will have to wait a few days before she can fit me in again. Emily Harris is 91. I am beginning to believe that many mountaineers of her generation drank from the same strange mountain stream that has kept them so active.

Harris joined the Mountaineers in 1925, shortly after arriving from Philadelphia. "I didn't know people," she says, "but I met quite a few teachers and librarians, many of them had been Mountaineers for quite a while. I began going on Mountaineers day trips in the fall of 1925."

Like most Mountaineers, Harris was not interested in first ascents, but rather the congenial companionship that the Mountaineers offered. She especially enjoyed the large summer outings, the winter ski trips to Mount Rainier (she met her husband, Ernest, on an outing) and the Mountaineers plays.

"I became interested in the plays," she says. "We were very amateur, but we put on plays down in the Forest Theater. I was never the heroine. Oh, we had lots of fun. It's a beautiful forest theater, those great big original trees. And that was a whole different group, people who didn't do a whole lot of climbing but were musical or enjoyed the acting. That's continued, rain or shine. And sometimes they've had it when it rained. I remember when the heroine had to lie down and she had a beautiful costume. It was right in puddles. We all just gasped, because we hated to think of what it was doing to her beautiful costume. But that went right along with being a good mountaineer."

To Emily Harris a good mountaineer was not necessarily the best climber, but one who shared food on the trail, identified the plants and birds, put on a clever campfire skit, or carried on in the rain. "When I joined the Mountaineers," she says, "you had to have two people sign your card, so it made for a group that was extremely reliable, that you could depend on.

«Our sleeping bags we made ourselves They were made of a waterproof, lightweight material. I made two big quilts. They were wool down and their cover was a very thin cotton covering. We would have quilting bees and have our friends

come and help us tie the insides to hold it together so that it didn't all slide to one side. But that made it very light. I had two of those quilts and I would fold them certain ways and put them in the sleeping bag. »
—*Emily Harris*

The Mountaineers today is so much different, much larger. As I understand it, anyone who wants to belong just signs an application."

▲

It seems that the Mountaineers had their Snoqualmie Lodge crowd, the Meany Hut bunch, and the Kitsap Cabin group.

I went over to Kitsap Cabin quite a little after I joined the Mountaineers in 1925. I was on the Kitsap Cabin committee for several years. People would take the little Virginia V boat, go over, get off and hike up through the woods to the cabin. We would order food which would go over on the boat with us and we would have to take it up to the cabin. We had committees among the groups that were there, and they prepared the dinner.

We worked on building the Forest Theater and enlarged it and the cabin also. The men worked on the hard labor and we went over and cooked for them and we had some awfully good times. We put on Halloween parties that were really remarkable things.

Did you get out in the winter?

That was the beginning of an interest in skiing. The Mountaineers had a lodge at Snoqualmie. It was a beautiful cabin, log, and with a lovely big fireplace. When the Mountaineers started to do some skiing they went up there in the winter and used it for overnight sleeping and skiing around in that area. They wanted to do more skiing, so they made trips from there over to Meany.

Of course I went on the winter outings to Paradise. We went over to Tacoma and took the bus from there into Ashford and on into Longmire. From there we had to go up the trail to Paradise. The food had been taken ahead so that we never had to cook. There would be probably a hundred people. The first floor of this building had a huge stove and they put big chunks of wood in it. That was where the wash basins and toilets were. The floor above it the women had. There were small rooms, and we used double-decker bunks with army blankets that were very heavy. The men were on the third floor.

The majority of the people when I first went up were using snowshoes rather than skis. When I went up the first time I took both snow shoes and skis, because I wasn't a skier by then. It was really a problem getting up the mountain, so I had to use the snow shoes. It was hard work because all your clothes were on your back. I remember getting up to Narada Falls that first time and they said, "When you get to Narada you can have some hot tea." There was a little house there and you could have tea. We got there and a group of Boy Scouts had been there just ahead of us and had used up all the hot water. The only way you could get water was to melt the snow, so we had to go on without our tea. But those trips were just wonderful.

We would go up the day after Christmas and be up there until the day after New Years. Of course there were a lot of school teachers who had vacation. A lot of people planned on it—I was a social worker.

Some of the boys would go over on skis to Pinnacle Peak and fix a bonfire in the saddle of Pinnacle for New Year's Eve. We had some people who had lots of initiative and good ideas, so there were some very clever stunts put on at the campfire. The Mountaineers, in those days, were very different. If you left your skis and mittens and poles outside and you went in to lunch, they were right there when you came back out. Nobody ever stole anything.

Did you get to know Edmund Meany at all?

Yes, on my first summer outing. It was in the Olympics. We went in to Port Angeles and hiked in from that end. I went in for two weeks. We had a big pack train. Mr. Meany was not only an important figure in the Mountaineers but in Seattle as well. He was a professor at the University of Washington. He taught history and was particularly interested in the history of the Northwest. He wrote about that, and the Mountaineers were an important part of that as far as he was concerned. He was tall and impressive. Everyone was fond of Mr. Meany and respected him.

The one trip I went on when he was still president, was in from the Olympics, the summer of 1926. His son Ed (We called him Ned) was along and they camped together. I think that was a wonderful thing for them.

When you climbed Glacier Peak and other mountains did you use an alpenstock?

I never owned an ice axe, but some of the men had ice axes. The alpenstock was very helpful in pumice and slipping gravel, and of course if you were coming down a steep slope it was helpful. In the old days almost all the people had alpenstocks. I have still the alpenstock that a Mountaineers friend gave me. It was very substantial with a spiked thing on the end.

Did you meet your husband on a Mountaineers outing?

Yes, he was a skier, and I met him on some of my early ski trips. On the trips you might have rain or extra cold or be late getting in. You learned to know who was a good sport and who wasn't. That's how you got to know people. That was the thing with the old-time Mountaineers. We always had a rear guard. They always stayed in the rear until everybody was back in. I mean they never left anybody out on the trail.

They told one story—and this was before my day—about a couple of oldtimers. It was in the Olympics and they had a pack train and something went wrong with the pack train. So they didn't get into camp at all that night. They had no dinner, because the pack train had all the food. On these long trips you would always have a nosebag lunch, so they'd eaten most of it, but some people had food left over. They all had some prunes left. They divided up the prunes, and that camp was then called Three Prune Camp. And as I understand, that was really put on the map. It just showed that the people on those trips would share their last crumb with you.

What sort of clothing did you wear on these Mountaineer outings?

I had long johns. We wore those even a little in summer, because after you'd been hiking, you'd be damp and the wool would absorb the moisture, and at night it would be colder. So we wore knickers, and wool socks that came up towards your knee, and the mountaineering boot. There was always an argument about what nails you should use. I still have my old boots. They came well up my leg, halfway to my knees I suppose. They had caulks in the instep so that if you were going over a stream on a log, the calks could go into the logs at your instep.

Today many climbers wear plastic boots.

Well, of course, I have seen the ski boots that my grandchildren wear, and those boots are just appalling. We didn't pay the money for our outfits. I had a parka that had a hood and came all the way down halfway below my knees. They had what they called mountaineer cloth which was something that someone had developed. It was part wool. Our sleeping bags we made ourselves. They were made of a waterproof, lightweight material. I made two big quilts. They were wool down and their cover was a very thin cotton covering. We would have quilting bees and have our friends come and help us tie the insides to hold it together so that it didn't all slide to one side. But that made it very light. I had two of those quilts and I would fold them certain ways and put them in the sleeping bag.

How did you learn to climb?

I don't recall that I went to any class. You would go with some of the oldtimers so that you could learn how things were done. They were very helpful. My nickname was Cornie and one of the men, Pete, said, "Now Cornie, you stop at noon and take off your boots and socks and put your feet in the stream where we stop to eat lunch. Get your feet in that cold water and then get your socks and boots back on, and that will help more than anything else to prevent you getting blisters." These were oldtimers who had been on many a trip. It wasn't a formal class.

The only thing I have against Pete, is on that trip—I'm real short and I was short then too—they were doing some real climbing. We went up to High Divide. And of course there is a whole row of peaks along there, and he said, "Oh, you ought not to try one of those that I did," because my legs were so short and it was rock climbing and you had to reach. So I only did that one peak. After we got back I went on a real small trip over into Eastern Washington with two or three of the men who had been on the summer outing and we climbed something that nowadays they say it's so bad they don't do it anymore. It's called Cathedral. And I managed to get up it and then I felt sorry that Pete had stopped me from doing some of those peaks in the Olympics.

CHAPTER

2

HAROLD ENGLES

H arold Engles never took a climbing class and doesn't claim to be a mountaineer. For over 40 years, Engles worked for the Forest Service, where mountaineering was just part of the job. He began working in the forests in 1919 and, in 1927, became district ranger in Darrington. "The rule was that you were supposed to put seventy percent of your working hours in the field, and we did. I was gone sometimes ten days, locating trail, roads for timber sales, checking the condition of the sheep herding ranges."

«I think my friend, Glen and I have made a little headway with some of the people we hike with and meet on the trail. We kind of let them know that you don't have

to quit hiking when you're fifty or sixty years old. A lot of people we meet are interested to know that we're still hiking after we hit 70.»
—Harold Engles

Very often Engles' work took him to the tops of mountains. In the fall of 1929 he and his foreman, Harry Bedal, left the rest of the trail crew and headed off in the direction of Mount Three Fingers to check out the possibility of building a fire lookout on one of the summit spires. They scrambled to within 15 feet of the south finger's summit before being turned back by snow. That day they traversed the entire mountain and returned to Darrington. There was no trail. A few weeks later they made the second ascent of Sloan Peak, again looking for a suitable lookout site.

His 40-mile day hikes through the Darrington district made Engles a local legend. It was not uncommon for him to heft 150-pound packs or walk into Darrington and carry home a 130-pound sack of flour on his back. His arms are still veined and sinewy, his biceps knotted as if he were curling weights.

At 89 Engles walks, hikes, climbs or skis every day. He admits to slowing down a little the past few years but still plans to climb Three Fingers in 1992, when he reaches 90.

If you can't talk to Harold on the trail, the next best place is his front room. A picture window opens out onto a panoramic view of Whitehorse Mountain. If clouds obscure the mountain there are watercolors and photographs of Whitehorse as well as

7

many of Three Fingers. There are also a number of books and magazines, a few that might irritate Darrington loggers, like the Sierra Club magazine. An admirer of John Muir, Engles says, "I've spent all my life reading. I'm quite interested in everything. I read sometimes three books a week. My daughter works for the county library and she gets me books. For twenty years I read every edition of the *Atlantic Monthly*. I still take it, but it isn't as good as it used to be; maybe it's me. Now, my mind's getting a little like a sieve, in one side and out the other. The old stuff hangs tough, but the new . . . I maintain the brain's full when information runs off the top."

▲

Do you remember the first mountain you ever climbed?

It was in Oregon. So much of what I did for the Forest Service down there was hiking along ridges. In the '20s I worked on that trail from Mount Hood to Crater Lake, and in 1921 we climbed several mountains along there, but I don't think any of them had any names. Back in 1919 we were building trails on the tributaries of the North Fork of the Willamette, and on Sundays I'd climb back up in the hills.

Did you own an ice axe or alpenstock?

Back then I had a World War I trenching mattock. It's pretty much like an ice axe with a pick on one side and mattock blade on the other. I put a longer shaft on it. It was the size of a walking stick and I used it for an ice axe. I didn't have a real one until I went down to work at Mount Hood in the late 1930s. Then I had ice axes and crampons. I had instep crampons made just before I left Darrington. Harland Eastwood was in this outdoor sports business. He had a pair and gave them to me. They had four spikes. They worked pretty good. I used them on Three Fingers before I went to Oregon.

Incidentally I was down to Mount Hood a month ago. I went down there a year ago for the fiftieth anniversary of the dedication of the Mount Hood Lodge. I was on the honor guard then. And now those of us left have an annual meeting. It's kind of nice except that the ranks are thinning. Fifty years takes a big chunk out of them. There were fifty-two originally.

When you worked down at Mount Hood, you must have climbed the mountain.

A few times. I think once I climbed it every day for almost twelve days. We camped in the crater; we were going to build a new house up there just before World War II. We hauled 3 1/2 tons of material up there. I think it must still be up there.

But you never got up Rainier.

We went up the Hazard route and one of the fellows got sick and I didn't like it, so I stayed with him at the camp there, Camp Hazard at about 11,500 feet. The rest of the party didn't get back down until 6:30 p.m. and we ended up crossing the Nisqually in the dark and those doggone crevasses.

You have an "Over 70" hiking group.

There's George Freed, Glenn Mackey and a few others. By the way, I think my friend, Glenn and I have made a little headway with some of the people we hike with and meet on the trail. We kind of let them know that you don't have to quit hiking when you're fifty or sixty years old. A lot of people we meet are interested to know that we're still hiking after we hit seventy. A couple of years ago we tried to climb Sloan in a day, and I decided to turn around at the glacier. Turned out later I had a bad tooth that needed work. But Glenn and a friend of his made it to the top.

Did you ever have any bad nights in the mountains?

I had bad nights when we were out fighting fires, but otherwise not so bad. I remember spending one night off the trail. I wasn't really lost. I was out locating trails, and you really didn't get lost because you were off the trail all the time. There was no trail.

You didn't carry a tent. What did you use for shelter?

Downed logs, rocks, trees.

What were your meals like out in the mountains?

When we had a trail camp we had beans, rice, potatoes as long as they lasted, dried fruit, cheese, bacon, ham. But on short backpacks we just took sandwiches. At the trail camp we would have a big stove. Most of the time, when we were out on a fire, we wouldn't have a stove. We'd build a fire, take a back log, get it good and hot and place hot rocks around it. Then we'd mix dough up in a frying pan. You might have twenty frying pans of bread going. You'd cook the bread just like you'd fry it and then lean it on the log and let the outside brown. It was pretty good.

Another thing we had as much as we could was butter. You'd keep it by putting it in a burlap sack and soaking it. In 1922 they came up with canned butter. It came in two-pound cans and was pretty good, but it could get pretty strong. We also had canned tomatoes. Sometimes we had them for dessert, kind of rough but all right.

For many years the Forest Service was actively involved in mountain rescue. What was the most difficult rescue you were ever involved with?

I probably had the hardest time up on Whitehorse back in 1930 because I was alone. Two guys were hiking up and one of them fell. His partner got him to where he could get some scraps going for a fire. As soon as daylight came he took off, got to a telephone about 5 a.m. I took off and left word at Clear Creek Guard Station to have people follow.

When I got up to the guy I fixed him up the best I could, and then I had to pack him out on my back. I slid with him on my stomach on a couple of steep stretches. There was no trail. I just had to find my way down. I probably carried him out a mile before we were met by the rest of the rescue team. I told the crew where I'd try to get to. And who should we meet at the end of the trail, but Dr. Blake, the local doctor. It was lucky for us, because the guy was in pretty bad shape. Afterwards he came up to thank me, and I asked him how much he weighed and he said 168 pounds. That's not big but it's not small.

So most of your climbing was done on the job.

I didn't think of what we did on Three Fingers or Sloan Peak as climbing, just places where we should go up and check out. It was interesting going out into the mountains where there were no trails. We had to figure out the trails. I remember hiking up White Mountain, Kodak Peak and Red Mountain checking for lookout sites, but I never got sold on them. I wasn't really a climber, never will be. I just liked the mountains.

During the winter did you have much chance to ski back into the mountains?

Well, one winter I went up to Goat Lake and spent a week up there. I took the railroad speeder up the Sauk a ways, but it was still quite a ways to go, past Bedal and Elliot Creek to the Goat Lake Trail. I was able to get up on some of the ridges. I might have gotten as far as Ida Pass. At the time I didn't think that there might be any risk. But I spent a lot of time in the mountains by myself snowshoeing. I had a pair made of vine maple. You could make a pair in about a day.

You made some of your packs as well.

I made a packboard to carry fire pumps. I used two Model-T innertubes for padding in the back and it worked. It was a big pack, weighed close to 165 pounds. I couldn't lift if off the ground.

The standard pack we carried in the Forest Service included five blankets and a tarp, thirty pounds. Of course in the summer you only had to carry one blanket. The first down sleeping bag I ever saw was in 1931. One of the supervisors got one out of Montana and showed us. I bought it from him. It had pack straps on it so you could carry it separate. I bought it for $5.

Did you ever meet Bob Marshall?

We spent a couple of hours working on a hiking trail. I've got a picture of him hiking up on the Crest Trail. I don't remember much about him, except that he was a heckuva nice fella. We both had something in common. We both liked to hike. I remember we scheduled a trip together, about a forty-mile day hike. He died about three months later on a railroad train, and we never got to make the trip.

Did you get out much this past summer?

Yeah, we tried Three Fingers but we turned back at Tin Can Gap because of the weather. I'll be perfectly frank and say the last two years have taken a bite out of me. Up until that time I was perfectly satisfied, although I'm still getting around. I don't mean I can't go. I just don't like getting tired. You know where I feel it the most is in the legs. Well, I'm eighty-eight. That's up there. I believe I was doing fine at eighty-five. Then at eighty-six it began to crowd me. At eighty-seven it was more so. I'm beginning to think there comes an end to getting up in the mountains. Well, you may not have to stop, but you have to accept the fact that you can't do certain things. But I think getting out in the mountains is the best form of exercise. Walking is good, but climbing is better.

Norval Grigg would not count himself in the first rank of climbers of his generation. He freely admits that he was not the climber Art Winder was, or Forest Farr. But they were among the best. Grigg was a capable partner who made first ascents of Three Fingers, El Dorado, and Dome Peak.

Grigg's interest in mountaineering grew out of long walks he took with Winder when the two were in high school. "We did a lot of hiking together walking back and forth to Ballard High School. But that wasn't enough for us, so weekends we liked to walk someplace. Once we got ambitious and hiked the railroad tracks all the way to Everett from Ballard and took the Interurban home. My parents didn't seem to mind our adventures one bit. We weren't boozing or changing girls, things like that."

Grigg was a connoisseur of the latest climbing equipment, and the best in climbing cuisine. His meticulousness sometimes made him an easy target for good-natured jokes, but very often he was the cook on climbs and his partners didn't complain too much at dinnertime.

We called those days BI, before iron. What's a piton? Something we read about in the British alpine journals. What are crampons?

Those were those funny little things with spikes that you stuck in the calf of your leg if you weren't careful.
—Norval Grigg

Like many of his climbing friends, Grigg curtailed serious mountaineering after taking on the responsibilities of home and family. Unlike some of his friends, he seems to have no regrets about that choice.

Grigg has thought about our upcoming conversation for a long time. Shortly after sitting down in his Seattle apartment, he begins a monologue that is only rarely interrupted by a question from me. Usually he will reply to my questions, "I'm getting to that." And he does. Grigg speaks slowly, precisely and makes effective use of the pregnant pause to cue the listener to a punchline. He relishes the telling of a story.

Norval Grigg: I joined the Mountaineers in 1925, while I was in college. For a couple of summers I worked for the Forest Service, up in the old Silverton Ranger District, doing various things like taking supplies up to the lookout on Pilchuck. I filled in when they needed me. I put up new lightning protection and new windows in that all the city sports had broken, kicked out. Even then they were doing that sort of thing. Art Winder came up to Pilchuck and spent a few days there. We took off and went up and climbed Vesper Peak and made a traverse over to, and presumably a first ascent of Sperry Peak; at least so Beckey records it.

At this point did you have climbing equipment?

Climbing equipment, what's that? Art and I started skiing in the winter of 1926 and bought our first skis to learn balance and control. No ski poles, just yourself and skis. That was for the birds, so I went in and bought myself a pair of ski poles the next weekend. In 1928 the Mountaineers built Meany Ski Hut at Martin on the Northern Pacific Railroad. Some of us evolved the Patrol Race, from Snoqualmie Pass to Meany and Andy Anderson and I donated a trophy.

I was then working for the city engineering department as a computer, a pretty darned good job in those days, $150-200 a month. It enabled me to buy an ice axe, a Simond, from Chamonix, which I still have. I bought it at the Outdoor Store, which was the place where you got all your outdoor equipment. In 1929 I made my first climb of Mount Rainier with my ice axe. By this time I had bought a sleeping bag, as well as ski poles from the Outdoor Store. I used to go down to see Mr. Lauridsen and go through the catalogs and make a list. They'd order from Fritsch in Switzerland. It was all good equipment, first class. From my experience with the Forest Service I had learned the value of good equipment. I always sacrificed something to get the first-class equipment.

At this time I made my first ascent of Mount Shuksan. Shortly thereafter we made the first ascent of Three Fingers. We got into the Monte Cristo District and made quite a few climbs, but Three Fingers was always a magnet. You couldn't miss the mountain if you were going up to Baker to ski.

You were using ropes on these climbs?

We had a rope on the climb of Three Fin-

gers, because we had done some climbing around and knew that a rope was necessary to help you get down. You could always climb up, but it was hard to climb down; better slide down on a rope.

What sort of rappel method did you use?

We didn't know what a rappel was in those days. We just looped the rope over a knob in the rock or something. We just had two strands of rope and we'd slide down. You had to have sure hands and sure feet. The rope we used was good manila rope, half-inch bought at Pacific Marine Supply. The second rope I bought was a Goldline from REI much later. I used it as a fire escape when we lived across the street on the top floor apartment.

We called those days BI, before iron. What's a piton? Something we read about in the British alpine journals. What are crampons? Those were those funny little things with spikes that you stuck in the calf of your leg if you weren't careful. I had a few detachable climbing aids as early as 1930. They just strapped on to your instep, but they helped.

What did your non-climbing friends think of your climbing?

We were regarded as semi-damn fools who should have picked some other way to burn off our energy. If you couldn't put it into work, then do something sensible.

Most of our climbs were overnights, but occasionally we would arrange for week-long trips during our vacation. We did a week trip up Glacier Peak using pack horses. Edith Bedal led the train. We took her to the top. She wanted to go. She was a very capable girl. Once we said yes, she got into her saddle bag and picked out a little box of screw calks and a little screw driver and put some calks into her boots, so she could go up the snowfield.

I have been told by some of your friends that you were a connoisseur of good camp food.

That goes back to my trail crew experience in 1925 and my two summers at Silverton. We didn't have a cook in the bunkhouse. We did our own cooking. In the planning of a trip I always thought that cooking was important to success. I had a double-ought Primus stove and still have it. You can't buy Primus stoves anymore. I guess they're called Optimus now. We usually figured for an extended trip $.15 per meal per person. And that was lots of bacon, ham, lots of goodies, lots of raisins. We ate well and had plenty of it. An interesting story.

We had none of this modernized food which I see long listings of in the REI catalog. The first concentrated food I ever bought was Herb's Wirtz, a contribution of the German military prior to and in WWI. It was a concentrated, hard-as-brick mixture of peas and carrots compressed into a stick. You got your pot and boiling water and hammered the stick and broke it up into the boiling water. In twenty minutes you had pea soup.

It doesn't sound too appetizing.

Darn good, if you're hungry and like pea soup. A lot of cooking was good planning. You always wanted to have enough. I always had a fifteen-ounce packet of raisins hidden in my pack. I never told anyone, just in case.

What was your hardest climb?

From a technical standpoint, one of the hardest climbs might have been Buckner going up from Park Creek Pass, going up the cliffs above the glacier. The route leads up from Ripsaw Ridge. Incidentally, that's a name Fred Beckey never liked. We named it Ripsaw Ridge, but he liked to call it the Set of Marching Gendarmes, something like that.

Who were the best climbers of your generation?

Art Winder and Forrie Farr. Now remember, when iron came in you got into a different category. You've got to give Wolf Bauer a lot of credit for that, because he introduced a lot of what he had learned from European climbers. Another one was Hans Grage. He went outside the Mountaineer's ski hut up at Stevens Pass one day and all the snow slid off the roof. Somebody wondered where Hans was, and they went outside but couldn't find him. They saw where the snow had slid down from the roof. He perished right there.

What do you think of today's climbers?

Oh, I would say that a lot of it is sensational, spectacular. Sometimes I wonder what good it accomplishes. I'm speaking frankly. I always figured that if there was a route up a mountain, pick the easy one. Why turn around the backside and try to find a hard one. Of course I realize that isn't the sporting way to do it. But mountains are mountains.

You mentioned in passing that you had severed

your ties with the Mountaineers in 1941. What caused the divorce?

I had always enjoyed and appreciated Snoqualmie Lodge. I had thought it a fine lodge, a fine retreat, and you had to expend a little effort to get there. Forrie Farr and I had been caretakers for a few months in 1932-33. It was a good, comfortable place to spend between Christmas and New Years. You had a congenial group of people, sometimes forty, and it could handle more than that. I couldn't afford my own rustic retreat.

During the '30s I noticed a group swinging their weight around in the Mountaineers—if I may express it that way—that said that every activity had to pay its own way; local walks, all the cabins. They had big seances, pow-wows and looked at whatever the expenses were, and a lot of expenses went to pay caretakers. We didn't pay them much, but it was a job and in those days a job was a job.

The leaders decided that they were going to dispense with the caretaker at Snoqualmie Lodge. The actual amount of loss was no more than $100-200 a year, and things were getting better. The Mountaineers weren't poor. I and several others wrote and expressed our opinion that it was being penny-wise and pound foolish. I said, "No lodge, no Grigg." About the only reply I got was, "Sorry Grigg, no lodge." So a few of us sent in our resignations. I made my last trip to the lodge and moved all my gear out. Some of us had made 150-200 trips apiece up there.

They closed the lodge in 1940. I flew over the lodge in 1944 in a B-17 and it was kind of high, but I could see where it was. About then I heard the lodge had burned down. A chap, who had been dedicated to the lodge, went up there to spruce the place up. He put all the debris in the fireplace, started a fire. A hot coal got on the roof and caught the hemlock needles on fire that had accumulated over the years. He climbed up on the roof with a squirt can but fell off. He devoted himself to saving things that should be saved. That was how the lodge register was saved. The lodge, though, burned completely to the ground.

The fire seems to be almost symbolic of the end of an era, for you and your group of friends who used the lodge. By the 1940s that group was breaking up, couples were moving to other parts of the Northwest, most were doing less climbing.

The Mountaineers and lodge provided a

nucleus for our group, which kind of formed a group within the Mountaineers. That always annoyed a lot of other people, but they had so much fun. Some of the people who went to the Meany Ski Hut said they had too much fun.

Coming home on the train one time, a nice, elderly lady, a Mountaineer from the beginning, said to me, "Norval, don't you ever dare bring your phonograph up to Meany." I said I wouldn't think of it. She said, "Well, if you want to, you go and ask Dr. Meany for his permission." He was still president and had given the land for the ski hut. You see I had packed a phonograph to the top of Silver Peak one time, just, so to say, for the hell of it. I wanted to hear a good Schottische and a Scandinavian waltz up in the mountains. It sounded good, you have no idea how good.

I guess that's what made your group a little bit different.

We were all about the same age, nobody was rich and nobody was truly poor, a case of even-Steven in likes and dislikes. And I'll mention something else. The Mountaineers had a rule, a very good rule; no liquor. Now I know that Mountaineers men carried liquor on trips. John Lehmann, on the Three Finger's trip, told us about having a spot of rum or whiskey after climbing a peak in Canada. There was never a punchbowl at any party or gathering at Snoqualmie or Kitsap lodges, but there was liquor there sometimes. I know, because I packed a bottle of it, but it was always very surreptitious. Not everybody was in on it. It was kind of being more devilish than anything else.

CHAPTER
4

GERTRUDE SHORROCK, KENNETH AND PRISCILLA CHAPMAN, JIM MARTIN, DOT AND FOREST FARR

*J*im and Lucille Martin, Forest and Dot Farr, Kenneth and Priscilla Chapman, and Gertrude Shorrock have known each other for sixty years. They were part of a close-knit group within the Seattle Mountaineers and more free-spirited than the general membership. For almost 15 years their social calendars were crowded with Mountaineer events: hikes and climbs from Snoqualmie Lodge, ski races at Meany Ski Hut, meetings and dances at the Mountaineers' clubroom, and plays at the outdoor Forest Theater. In the 1940s the Farrs and Martins moved to Portland, The

«We were regarded as a bunch of upstarts by some of the Mountaineers. We were kind of brash. We did sort of odd things, you know, like drink wine, things of that sort. I think there were people who felt we were sort of cliquish. »
—*Dot Farr*

Pictured above, left to right: Gertrude Shorrock, Kenneth and Priscilla Chapman, Jim Martin, Dot and Forest Farr.

Chapmans settled in Everett and the Shorrocks in Snohomish. They had last been together at Art Winder's funeral in 1987.

On a Thanksgiving weekend, the seven friends gathered at the Martin home in Portland, Oregon—just down the street from Reed College. Between hugs and handshakes, the stories began to spill out. Great climbs, bad camp food, practical jokes and impractical gear, adventures and fiascos. It could almost have been a Wednesday night meeting at the Mountaineers' clubroom. Only death had intruded into this close-knit circle of friends.

Gertrude Shorrock's husband, Paul, was missing from the group at Martin's that afternoon. Paul died in 1976. He was a delightfully eccentric man who taught English at Snohomish High School for three decades. Once a year he would lead the student body in a rendition of *McNamara's Band*. Paul and Gertrude met on a Mountaineers' outing, as did the other couples. The Shorrocks spent several summers as park rangers at

14

Mount Rainier and Paul often showed up at teacher orientation days with his uniform on. A bit naive, effusive, with emotions bubbling to the surface, he would let go with lusty "Bravos" at Seattle Symphony performances. Paul was a teacher students poked fun at but remembered fondly as adults. Among his friends Paul was an easy target for pranks. "Paul was the butt of an awful lot of jokes," Forest Farr commented, "but he was good natured about it."

"He never knew when he was being kidded," Gertrude replied. "I don't know whether he didn't know or pretended not to know. There was the time at Meany Ski Hut when they decided to change the men's and women's quarters. Someone remembered that Paul was coming up on the late train that night, and when Paul came in and tiptoed into these quarters and was undressing he began hearing these giggles. He wondered what was going on and suddenly he grabbed his clothes and dashed out."

"He probably still enjoyed the joke," Dot Farr said.

When Paul talked about his climbing days, he usually prefaced it with some sort of self-deprecating comment ("Of course, I really wasn't much of a climber by today's standards") and then he might recall the time he returned from a climb of Rainier and was convinced by the young Whittaker twins to literally turn around and climb the mountain again with them.

With the exception of Lucille Martin, everyone sitting around the dinner table enjoyed climbing mountains. Forest Farr was one of the best climbers of his generation, with first ascents of Dome, Three Fingers, Chimney Rocks and Big Four to his credit. Jim Martin and Kenneth Chapman were first-rate mountaineers, and during an age when most women alpinists deferred to the men, Gertrude Shorrock, Priscilla Chapman and Dot Farr followed their husbands on many rugged Cascade climbs. Today they would most likely be leaders. But first ascents were rarely mentioned, only when I brought them up. Their importance had diminished over the course of 60 years. What had not diminished was their affection for one another and the shared knowledge that they had been a part of something unique.

▲

Priscilla Chapman: Kenneth and I climbed Mount Pugh on our honeymoon, and I said that on Seattle Mountaineers outings it was the men who did the cooking. He said that when he went with the Everett Mountaineers, it was the women who did the cooking. There we were with nobody cooking.

Forest Farr: Well, who did the cooking?

Priscilla: Guess. I had to learn how to cook.

Jim Martin: When Bill Degenhardt, Herb Strandberg and I were up in the Southern Pickets, we made some first ascents on several tooth-like peaks. Bill had figured out the commissary beforehand, just the exact number of days; two weeks away from Newhalem. It was all measured out. Bill was a great dietician. Sometimes we'd have boiled rice. When it was ready, he would put some of it off to the side to get cold and he'd stir chicken into it. When we were finished with that he'd throw a handful of raisins into the cold rice for dessert. That was efficiency.

I remember the day he boiled lima beans in a bucket hanging over an open fire. When he got ready to take it off, the pail came loose, and he dumped the pail right into the fire, almost put it out. Here was Bill sitting next to the fire with that pail picking these beans up, brushing off the ashes. He picked up all the beans, put 'em back into the pot with more water. He was that talented.

After two weeks of climbing in the Pickets, Bill wore the seat out of his pants. When we got within a couple of miles of Newhalem, he sat out on a rock, took off his high-topped boots, and his pants and sewed a bandanna on the inside of his pants.

Gertrude Shorrock: It was Paul who came into the lodge at Mount Baker wet and backed up to the fireplace. He was getting dried out when he began to sniff something. He said, "Something smells like it's on fire." He stood there and said it again. Everybody knew it was his pants, but nobody would tell him. It finally burned through to the skin, and he yelled, "It's me!"

Jim: Gil Erickson always smoked a pipe.

15

One time he set his can of tobacco down, and I think Art Winder and Jiggs Grigg picked up the can, found a piece of old rubber hose, ground it up in the kitchen grater and put it into the can. Later in the day Gil refilled his pipe. Everybody else could smell the burning rubber, but he kept on smoking.

Gertrude: Once we started for the lodge on a Saturday night in Bill Maxwell's car. Paul and I were in back. Bill and Jiggs had brought the sandwiches. Paul and I had ours in the backseat. Paul worked and worked on his sandwich and finally said, "This is awfully tough beef." They had put innertubing in Paul's.

Dot Farr: They were such kind hearted folks.

Where was Meany Ski Hut located?

Jim: Stampede Pass where the Northern Pacific goes through at the east end of the tunnel. You had to hike to get to it. When I see the price of ski boots and skis these days, I think back to my first year with the Mountaineers in 1926. I spent New Year's weekend with the Tacoma Mountaineers at the guide house at Mount Rainier. I was just a kid in high school, but I washed dishes alongside one of the University of Washington professors, and I thought, "Hey, this is a great organization." On that trip there were only about six with skis. The rest had snowshoes.

Gertrude: Paul told of a winter outing to Paradise in 1922 or '23. They took the boat to Tacoma, a train to Longmire, stayed at Longmire overnight and then hiked to Paradise. Joe Hazard was leading the trip and said, "Anybody who brings skis, I'm not responsible for." At that time everyone used snowshoes.

Dot: When you look back at some of those old Mountaineer annuals, the cost for a whole weekend at the Meany Lodge was only 45 cents which included the food, really wonderful meals.

Did you have dehydrated food back then?

Jim: Well, there was Herb Wirtz's soup. It looked like a stick of dynamite.

Dot: It tasted like it too.

Jim: The year I was the chairman of the Meany Hut committee, the secretary was Muriel Johnson. She worked at the Northern Life Building, just a block from my office. I would drive up to the lodge every weekend and decide how many pounds of meat to take up there. After several weeks of this Rex Reston joined the Mountaineers,

and he'd drive with us. One Saturday morning—we worked half days then—I called Muriel at her office and told her I'd meet her at twelve sharp. She said, "Jim, I forgot to tell you. Rex called and he's going to drive me this weekend. Two months later they were married."

It seems that one of the chief functions of the Mountaineers was that of matrimonial agency.

Dot: Well, look at this whole crew.

Jim: There was a period when about ten men and ten women, who had more or less gone with each other at different times, just changed partners.

Gertrude: Hugh Sullivan was the first man I dated. After Hugh, I dated Carl Lindgren. Carl took me on a climb where I met Paul and dumped Carl.

Jim: I can tell you how Lucille got in the Mountaineers. Do you remember the Mountaineer Players? I just didn't get involved with the Players at all. I was out in the mountains every weekend, except my mother's birthday and Christmas. Sometimes I would leave Christmas night. Summer and winter it was skiing and climbing. One summer I was roped into trying out for a Russian skit.

About eight days before the show the gal who had the lead just lost her voice completely. One of the girls in the cast, Lois Boyd, said, "There's a girl who works in our building. She's not a Mountaineer, but she could learn the part in eight days." The next rehearsal there was Lucille with the script being shown where to move. I thought, "Boy, this is going to be some show." But on the night of the show it looked like she had been in the cast right from the beginning. I had to do my little Russian dance—I can't squat down like that anymore.

That was the first time I saw her, but I kept on with my skiing and climbing on weekends. A year later I went over to Kitsap for the Spring Play and the gal with the lead was Lucille. It turns out they had given her a membership for saving the Winter Skit. I was so impressed I went over the next Saturday to Kitsap. The cast would sit around the fire afterwards and sing. I tried to get a date. I'd wait to see how the snow was for skiing, and it took me the longest time to work in a date, but I finally did.

Forest: Most of our climbing was done on weekends. We'd tackle practically anything on a weekend, almost run both ways. At one time we talked about climbing Glacier Peak on a weekend.

Gertrude: We took the train to Barlow Pass to climb Sloan Peak. The members of the party were John and Chris Lehmann, Tommy Jeter, Paul and I. We got on the little Hartford Railroad Line, a flat car. We had to sign a waiver saying that if we were killed it wouldn't be their fault. We had gotten as far as the Big Four Inn when it seemed like the car stubbed its toe, gave a couple of lunges and then rolled over the bank onto its side. It was an open car, and we had all this food, packs for a three-day trip. It was just one great jumble. I seem to recall that the car had rolled over, and we dropped down quite a steep embankment. Everybody was able to get out of the mixup. Paul stood up, looked at Big Four and said, "Well, if we can't make Sloan, we can climb Big Four."

Everybody trooped into the hotel, just looking messed up. There was a nurse who bandaged Tommy Jeter's leg, but Mabel McBain was hurt enough that she didn't think she would make the climb. By the time we got organized we had to hike all the way to Barlow Pass. We met the packer who had trouble with one of the horses. We got lost in the dark and finally had to camp in a dry river bed.

We were up at daylight the next morning, had a little breakfast and started up Sloan. It was steep and there was a lot of brush-fighting, but we finally made it. Coming back that night, we weren't sure of the way and I stumbled once in the dark, fell and hurt my arm like anything, but nobody paid any attention. By that time it was every man for himself. We finally got back to camp and I just crawled into my sleeping bag. I didn't care whether the men had anything to eat or not. The next morning we reached the railroad car which was back up on the track. We all got on and had to sign the slip again. On the way down, one wheel on the car was just wobbling. I said to Paul, "That wheel is coming off," and he poked this rather noncommittal driver and said, "Pardon me sir, but I think this wheel is coming off." He replied, "It has to be put on that way. That's how the tracks are." The whole trip seemed like one catastrophe after another.

Kenneth Chapman: John and Chris Lehmann were instrumental in the Everett group. They asked me to go on some trips, so I joined up there. We didn't gibe too well with the Seattle Group because in those days we were far apart. Thirty miles was a long ways. We did tend to feel a bit provincial, because we stayed up in the Stillaguamish area. There were so darn many mountains up there, that we never ran out of them.

Forest: You had all the good mountains up there.

I was real curious about one of your climbs in that area, the first ascent of Dome Peak. Did you know that when you climbed Dome there was a bit of competition over who had actually climbed the highest peak on Dome?

Forest: No, I didn't know that. There was another group coming in from the east. We weren't conscious of that . . .

Dot: I don't think you guys ever climbed competitively.

Forest: Oh, I don't know. When we went into Chimney Rocks, there had been several parties that had been turned back, and we thought we ought to get in there and try pretty soon.

Dot: But, I mean, you weren't racing with anybody.

There couldn't have been that many people climbing at your level at that time.

Dot: A lot of their climbs were pre-piton.

And you used the standing hip belay?

Jim: There were a lot of places where there were no natural belays or because it was easy to do. The belayer would stand up in a good, secure position.

Did you ever have to hold a fall with the standing hip belay?

Jim: No, I never had a fall. We usually had several layers around the shoulders, and we were always looking for natural belays, like rock horns.

Forest, what was the hardest peak you ever climbed?

Forest: I suppose Chimney Rock was the most exposed. Without any aids at all it was probably the hardest.

You mean you didn't even have a rope?

Forest: We did, but we didn't bring it to go up the mountain. We just decided we'd have to do without it, because there was really no place to anchor the rope. It was a steep chimney. I've probably stood on a few spots that were more hair-raising, where you kind of get stuck, but after you get over it . . .

Priscilla: You forget all about it, until you've got to come back down.

Forest: We climbed very fast. Art Winder was a very fast climber and sure-footed, nervy. He almost danced on rock. We walked over stuff that a lot of people wouldn't even look at. Art and I climbed Big Four one time. I believe it was the first ascent. It was one of those really hot days up in that valley in the middle of summer. I remember Art had a scar on his wrist where he'd touched a rock hot enough to burn him. We had plenty of water and chased a couple of goats all the way up the mountain. We didn't have much rockfall to worry about. On the way down we came to a place, a big smooth rock, about eighty feet wide and smooth all the way down. So Art slides right down this thing, must have been seventy feet of it. I looked at it for a little while and then went down after him. But I never would have tried it if he hadn't done it first.

Priscilla: I remember climbing Mount Thompson. One young man in the group was a sailor. His mother had told him if he ever got to Seattle to be sure to look up the Mountaineers and go out with them. He didn't have any equipment, and I don't know who was in charge of that trip, but they let him go. Somebody lent him some boots, but they weren't very comfortable, so he had to sit down and rest his feet every once in a while. We were caught after dark off Rampart Ridge and stayed overnight. We sort of laid around on a little gravel spit in the middle of a creek.

Gertrude: Paul was on that trip, and I was back at the lodge, and I had to be back at work the next morning. We sat up all night at the lodge waiting for the group. Jiggs took me to Hyak to the train the next morning and gave me money to get me to Seattle where I got a taxi to the Seattle Times. I worked all day in my mountaineer clothes.

Word got back that I had just got in and there was a mountaineer party lost up there. Well, I knew that the Mountaineers would hate me for life if it got in the paper because they prided themselves. I talked to this fellow and told him, "You just can't print this." He said he'd hold off until noon, and Paul called me just before noon.

Priscilla: The way I told it, it was the night that the Mountaineers Mother's Club was formed, because all the mothers were calling all the other mothers. We came out and met a party that was just starting out to look for us.

What did your non-climbing friends think about your climbing?

Dot: We didn't have any.

Priscilla: I remember taking some of my Mountaineers friends to sorority parties at the University of Washington. That went over like a lead balloon.

I get the feeling that your social life revolved around the Mountaineers.

Gertrude: Oh, it did. Absolutely! After we all got married we had that supper club, the Gorge Society.

Dot: What I think we had was that we were all pretty much the same age.

Gertrude: I think what we had was kind of unique.

Dot: The girls were always chasing the boys, naturally.

Forest: In the winters we'd go up to Lodge Lake after the Mountaineers clubroom meetings on Wednesdays and go ice skating.

Dot: We must have had awfully good employers, because we'd skate up there all night and come back in the morning to go to work.

Kenneth: I'll never forget the first night I was up at the lodge with Priscilla. There was a terrific wind storm, blew trees down over the road. Gertrude was the life of the party.

Gertrude: I was? I don't remember being the life of the party.

Kenneth: We couldn't get out 'til the next morning. I remember Priscilla took me down to the waterfront where I caught the Soleduck to Anacortes, got in about 5 a.m., took a shower, got dressed and went to work.

Were some of the oldtimers still around when you were in the Mountaineers?

Forest: Edmund Meany was still president when I joined. He presided at the meetings.

What did he think of your crew?

Dot: Well, I think there were several ways of looking at our group. We were regarded as a bunch of upstarts by some of the Mountaineers. We were kind of brash. We did sort of odd things, you know, like drink wine, things of that sort. I think there were people who felt we were sort of cliquish.

What did the Mountaineers think of the Mazamas?

Dot: There was a certain amount of rivalry.

Forest: One of the things was that the Mazamas had a lot of bad luck having people killed on trips.

Jim: They used to take huge numbers of people with just one leader and then lose control. Eldon Carney and I ran into a group of Mazamas on Mount St. Helens one 4th of July weekend. The Mazamas had a big party on the mountain, and on the way down, the leaders had let the group glissade down any way they wanted to. The upshot was that by the time we got to our camp, they were still trying to round up their party. They had climbers in canyons and gullies all around the base of the mountain. It was almost dark. I remember helping a young engaged couple try and find a diamond engagement ring they had lost in the grass, but we never found it.

Forest: I think the early Mountaineers were pretty disciplined as far as their trips were concerned. They usually had a leader and rear guard. You stayed in line and you kept track of everybody.

Lucille Martin: Larry Byington didn't take me on a trip up Chair Peak because my shoes weren't good enough. I was really glad he didn't. I was very inexperienced.

When you were active mountaineers, could you have imagined the sort of climbing that's being done today?

Forest: We always used to read every book that was written on climbing and skiing. We didn't know much about modern climbing; pitons and carabiners, all that sort of thing. We had a rumor coming along about those things about the time I quit.

Jim: Nowadays they have grades 1, 2, 5 or 6 in Beckey's guide book. It's all Greek to me.

Well, it seems, listening to you all talk that there couldn't have been a better time in the world.

Gertrude: That's kind of the way we feel. We had a wonderful time. It's kind of remarkable that as many of us have kept in touch as well as we have.

Jim: I can truly say that my life, social as well as mountaineering, was all tied up with the Seattle Mountaineers from the time I left school until I transferred down to Portland.

Lucille: Well, what a well-preserved group.

Priscilla: Those of us who have lasted this long have to be.

Gertrude: We all had such a healthy youth, all that exercise.

Lucille: I figure if you've made it this far, you might as well as crow about it.

1

— Robert H. Hayes Photo

2

— Tom Miller Photo

3

4

5

6

(1) Forest Farr, Don Blair, Norvall Grigg at base of southwest peak of Dome before making first ascent July 5, 1936. (2) Mount Logan from summit of Goode, first climbed in 1926.

(3) Jim Martin in southern Pickets, 1931. (4) A dramatic overlook, Chimney Rocks in the background. (5) Early-day rock climbers, bottom to top: unidentified, Max Maxwell, Paul Shorrock, Lawrence Byington. (6) Bill Degenhardt, Evelyn McAlpin and Jim Martin on top of Glacier Peak. That summer, the trio climbed Rainier, Glacier and Olympus in one two-week vacation.

1 — Paul Shorrock Photo

2 — Robert H. Hayes Photo

3

4

(1) Mountaineers take sun in grassy meadow. Standing, third from left: Paul Shorrock. Next: Lawrence Byington, with Helen Spellar and Edna Grigg in back; Evelyn McAlpin at far right.
(2) Southwest peak of Dome as viewed by first ascent party: Forest Farr, Don Blair and Noval Grigg, 1936.

(3) Mountaineers outing above Paradise Lodge, Mount Rainier. (4) Winter outing, probably at Snoqualmie Pass Mountaineers lodge.

*I*magine the panorama of unclimbed Cascade peaks awaiting mountaineers in 1930. The thought is intoxicating to any climber who has had to settle for the occasional 10th or 12th ascent of a mountain or simply being able to scribble his name on the same piece of paper as the original summiteers.

I could have had the pick of all my favorite Cascade peaks in 1930: Dome, Three Fingers, El Dorado, Big Four, Challenger, Bonanza, Redoubt, Chimney Rocks, Goode, Forbidden, among others. But would I have been quite so bold without crampons, carabiners, pitons, and at least a goldline rope?

The best climbers of the early 1930s had intense ambition, an affinity for exposure, a new athleticism and improved access to the Cascade interior, but they carried little more on their backs and feet than odd lengths of manila rope, rubber-soled shoes for rock climbing, tricouni-nailed boots for snow and ice, and long wooden ice-axes.

When Forest Farr, Art Winder and Laurence Byington made the first ascent of Chimney Rocks in 1930, they did so without ropes. Instead of kletterschue they had tennisschue—or in the case of Byington, bare feet—and they employed a technique called the "back and heel method" when grunting up the sometimes-overhanging chimneys. They crossed the icy Chimney Glacier without crampons, their only purchase tricouni nails and laborious steps hacked from hard snow by their ice-axes.

European climbers had been using carabiners, pitons, ice-axes and crampons for decades. As early as 1910 they had perfected the Dulfersitz rappel, though I'm not sure anyone really perfects, or wants to, that rope-burn rappel. In 1930 Northwest climbers were heading to

the hardest Cascade peaks equipped with virtually the same equipment and techniques employed by the founding fathers of the Mountaineers. Big Four, Three Fingers, El Dorado, Dome, Terror, Colonial and Snowfield all were first climbed without fancy equipment by the likes of Farr, Winder, Norval Grigg, Don Blair, Herb Strandberg and Bill Degenhardt before 1935.

It would take a bit of a revolution by a group of "outlaws" within the Mountaineers to give Northwest climbers a taste of state-of-the-art climbing. One of the ringleaders of the little revolution was Lloyd Anderson, who later in the decade would further shake up the mountaineering establishment by founding the Recreational Co-op (REI).

Lloyd Anderson climbed with a passion and intensity that set him immediately apart from most Northwest climbers. In his first two years of climbing, Anderson summited on the six major peaks and all 20 Snoqualmie Peaks. At the time Mountaineers policy dictated that climbers must check in at the Snoqualmie Lodge before making a pin peak climb in order to get credit for the climb. There was also a fee involved. Anderson, and many of his climbing companions, balked at the extra expense and time involved in the procedure. The country, after all, was in the throes of a Depression. And there was simply not enough time in the day-and-a-half weekend allotted to most climbers to climb and check in at the lodge as well. Often they were climbing two or three peaks on a trip.

Those climbers banded together as an informal climbing group within the Mountaineers. In 1934, they decided to begin their own formal climbing classes. They asked a young, but experienced climber with a knowledge of European technique, Wolf Bauer, to give instruction. He agreed. The class that first year consisted of loosely-structured demonstrations, but it caught on. In 1935 Bauer taught a formal class and the Mountaineers climbing course, most likely the first of its kind in the United States, was born.

The course proved immediately popular. The Mountaineers leadership could no longer ignore it and the classes became an integral part of the Mountaineers program. By the end of the decade, the rebel climbers had become the establishment, controlling the Mountaineers board of directors and its presidency.

The 1938 climber's course outline appears to bear few changes from the present-day course offered to hundreds of Mountaineers each year. One outing looks rather intriguing though; It reads,"Southend Gravel Pit (Imitation Snow)."

The 1937 written exam for the basic climbing course contained questions that still show up today, but there were a few . . .

One question asked, "Before a climb bacon and eggs make a good breakfast, true or false?" Students were expected to know that "Berg-Heil" meant (1) the name of a mountain (2) a mountain greeting or (3) a type of avalanche. And a fill-in-the-blank stated, "To clean a frying pan easily mix a little _____ with the grease."

The climber's group came up with The Mountaineer's Ten Commandments, taken from other climbing manuals and supplemented by Wolf Bauer. It is an odd mix of common sense and early Mountaineers homilies, with a stodgy moral tone and a goofy sense of humor:

II . . . You should not overload your stomach with fancy concentrated foods . . .
III . . . A man's word is not good on the end of a rope.
V . . . You should hold mountain comradery in high honor . . .
VI . . . Thou shalt not steal. You shall not take from others their mountain peace through shouting. The people you meet are not lonesome for your voice and company . . .

X... You shall not desecrate the mountains through speed manias and record crazes. You shall find their peace and soul.

None of the hotshot almumi from the first climbing classes would admit to suffering from a slight case of speed mania or a touch of the record crazes. But Anderson, Bauer, Jack Hossack, Phillip Dickert, Agnes Dickert, Ome Daiber, George MacGowan, and even the likes of Farr and Winder, got to the tops of a prodigious number of important Cascade Peaks in the 1930s. There was no Depression when it came peak-bagging.

Bolstered by the newest in ironmongery and technique, Wolf Bauer and Jack Hossack climbed Ptarmigan Ridge on Mount Rainier, the first ascent of Rainier's forbidding north side. They were followed a few weeks later by Ome Daiber, Arnie Campbell and Jim Borrow who first climbed the now-classic Liberty Ridge. Neither of these climbs would be repeated for another 20 years. In 1936, Bauer, Hossack, Phillip Dickert, Joe Halwax and George MacGowan made the first ascent of Goode. Lloyd Anderson made first ascents of Triumph in 1938, Sinister and Despair in 1939 and Forbidden in 1940.

The Mountaineers did not have a monopoly on first ascents or even the best climbers. In 1937 a group of Boy Scouts interested in mountaineering, an activity deemed too dangerous by the overly cautious national organization, abandoned scouting to form their own climbing club, the Ptarmigans. In contrast to the Mountaineers, the Ptarmigans had virtually no rules and practiced the purest form of democracy, which often resulted in roaring arguments on climbs. They headed for the last blank spots on Cascade maps: the Northern Pickets—including a first ascent of Fury—the Redoubt Range, and the classic traverse that bears their name, the Ptarmigan. Among the members were Will Thompson, Calder Bressler, Ray and Ralph Clough, Bill Cox and Tom Myers.

On the east side of the mountains climbers had their own club, the Cascadians. In 1935, Les Maxwell, Fred Llewellyn and John Vertrees made the first ascent of the west ridge of Stuart. Two years later Louis Ulrich, Edward Rankin, and John Riley climbed the Stuart's northeast buttress.

Local mountaineers also began to make names for themselves outside of Washington. In 1939 George MacGowan and Jack Hossack climbed the Northeast Couloir of the Grand Teton, a fast first ascent on a difficult route. In 1941, Lloyd Anderson, Tom Campbell, Lyman Boyer, and Helmy Beckey made the first ascent of the South Howser Spire in the Bugaboos, and in 1943 Helmy and Fred Beckey made the second ascent of Mount Waddington in the Coast Range.

Lloyd Anderson and his wife, Mary, were at the center of another small mountaineering revolution in 1938 when they founded Recreational Co-op. Dissatisfied with the quality and price of much of the climbing equipment sold in such stores as the Outdoor Store (The Mountaineers store of choice), or Cunninghams, 25 climbing friends met in the Anderson living room, leafed through Swiss and Austrian climbing catalogues and ordered equipment. Members paid $1 for membership and received a yearly 15 percent rebate on purchases made. For many years it was simply friends choosing and the Andersons ordering. During World War II, the Co-op operated out of a gas station, although members could always count on Lloyd and Mary to open their doors when the station was closed.

With the outbreak of World War II, many Northwest climbers defended their country while honing their climbing and skiing skills as members of the legendary 10th

Mountain Division. For many area climbers, the service allowed them to climb in the Rockies or West Virginia's Seneca Rocks. Fred Beckey's climbing log for 1943-44 shows climbs only in Colorado where he was stationed with the 10th Mountain Division. After the war Beckey, like many other soldier/climbers, returned to the mountains with a vengeance. In the two years following World War II, he redefined the word prolific with over 15 first ascents in the Cascades, Olympics, Alaska Coast Range, and Sierra Nevada. And in the process Beckey would be declared foolhardy by the generation that had been called foolhardy by the generation that had been called foolhardy . . .

▲

CHAPTER

5

LLOYD AND MARY ANDERSON

I first visited REI in the summer of 1961. At that time it was crammed into a space in downtown Seattle above the Green Apple Cafe and the Roosevelt Theater which showed adult movies. I remember the smell of freeze-dried food and also the sight of Jim Whittaker helping customers—he was much taller then. My parents loaded up with far too many Seidel's Vegi-rice Beef dinners because they were the cheapest.

«I thought if we had 100 people, we'd have enough to do a little business. I never dreamed it would grow like it did. But it never

stopped growing. It still hasn't. I don't quite agree with expansion as fast as it is expanding now. But then that's all right as long as there isn't a depression.»
—*Lloyd Anderson*

Lloyd and Mary Anderson may very well have been working at the store that day, but I would not have recognized them. Another decade would pass before I would even begin to understand that, without Lloyd and Mary Anderson, numbers one and two, there would have been no REI.

For many years REI was simply called the Co-op, and it was located in the Anderson living room in West Seattle. The warehouse was their attic. The Co-op's customers were Mountaineer friends, who like the Andersons, were looking for climbing equipment that was simply not found in Seattle stores or just too expensive for most Depression-era climbers. Membership was a dollar and members received yearly dividends according to their purchases.

The Co-op **was** Lloyd and Mary (often assisted by their two daughters) during its first years of existence. Lloyd worked at City Transit until leaving to work full-time at REI in 1960. He also climbed mountains, lots of them. During his 50-year career, Anderson climbed 450 mountains, made 19 first ascents and was an active member of the Mountaineers. Lloyd and Mary were instrumental in starting the first climbing class, perhaps the first ever offered in the United States, and, in the process, radically changed the structure of the Mountaineers. Lloyd always considered himself a bit of a revolutionary who didn't mind shaking

24

up the status quo. The interview takes place in the Anderson home in West Seattle.

Mary and Lloyd are gracious, but initially seem reserved, as if trying to gauge our intentions. At one point, though, Mary smiles and the room thaws measurably. She offers to show Cliff the famous attic that served for so many years as the Co-op warehouse. While they are gone, Lloyd pulls out his bound collection of climbing notes, photos, mountaineering course outlines, summer outing food lists. It is an impressive document. Later Lloyd and Mary give us a tour of the house which Lloyd built himself over a period of several years during the Depression. Their yard is lush, green and neat. Their elaborately terraced garden takes advantage of every available square inch of the yard.

A bad hip has kept Lloyd from the mountains in recent years, but he and Mary have discovered lawn bowling. "This is a new avocation," Mary says. "I first saw it in Vancouver and thought, 'Gee, that's something I might be able to do.' I could never take part in any sports due to the limitations of having had polio. I took Lloyd over and said, 'I want you to see this.' Well, it happened to be a women's tournament, and they all wore skirts and hats and it was rather formal. We got there at the end and they were down on their hands and knees measuring to see which ball was closer. Lloyd took one look and said, 'Looks like a stupid game to me.'

"Later in Seattle I managed to get Lloyd to watch a game a friend of ours was playing in. When we got there, there were two Mountaineers friends who had gotten to the same place Lloyd was; where they couldn't climb mountains anymore. The two men rushed up to him, threw their arms around him and said how glad they were to see him. Well, he was smitten from then on. Lloyd never does anything by halves."

▲

Lloyd Anderson: I got into the Mountaineers through the Tillicum organization at the University of Washington, which at the time was a radical organization that, you might say, was opposed to fraternities. We even elected the president of the student body, and the fraternities were so mad about the thing that they burned him in effigy. T. Davis Castor was in the Tillicum group and was also a Mountaineer. He showed me an application and in 1929 I joined. When I joined I became part of a radical group that didn't agree with the old Mountaineers either.

Mary Anderson: It was at this time that the climbers course was started. Wolf Bauer started off with notes he had collected. What he really did that was most important, I think, was to let people know that there was mountaineering of a different caliber somewhere else. And that's what he brought to his lectures. He said, "I know these techniques. I have done them." And if people wanted to learn he was perfectly willing to show them. Along with this he showed that there was equipment that we didn't have.

Lloyd: Our climbing group was really on its own for a while, sort of an offshoot of the Mountaineers, kind of an illegal group. We conducted our climbing courses at the Mountaineers clubroom, but there was a committee of 33 that tried to stop us from doing some of the things we were doing.

At that time, in order to climb the major peaks, you had to do it through a summer outing with the Mountaineers. You couldn't go out on your own on the Cascade peaks. You had to go to the lodge to climb. Our climber group didn't bother to go to the lodge. We listed our trips and did our climbing directly from Seattle. We finally got four or five people elected to the board of trustees so we had a voice. Either that or we were going to have to start our own club.

Our goals were just not their goals. A whole bunch of oldtimers in the Mountaineers resigned, and we got control of the board of trustees. We fired the caretaker at the Snoqualmie Lodge, and if they needed a cook they could hire one when they needed one. So we had a revolution in the Mountaineers.

Were you involved in the planning of that first climbing course?

Lloyd: Actually Wolf didn't have an outline for the first climbing course. He just had some field trips, and then he left us. So I made the outline for the first climbing course after Wolf was gone. We made an outline and assigned instructors to teach just certain parts of the course.

Did you then create a book after coming up with the outline for the course?

Mary: After Wolf left, topics were assigned to various people. One night a man was speaking on clothing and he was expounding on nightcaps and this and that, and people began to be disturbed. It was decided after that that somebody needed to supervise what went into the lectures.

Lloyd: Agnes Dickert kind of wrote up a text after each of the members of the climbing group wrote their section.

You were in essence creating as you went. There wasn't a great American climbing tradition to draw from.

Lloyd: We had books from Europe that talked about mountaineering technique, but we didn't have anything like a class. No one had ever done that before.

Prior to that skills had been taught by example.

Mary: You went out with Mountaineers or the Mazamas. There would be a leader and the people would sign up for the climb. Lloyd took forty people up Rainier.

Lloyd: There was one peak, Whitehorse, where I had eighty people.

Mary: We climbed Rainier, forty of us, in a lightning storm. It was a huge one. The Seattle papers called it the most terrific lightning storm Seattle had ever experienced. I kept thinking about our two kids at home and wondering if I would ever see them again. We could hear rocks coming off the Prow and lightning was going off the ice axes and tips of crampons. There was St. Elmo's Fire everywhere.

Were you a mountaineer when you met Lloyd?

Lloyd: She wasn't. When I was still going with her I'd take her on hikes up along the Skykomish River.

Some awful mistakes are made by men trying to impress women with their climbing prowess on the first date. It often becomes the last date.

Mary: I was invited once by the Seattle Chamber of Commerce to give a lecture on how men could introduce women to the mountains. That's what I told them. Do it slow. The first real peak I climbed was St. Helens.

Lloyd: The one thing I didn't know about

Mary at the beginning (sometimes she would stumble or come down wrong on a glissade and I'd have to block her because she was supposed to stomp her feet in) was that she had infantile paralysis at five and didn't have full use of her feet. She didn't tell me at the beginning. When we would be glissading down a mountain she would get out of control, and I would block her off to keep her from hitting the rocks.

Mary: I can't walk on my heels, and everyone would yell at me, "Dig in your heels, dig in your heels." I hated it.

Lloyd, you made several first ascents in the North Cascades.

Lloyd: Well, it was just that there were all kinds of first ascents to be made when I started climbing, although I wasn't interested in making first ascents like others. I made nineteen, plus or minus a few. I could have made twice that number easy, but I was interested in promoting mountaineering through our climbing course.

What was the hardest peak you ever climbed?

Lloyd: The south tower of Howser Spire in the Bugaboos. That was a first ascent in the Bugaboos. The Sierra Club had a group up there. We had climbed some of the other peaks for practice, and we saw them camping below us and knew they were coming in to make a first ascent of an unclimbed peak. So we got up early the next morning, five o'clock, and headed for the peak. We took over fifty hours on that peak. We took a big trail lunch and thought we'd get back that night. But we never got back that night. We didn't get to the top of the mountain. We had to bivouac about three-quarters of the way up the peak, and we just about froze to death. We had a little bit of food left. There was a rat up there, and we had to put our food in our sleeping bag because he was plundering what little food we had. The next day we were left with sugar cubes. We got to the top at 4 p.m. the next day, and we had to rappel down the mountain in the dark. We didn't reach camp until daylight.

There was some hard rock climbing on that peak. I'm not a rock climber, although I had to lead up on some of the route. Lyman Boyer did the rock climbing. I couldn't have climbed on the rocks that Lyman did. You had to hold on with your finger nails. I think he put in a piton or two to help. In those days we didn't have lug soles.

We wore felt soled shoes. They were sort of like tennis shoes.

When you first climbed the west ridge of Forbidden with Fred Beckey did you have the sense that it would someday become a classic climb?

Lloyd: I didn't think it was that important. I didn't think it was that hard a climb. We had to be careful on the ridge. It took us two years to make the ascent, but I don't know why it's listed so high.

I remember one time I got the Beckey brothers to help me scout out Mount Cruiser in the Olympics. I was supposed to lead a climb and I hadn't climbed the thing before. Fred didn't have the right route to start with. He didn't know anything more than I did about it. So he was going up a vertical place, and I was supposed to belay him. I said, "I can't belay you because if you fall, you're going to take me with you." Then he said, "Well, just get out of the rope." So he climbed up and finally pulled me up. He climbed like a cat. I don't know how he hung on. It wasn't even the right route. We found the right one when we came back down and I climbed it. I put in a piton and anchored to that. When I reached down to test it, the piton pulled out in my fingers. It was kind of a shock to be belaying and find out I didn't have any security.

You two were very much involved with the Mountaineers summer outings. Tell me about them.

Mary: They are nonexistent today. If you read the Mountaineers ancient history, the summer outings were the big event of the summer. You would go with pack train, big parties of people. They traversed around Mount Rainier, went into the Olympics. There was a whole mass of equipment that was summer outing equipment and no other group in the Mountaineers was allowed to use it. It was really a vacation for everybody. It was the one way people could get out into the wilderness. There was singing and the goodnight song. I don't even think the Mountaineers know the Goodnight Song anymore. The summer outings finally died out when roads and cars made places more accessible, and maybe because no one wanted to take over the responsibility.

When did you get the idea to start the Co-op?

Mary: There was a store in Seattle, the Outdoor Store, and that's where the Mountain-

eers went for equipment. There was also Cunninghams, but their prices were beyond our meager resources. We knew that Wolf knew the prices of equipment in Europe, and there was another man in the Mountaineers who said he would translate the ads in the European catalogs. So we thought, "We'll buy Lloyd an ice axe." And that's how it got started. Once you buy one for yourself and go on a trip and somebody sees it, they want it.

That must have made you a popular couple.

Mary: I don't know whether that made us popular or not. It made the Mountaineers very angry because here we were not patronizing the Outdoor Store. There was a lot of push and pull. After enough people decided they wanted something, we said, "We'll send in an order." For two years we did that just out of the goodness of our hearts. We would send in the money for the order, the order would come and everyone would sit in the living room and unpack the package, pay their bill and go home happy. But eventually it got to be more than we wanted to deal with.

So initially there was no name, just the Andersons sending out the orders.

Mary: That's right. At one point a woman wanted some equipment, and by this time I guess we were probably charging a membership fee. At any rate she wouldn't join because we were unincorporated. She didn't want to be a part of any organization that wasn't incorporated. She might be liable. So that's when the incorporation started.

So REI had its origins in this home?

Mary: Right here. The attic used to be the warehouse.

Was it always called REI?

Lloyd: No, we started out as Recreational Equipment Cooperated. But we had a problem with the word cooperated when we incorporated. If we incorporated as a profit organization we couldn't use the word cooperative. We ran unincorporated for fifteen-twenty years. I wasn't so concerned about liability, but I would be now, because if somebody gets hurt they try to sue you for everything you own.

In the beginning did you order everything from Europe?

Lloyd: We had to deal with some businessmen in town to get certain wool clothing. They were a little skeptical. They were concerned that we'd come in and cut prices and their regular customers wouldn't have anything to do with them. But after we got to have a volume of business, they weren't so concerned.

After a while you moved from the house to a gas station.

Lloyd: Yes, and it was open whenever the gas station owner was there, at least six days a week. He wasn't a mountaineer, but he was honest. We paid him five percent on his sales. He'd write a slip or something, and that's how I could keep track of the dividends. And if he wasn't open, heck, people would come out to the house. After the gas station we operated up overhead on the corner of Sixth and Pike. It was too much business in those days.

Mary: In 1959 Lloyd and I made our first trip to Europe. We first went to the factories we had already established relationships with, but we also went to every sporting goods store we could find. Any time we saw a piece of equipment that was different from anything we had, we just decided whether it would be something worthwhile or just a gadget. After that trip the equipment changed, because we could actually see what we were buying. Prior to that we had been buying from the catalogs.

Lloyd: It wasn't as complicated as it is now. In those days we had pitons you drove in with hammers. Have you ever seen the complications of the present REI bulletin that they put out? When I look at the climbing equipment, I wouldn't even know where to put it. It's terrible.

Was any equipment being made in the United States in the early days of REI?

Lloyd: There was no equipment being made in the United States.

Mary: Probably Chouinard was the first.

Lloyd: We had a man in Seattle making ice axes, although he wasn't there in the beginning. During the war when I couldn't get equipment, I went back to Roy (his hometown) to a blacksmith there, showed him an ice axe and he made ice axe heads. I bought the hickory and made about a hundred ice axes that I used for rental. He also made pitons. We couldn't get any of that from Europe during the war. So maybe the first ice axes made in the United States were made in Roy, Washington.

Mary: We made carabiners for awhile. We still have some parts left.

Did you ever imagine that REI would become such a dominant force in the outdoor equipment field?

Lloyd: I thought if we had a hundred people, we'd have enough to do a little business. I never dreamed it would grow like it did. But it never stopped growing. It still hasn't. I don't quite agree with expansion as fast as it is expanding now. But then that's all right as long as there isn't a depression.

CHAPTER

6

WOLF BAUER

Wolf Bauer moved to Seattle from Germany in the early 1920s. He was ahead of his eighth grade classmates in all subjects but couldn't speak English. As a result Bauer was put in the first grade. Each month, as he became more fluent, he was promoted a grade. By the end of the year he found himself back in junior high. It was perhaps the only time in Bauer's illustrious life that he had to catch up. More often than not Wolf Bauer has been the leader.

Bauer brought from Germany a knowledge of European technique in mountaineering, downhill and Nordic skiing. Energetic and enterprising, he was generous with his time and knowledge. In 1934, while still an engineering student at the University of Washington, Bauer started the first mountaineering course in the Northwest, and perhaps the United States. A champion skier, he competed in the 1936 Olympic ski trials at Mount Rainier and the second Silver Skis race, a grueling downhill race on Mount Rainier from Camp Muir to the Paradise Lodge. During that time Bauer also made important first ascents in the Cascades—Ptarmigan Ridge on Mount Rainier and Mount Goode. 1948 was an especially busy year for Bauer as he helped found both the Seattle Mountain Rescue Council, the Washington Kayak Club and the first kayak courses in the Northwest.

As he nears 80, Bauer protests half-heartedly that he is trying to retire, but he is probably busier than ever in his role as shoreline-resource consultant, where once again he is exploring new territory, waiting for the crowd to catch up.

When I first meet Wolf Bauer at his home on Vashon Island, I am struck by two things: his incredibly white, bushy eyebrows, and the equally incredible shiner. It is a doozy—beneath the bushy, white eyebrow, nothing but black, purple, red and swollen. Before we have settled into chairs, he explains that he fell while downhill skiing. The tip of his ski flipped and whacked him in the eye. Bauer, who retains a soft German accent, laughs and says that he still likes speed and skis like a

« For a number of years I didn't want to put in a piton. Putting in a piton was almost blasphemy, only to be put in as the last thing, never as direct aid. What I was out to do was climb more difficult routes on mountains that had already been climbed. I wasn't out for first ascents—new routes, yes. »
—*Wolf Bauer*

29

racer. He has recently taken part in a senior ski race where he beat all comers, many of whom were 25 years younger.

▲

When you came to Seattle was there much skiing being done?

No, it was a few Norwegians. The Mountaineers were the basic catalyst. Then came the Seattle Ski Club. I was in the first slalom race held west of the Mississippi in 1929. It was held up at the Meany Ski Hut. I remember well playing hookey on Friday because we had these races up at Meany and doings at the Snoqualmie Lodge. We'd take the train up and it would stop at the tunnel and we'd have to hike up from the tunnel. So you had to take the train in the afternoon before school was out. I would pack my skis onto the streetcar, and I remember one conductor asking me what they were. Or an old Swede would come up to me and say, "Oh, I ain't smelled der Klister vax for a long time."

In the '30s we started to do a lot more racing. We initiated the Patrol Race. But skiing at that time was more closely related to mountaineering.

Tell me about the Silver Skis race.

It was a race from Camp Muir to Paradise, the longest downhill race in the country. It was put on by the Seattle P.I. I raced in the second one in 1934. We all started at one time. There were sixty-nine of us in one line, and we all funneled down two miles to the first gate; there were only three on the entire course. And I'm telling you it was hard crust, wind-whipped into a regular washboard. We got into sixty-mile-per-hour stuff and then started to cartwheel. There was no way you could turn in that stuff. We didn't have edges. I had a shop in Seattle grind off the tip of a band saw, punch holes and rout a groove along the edge of the ski and put the tip of the saw in. They were in one piece and of course they popped screws on one side if you flexed too much. But I figured for that race it would be a real help in the crust.

I had also put shellac on, and wax on top of that, but it wore off before I even got to the first gate. I did a complete cartwheel and thought, "Oh My God!" It knocked the wind out of me and when I looked up there was nobody around me. I could see others behind me doing the same thing, so I thought I still had a chance. But my poles were gone, my goggles were gone. I had practiced skiing in a deep crouch for a month so I could hold it for a long time, way down deep, and didn't need poles. When I got up and ready to go I could see one of my ski tips was broken. The only thing holding it was the steel edge. I kept my weight off it and came in fifth.

At one point during the race I was told I was in third place, but then I got into the flats where the snow got sticky, and I started to run. Hans Otto Giese was in front of me. He was staying in the track that several other people had taken through the flats, and he was pumping. He was a cross-country champion. I heard the Mountaineers yelling, "C'mon, Wolf, we know you can do it." And I yelled, "Track", but he wouldn't step out, so I ran past him without ski poles, past this champion cross-country skier. He never forgave me. Five years ago we were at a meeting, and I reminded him, and he still didn't have a sense of humor about it. He sort of muttered, "I'll never forget that."

The race dropped 5,000 feet in 4.5 miles, and we did it in 7 1/2 minutes. Only forty-four of sixty-nine finished. I entered about three of those races, but that first one was the only time they started everyone at once.

When did you join the Mountaineers?

The Mountaineers selected three Boy Scouts each year to get three years of free membership. In 1927 I was one of those selected, not necessarily because of my character, but because I knew how to ski.

Seven years later you started the Mountaineers first climbing course.

Well, I was lucky. I had a hero in Bavaria who was a very good climber and guide and had also become a movie actor. He was in several movies that had to do with mountain drama. I wrote to him from Seattle and asked if he could send me some books on climbing technique. He sent me some books and also got me in touch with a publisher over there. I scraped money together and bought all the German books I could; pamphlets of all kinds that had to do with winter mountaineering, bivouacking, avalanches.

Was there anything comparable being written in the States at that time?

No, there was nothing like that. People like Forrie Farr, Art Winder, Norval Grigg had learned climbing the hard way, their own way. They had never seen a piton before. They were doing shoulder belays. They were older and were in sort of a clique. They kept to themselves. When I got in, they would never teach me anything. I was just an upstart, a kid. They believed you had to learn it yourself. It was because of that I felt somebody should be teaching mountaineering techniques and not holding it to themselves. That's what got me into it.

Jack Hossack was in my first class, and he and others became the first teachers. What I would do is read these German books, on the weekends practice this stuff, and the next week I would be teaching it at the clubroom. There was this big staircase and people would line up at the bottom and I would rappel down. The older group kind of hung around on the side and finally took up with us. I think they looked askance at first, but they knew already that everything they had learned about skiing had come from Europe. So they thought that if they are so far ahead of us in skiing they're way ahead of us in mountaineering too.

We had about twenty in our first class and it went over real good. So I taught a second course. The people who graduated from the second course became the instructors for the beginner's course.

To your knowledge, were there any other mountaineering courses being taught at that time in the United States?

I don't know. I'm sure the rock climbing section of the Sierra Club must have had a course. They were ahead of us in rock climbing, but we knew little or nothing about them. I was just thinking that it must have been a parallel development. They were exciting times.

It was shortly after you started the climbing class that you made the first ascent of the Ptarmigan Ridge on Rainier.

Jack Hossack and I climbed it in 1934. It was the first time the mountain had been climbed from the north side. You know when you live here that long, and you see that mountain out there, and the side of the mountain you see has never been climbed, that got to me.

Why did you choose that particular route?

It seemed to be the easiest route for the north face. I had tried twice before with Hans Grage. One time we got to 12,000 feet and he got sick, just before we got to the actual ice work. Hans was a heavy smoker and that did it. I'll never forget how we went down. I half-carried the guy. In those days we thought two was the fastest way to travel on the mountain. When Jack and I tried the route, my former wife hiked up with us to Echo Rocks. Then we gave her the signal that we were okay and were going on. She drove my Model A Ford around the mountain and was to meet us at Paradise. Well, it took a lot longer, about fifty hours. And we had no sleeping bags. We just had sleeping bag covers. We were cold but so exhausted that it didn't matter. We had a little Japanese stove and cooked tea.

The biggest problem with that route was rockfall. We had to expose ourselves to it. We got off to an early start but still had the ice stuff whistling past us. In those days we had no helmets. There were a lot of things we didn't have. When I think of it now I don't see how we did it. Jack saved me from going over at one point. I had knickers on. My crampons caught in a knicker, and I slipped, but he held me on glare ice. We didn't have the knowledge or sense to have at least three in the party. From that standpoint, it wasn't good safety practice as we look at it today. It was about twenty years before somebody climbed it again. And then they didn't use the same route.

Liberty Ridge has become the classic northside route on Rainier.

Yes. Ome Daiber climbed Liberty Ridge about two weeks after us. I don't even think he knew we had made the first northside climb. I put in the register, "The first climb of the north face", and that must have hurt them. I would have liked to see my route become the popular one, but I had to tell people that I wouldn't recommend it to anyone.

Was Ptarmigan Ridge your first big first ascent?

Well, I really wasn't after first ascents. I had a very different philosophy than a lot of people in those days. I was probably a little more juvenile and idealistic. I picked up through my books the idea that you didn't use the mountains as a climbing apparatus. For a number of years I didn't want to put in a piton. Putting in a piton was almost blasphemy, only to be put in as the last thing, never as direct aid. We used rock belays. What I was out to do was climb more difficult routes on mountains that had already been climbed.

31

I wasn't out for first ascents—new routes, yes.

Tell me about the first ascent of Mount Goode.

I had never been up there before, but you got to hearing about all these guys trying to climb it. It got bigger and bigger in your mind. Here was this chimney with a huge chockstone; the ideal thing. Climbers were always stopped there. The funny thing was that when we went up to climb it, there was a Canadian party that also wanted to be the first on Goode. It was one of those rare coincidences. We were on the same boat going up Lake Chelan and there was only one car to take you to the end of the road. Well, I had made arrangements for the car ahead of time. So we got to the dock and here were these guys with climbing gear. They were going to the North Cascades and that was fine. But slowly it came out that they wanted to be the first to climb Mount Goode. We didn't tell them what we were doing. It turned out we were trying different routes, and we got the car and a head start.

Jack and I were the lead rope and we got to the chockstone and had to make a finger traverse and do a swing around the chockstone. Then after that hard work it was just another fifty feet of crawling up on your hands and knees. So we were ahead and George, Phil and Don were still down below. They used a couple of pitons. So I told Jack, "I'm going to sneak up to the top. You stay right here above them." When they got up we sat there with sad looks on our faces. They said, "What's the matter?" We pointed to the top and a rock cairn I had built and said that those Canadians had beaten us to the top. When we got there they asked where the register was and we told them the truth. You should have seen the look on their faces.

What did you think about the next wave of climbers who used more hardware?

There were some who were using the mountains to do gymnastic tricks, and to me, that wasn't mountaineering. I knew the Beckey brothers when they were six or seven years old. His father was our family doctor. I remember babysitting those guys. He came into climbing after I got out of it. He asked me to go climbing with him many times. He wanted me to climb Waddington, but I was too busy with my work. So I never climbed with him. I was a little bit worried about some of his climbing, safetywise, but I think he's done just a tremendous job, and

I think he's had a good spirit and philosophy towards mountaineering.

Did you ever conceive of a time when people would make their living as mountaineers?

In part maybe. When I was seven or eight, living in the Alps, my friends and I used to walk down the village street imitating our heroes, the mountain guides. They were old guys, sort of bent over in a climbing position a bit like Swiss cows having one short leg and one long one.

When did you start the Mountain Rescue Council?

In 1948. I had seen the Bavarian Red Cross doing this thing in Germany, and they were just getting back to it after the war. A publisher of mountain books in Munich was just starting to get his business going from the ruins of his building, and he gave me some books. Otto Trott and Kurt Biehm translated the book into English. Otto Trott, Ome Daiber and myself were the nucleus of the group.

We started out with the Seattle group, and after about six years we brought in branches. Out of that came the idea for an association. My job was really to get the various agencies to cooperate. At the time there was nothing like that. You see, we needed the sheriff's office. We needed the Forest Service. We needed the Coast Guard even. In those days we used their helicopter, although they weren't supposed to go into the mountains. They did it on the QT, more or less. We had a heck of a time bringing it all together. For one thing, all the agencies were on different radio frequencies.

One time during a crevasse rescue I needed a saw. The Forest Service was right below us. We could see them with our eyes, and yet to reach them we had to have one of our radio men, who had a short wave, make contact with a ham operator in Seattle who phoned the Forest Service office in Seattle and they phoned the guy right below us. He then brought up the saw in a chopper. We had those sorts of problems to solve.

When we first started Mountain Rescue, we had three sponsors: The Seattle Mountaineers, Washington Alpine Club and the Ski Patrol. For the first couple of years our major job was selling our reason for being to the public and various public agencies. And we used Ome Daiber's name and fame. We told him that too. But that was right up his alley. If you look at some books on mountain rescue, you may see Ome swinging off a rope. And that was Ome. He liked being our front. Then as we rescued people, friends and relatives would donate money which we would throw into the kitty. I remember we had a hard time getting our first rescue truck, a four-by-four postal delivery truck. Over the years the Air Force would donate equipment that they loaned us for rescues.

Did you have regularly scheduled practice sessions?

We had conferences, which were really a highlight for us. The first one was at the clubroom at the Mountaineers. We had to give the Sheriff's Office and State Patrol an idea of what we were doing. At the second conference I decided to get out in the field and really show those people what we could do. At later conferences we invited groups from Oregon and B.C. We had people coming in with new ideas and we would test them. We learned a lot at these conferences.

How did the Mountain Rescue evolve into regional groups?

We decided that for efficiency, we needed a group that could get into the Olympics real fast, or up to Mount Baker, before we could get there. So Whatcom, Port Angeles and others were created. By this time I had dropped out of the association. My job had been to sell the idea. But many of the guys who got involved saw the adventure in it.

You seem to have been on the cutting edge of a lot of movements in the outdoor field; mountaineering courses, mountain rescue, kayaking and skiing.

To a large degree I was concerned with teaching safety. Anything that has a little hazard tied to it needs classes, needs to get away from the self-inflicted experience. I first called our mountain rescue organization "Mountain Rescue and Safety Council" because education and safety were part of what we were about. But the name was too long. And there was the idea of pioneering. With climbing and kayaking classes and mountain rescue it was a wonderful feeling knowing that you were starting something that is now going on by itself quite nicely.

From his handshake to his thick crewcut hair, everything about Jack Hossack seems solid. A snug-fitting wool sweater betrays no flabbiness, and he walks quickly and fluidly while giving a tour of his home on the Olympic Peninsula. Jack Hossack could easily be 53, but he is thirty years older. He hikes four miles every day in less than an hour. In the 1930s he walked three miles to work and back every day. His wife, Mary, who was an active Mountaineer herself, says, "Jack was always very healthy, and I was always trying to fatten him up. He was so thin."

« The first ice axe I had was a Chamonix, and it was light. As a matter of fact when Wolf Bauer and I climbed the Ptarmigan Ridge on Rainier, the doggone prong on that thing just about doubled back because we hit rock embedded in ice. Wolf's ice axe was the same way. We just took rocks and straightened 'em out again. »

—Jack Hossack

Hossack was one of a small group of climbers, including Wolf Bauer, Phillip Dickert, Lloyd Anderson and George MacGowan, that brought European-style climbing to the Cascades in the 1930s. Using new techniques and hardware they solved climbing problems that had puzzled climbers for years—the north face of Mount Rainier, and many of the rugged North Cascade peaks. The new style brought with it a new confidence, what oldtime Mountaineers considered brashness.

Jack Hossack remembers his first climb of Mount Rainier being a "breeze." He says pretty much the same thing about first ascents of Rainier's Ptarmigan Ridge, Mount Challenger and Goode, as well as the north ridge of the Grand Teton. Challenger was not very difficult, Goode had only one hard spot, and the Grand Teton was "nothing like a struggle." He will allow that Ptarmigan Ridge was a lot of hard work. There is no false modesty in his terse assessments. For him they are simply statements of fact.

Blessed with strength, style and an engineer's logical approach to problem solving, Hossack and friends paved the way for Beckey, Schoening, and the Whittakers.

Hossack, perhaps born a generation too early, could easily have continued to make first ascents well into his sixties. He climbed the North Ridge of Sir Donald when he was sixty, and a decade later he climbed 11,500-foot Mount Temple in the Canadian Rockies. He dismisses it as a walk up scree slopes, even though it was 10.5 miles of walking. When asked what peak he would have most liked to climb, he says, "I really wanted to get up Assiniboine. It's a thirty-one-mile hike. I doubt if I'll try it now. That's a real captivating peak." There is hint in Jack Hossack's voice that if the right circumstances arose, he might just give it a try.

▲

Do you remember your first climb in the Cascades?

Jack Hossack: I wanted to get into the mountains by the time I was ten, but my parents didn't have a car and there was no way to get there. I finally got there through the outdoor club at Franklin High School. Our first trip was a climb of Mount Baker. I don't even think I had an alpenstock.

I've always wondered how climbers stopped a fall with those things.

Jack: It's very effective. You use the point of the alpenstock just like you do the point on the shaft of your ice axe. You get pretty good purchase. As a matter of fact I used one for years. I climbed Mount Rainier with an alpenstock a number of times.

Most of the people going into the mountains in those days didn't have much technique. My folks gave me an ice axe when I was about twenty. They said, "If you're going to spend a lot of time in the mountains you may as well have this." The first one I had was a Chamonix, and it was light. As a matter of fact when Wolf Bauer and I climbed the Ptarmigan Ridge on Rainier the doggone prong on that thing just about doubled back because we hit rock embedded in ice. Wolf's ice axe was the same way. We just took rocks and straightened 'em out again.

When did you first start doing more difficult climbs?

Jack: I would say probably in 1934. Challenger may have been my first first ascent. It really wasn't difficult.

Cliff Leight: Did you drive those first pitons in on the summit pyramid of Challenger?

Jack: No, I think we just had a double-roped belay on a rock. The first pitons we had were pretty heavy, crude implements. The hardware you get today is in a different league altogether. We'd carry about five to six pounds of carabiners and eight to ten pitons and a hammer. We didn't

travel with anywhere near the weight that people carry nowadays. You see these guys with a belt just loaded. The climbing we did was child's play compared with what they do today.

But you had no guidebook when you went into Challenger. Were there any written descriptions?

Jack: Oh no, just a forestry map. That's all. There weren't any topographic maps available. Jim Martin, Herb Strandberg and Bill Degenhardt had been into the Pickets before, going up Goodell Creek. There was real satisfaction in getting up some of these peaks for the first time. Hermann Ulrichs had tried Mount Goode a number of times. You could see the marks, scratches in the rocks that showed how high he'd gotten each time. But we always enjoyed any kind of climb. It didn't have to be a first ascent to be enjoyable.

Mary: He was what I would call a peak bagger.

Jack: We made a first ascent on the Grand Teton during a Mountaineers summer outing. We were going to rest up a day while another group of Mountaineers was on Owen. George MacGowan, Jim Crooks and I said we'd head up the Teton Glacier and see what it looked like. We left the glacier and here's a nice looking ridge running up to the Grand. We took a look at that and it was so easy we were up the Grand before the others were to the top of Owen. It was a first ascent but nothing like a struggle. We had to make a few stands on shoulders to reach holds, but we didn't use a bit of hardware.

Mary: It was a very fast ascent. We were on Owen watching.

Norval Grigg said that on most of his climbs he didn't rappel but rather climbed hand over hand down the rope.

Jack: Wolf Bauer introduced the rappel, the Dulfersitz, and the new technique using the carabiner. The carabiner brake was much better. I've still got a rope burn from a Dulfersitz rappel we did on the Grand. I was careless and didn't get the rope under my collar. We were up there in a lightning storm and wanted to get down fast.

Did you ever have any close calls on any of your trips?

Mary: How about the last time you led a big Mountaineer group up Rainier via the Kautz? We had a party of forty-one and they had just gotten off the Kautz and it hadn't been more than five minutes and a horrific shower, not just a shower, but a huge chunk of ice fell off where the party had just come.

Jack: The Kautz Icefall is very strange. You can go up it and it doesn't indicate any movement at all. At other times, you never know, away she goes. We hadn't been off the icefall ten minutes when carloads of ice came down.

Mary: The old mountain still has a lot of clout.

Did you ever have a partner injured?

Jack: Not on a club climb. I got involved with mountain rescue when Wolf started it. A fellow by the name of Jim White got a bump on the head up in the Monte Cristo area. What made it bad was that we had a registered nurse in the outfit and she, of course, imagined the worst possible conditions. He had a headache and may have had a concussion. She said he shouldn't even walk but should be carried out. So we had to improvise a stretcher, cut poles down and use our jackets. We took him down over cliffs, belayed him down and got him down after hours and hours. She told him, now you make sure you get to a doctor, and if you feel bad go to a hospital. We heard later on that he went to a movie that night.

This didn't involve an accident but we got into trouble once for climbing Mount Rainier. It was one of our first trips and we stopped at the entrance to register. It was lousy weather. We weren't sure we were going to climb at all. At Sunrise we told the guy there that we weren't sure we were going to climb but were going to wander up a ways. The higher we got the better the weather got. We thought, "Phooey, we're not going to go back to Sunrise and register." So we made the climb and when we came back down the ridge, here were some rangers and they said, "The chief ranger wants to see you." We thought what now? He said, "You guys shouldn't have gone up without registering. Technically you're under arrest."

So we went down and the ranger said, "You folks have violated the law and we're going to give you a hearing Tuesday night at Longmire. The park commissioner will be there and you'll be tried."

We came up the following Tuesday and appeared before the commissioner. The chief ranger read the list of charges. I don't know how many there were, but we said not guilty to all of them. He said the biggest problem was that we weren't experienced, but we had done a lot of climbing. He said, "But I'm sure you're guilty of lack of experience because experienced climbers don't go out over glaciers." Well, we made monkeys of them, actually. Finally the commissioner said, "To prevent this thing from becoming a farce, we're going to fine you fellows $2.50 each."

Did you ever have any trips that were complete washouts?

Jack: We went up to climb King George once, which was right across the Canadian border, near Chilliwack Lake. The first boner we made was trying to cross the Chilliwack River. It was miserable weather and we almost lost a man trying to cross it. He got washed down the river. Finally we got across and worked our way down the other side of the river and found a bridge about a half-mile away.

Did you ever have a yen to do a big expedition?
Jack: Oh yeah.

Mary: I think you should have had the chance Jack. Dee Molenaar said when you guys climbed the Northeast Ridge of Sir Donald that you could have gone on a Himalayan expedition.

Did you ever climb with the Whittaker brothers?

Jack: No, they were just getting started. They were in the Scouts. I could never tell the Whittakers apart. I guess you can identify them a little more easily now, but they had more hair then.

When did you stop doing adventuresome climbs?

Jack: Probably when my climbing groups broke up. Climbers tend to have a little group or team. At least we did. People passed on or went on to other things.

Mary: You climbed the Northwest Ridge of Sir Donald with Dee and Maury Muzzy about twenty-two years ago.

Jack: That was a real fun climb.

So you've kept pretty active then.

Jack: I don't know how Fred Beckey can still be doing serious climbing. I mean, my muscles tend to cramp, my fingers cramp. I'd be afraid of being in a real tough spot.

Cliff: It doesn't seem to worry Fred much. He is still in real good shape. The one climb I did with him, a first ascent in the Valhallas, had six pitches of 5.8 rock climbing. Fred had no problem and led part of the way.

It was a horrible hike in there. He had his directions all screwed up. A good friend had told him the most direct route into this basin. We were going every which way, and we were lost in the bushes. We were laughing about these great directions.

Fred was up in Canada with a friend of mine a year ago in the winter, and they were looking over this map. Fred said, "This map doesn't have any detail. Who wrote this thing?" And my friend pointed to the bottom of the map and said, "Fred, you did."

Mary: We still hike a lot. Jack hikes four miles every morning in an hour. We do lots of canoeing.

Jack: About five years ago I went up Mount Temple, above Moraine Lake, but that's just a walk, about 10.5 miles and just scree slopes to the top.

Mary: Well, by the time you reach this age, if you're healthy, you feel as if it is sort of a bonus.

Jane MacGowan clearly remembers her first trip into the mountains in 1920. "Our first trip, long before we could afford a car, was to take the train and go up to Monte Cristo on that little, narrow gauge railroad. We rode in open cars. That was exciting. I saw for the first time Glacier Basin. We stayed in a motel at Monte Cristo. In fact there was a little bit of sporadic mining going on up there."

MacGowan's parents joined the Mountaineers a few years after its creation in 1906. Her mother was particularly avid.

« I was just plain and simple a peak bagger. I would never do it now, although there was a time I

would go in the worse weather if I wanted to get something. »
—*Jane MacGowan*

"Back in those days, the idea of mountaineering for women still involved wearing long dresses. Mountaineering then was really hiking on a rather modest scale. They'd hike out to Fort Lawton or something like that. I mean, this was rugged country. But both of my parents just loved mountains."

MacGowan joined the Mountaineers in 1929 when still a teenager. She is modest about her mountaineering skills. "Mountaineering was hard work for me," she says. "I'm strong and determined. I'm not agile." MacGowan did climb most of the major peaks in Washington and many in the Canadian Selkirks and Bugaboos.

She was not a leader. Few women chose to or were allowed to in those days. She met her husband, George, on a Mountaineers outing in the Selkirks and continued climbing with him until his death in 1954. George was among the best climbers in the Northwest during the 1930s. There were some climbs, like Sir Donald, that he would not let Jane attempt, and she agreed with his judgement.

Her children started hiking at an early age, and today MacGowan hikes with her grandchildren. Her home in Fauntleroy has few obvious reminders of her climbing days, but with very little coaxing, she shows us her ice axe and kletterschue, which after several decades still serve as her walking shoes.

▲

Jane MacGowan: We were all working at Boeing during World War II. I was working in tooling with George. Boyd Busey, a Mountaineer, was head of that department at the time. VJ Day came and Jack Hossack called up and said, "Let's go. We've gotta climb something."

Somebody said, "What?" Now we hadn't been able to do anything for four years except hike around here. We decided to climb Three Fingers. And George said, "That's kind of far for a day."

Jack said, "Oh, your grandmother could climb it." We got about ten together and got our food together. The trail was completely grown over up French Creek. We knew what we had to do, get up to Goat Flats. But with bucking the trail and being out of condition, frankly, we just staggered up to that little lake below Goat Flats. We plopped down, got up very early and got up to Goat Flats and climbed the north finger. I was just exhausted. We just weren't in condition. But we had to get down and out, and we were afraid we'd be benighted because the flashes started to run out late at night. But we finally made it out.

I joined the Mountaineers in 1929. I was pretty young. The reason I joined so young was because my parents were members with Edmund Meany. And so we kind of had mountains in our family. I started climbing before they organized the Mountaineers climbing course. My husband was one of the men instrumental in getting that started. So I was actually climbing before that, but not technically much, except just getting up there.

Who taught you?

I just signed up for climbs and went. I was determined to get my pins. I started doing the majors and the twenty mountains of the first and second pins. Some of them were quite hard. I did all that before I took the climbing course. You might be interested, but I'm number 26 in the REI.

I'm still a mountaineer and I still hike on a modified scale. Two summers ago I went to Europe hiking with the British in North Wales, Devon and Dorsett, Scotland, staying in the British friendship houses. They're beautiful old manors, marvelous old houses.

I'm not climbing. I'm hiking. I was on Rainier recently, hiking around, but I'm too old

for that and I know better. But you know ten or eleven mountain miles can get you a pretty good workout.

What were the Mountaineers like in the early days?

Oh, it was wonderful, probably one of the happiest times of my life. I don't think there were more than six-hundred altogether, and there weren't as many activities as there are now, but if you wanted a climbing group you just got one together. My favorite lodge was Meany. Every night there would be something going on. If nothing, old-time dancers. We always had a player and we really beat up the dust. Paul Shorrock was a great one at leading those. I took a few small parts in the Mountaineers plays, but it was an awful lot of work and rain pouring down on you. I think I was the Red Knight in Alice in Wonderland. I remember that papier mache armor, with rain pouring down through the helmet. I lost my interest in acting right there.

We were all more or less peak baggers at the time. It wasn't like it is now where you're climbing routes. We knew the Beckeys and all the great climbers. The Whittakers grew up here in Fauntleroy. We knew and marveled at them. I was just plain and simple a peak bagger. I would never do it now, although there was a time I would go in the worst weather if I wanted to get something.

I started out with an alpenstock. You couldn't get an ice axe. When we got the REI going, Lloyd Anderson immediately sent over to Germany or Switzerland and a shipment of ice axes came back. I still have my ice axe. It's an antique.

In Washington I climbed Shuksan, Whitehorse, Three Fingers, Stuart, Cathedral Rock, Constance. The hardest peak was up in the Bugaboos. In 1937, by that time I had climbed quite a bit around here, and I decided to try something different. I got two of my friends and joined the Canadian Alpine Club in the Yoho Valley. Up there we climbed President, Marpole. It was the first time I had a Swiss Guide. They brought him in from Lake O'Hara. Whew, he had quite a personality. All he ever said to me was, "A little more speed please." I hadn't had technique yet. So here I was trying to climb this ridge of the Marpole thing. I'd climbed Shuksan and things like that, but this was different.

The next year I went to the Selkirks and climbed. George would not let me climb Sir Donald. He was right, but I climbed all the others. That was when we became engaged. I met him up there. He was running the Mountaineers outing. The next year was the Tetons, and that's when George and Jack Hossack made that quite well-known climb on the northeast face of the Grand. Never been climbed before. They were so used to each other's climbing that they made it in record time. It's still spoken of. I was climbing Owen right across the valley, so we could see those two little specks.

After a while we didn't care about the big Mountaineers outings. Too many rules and too big. It's much nicer to go with a small group of your friends.

My husband died when the kids were seven and ten months, and I think the first campout after that Laurie was eighteen months. She was walking. I took them out all the time, with the Mountaineers. We had a real close group of friends and everyone took their kids. I took Doug into Lake O'Hara, when George was still alive. He had to hike eight miles and he was five.

Have you ever been involved in a climbing accident?

Not personally, but one of the worst was on Glacier. In those days you had to take about two days to get in from Lake Wenatchee. We had a pack horse, four men and myself and my mother. She loved to go on these trips. She wouldn't climb the mountain, but she was such a good hiker. So she went along, I guess, to make it legal for me to go on it. We camped at Indian Pass and White Pass.

The man guiding us was Ernest Fitzimmons, who was a well-known mountaineer and violin teacher in Seattle; very nice man. We climbed the peak easy enough, and we sat on top for a while, started down, glissading, not more than one-hundred yards from the top, when a rock avalanche broke loose and came down on us. With glissading it's terribly hard to look back and see which way these big rocks are coming. Fitz was being a gentleman and waiting for me to catch up. I glissaded a little more cautiously than the others did. And he was the one hit in the right hip and knocked way down the slope. Then the avalanche calmed down. Nobody else was hurt. But he had a badly fractured hip, the bone out, terrible. So what to do?

There were two men and myself and just off of the mountain, very remote from any help. No mountain rescue in those days. So we gave him all our extra clothes and got him off the glacier and onto a rock spur, and the two men told me to go on down by myself and get help, because they could haul rocks and make kind of a shelter. He would have frozen otherwise. Fitz never complained. He could take it. I hadn't been climbing very long. We'd crossed these crevasses so carefully on the way up. I was supposed to go down and they said, "If you see anyone alive, and they can come up here, bring them up, because two of us can't take him down."

I managed to follow footsteps, and the weather was nice, thank goodness. The crevasses were at such an angle that I was able to jump without too much trouble. I did get off toward the end, because we had climbed in the dark, and I was kind of anxious to get off the darned glacier, long before I should have. I heard a lot of sheep, and I figured that where there were sheep there would be shepherds. I tried to scream and holler and all that sort of thing. But nobody came out. I didn't know where the shepherds were. They had to be somewhere. So I took my ice axe and started poking the sheep, sort of stampeding them. By this time I was just scared to death, and when I saw the shepherds, I was even more scared, because they were actually Basque. They spoke French, and I'd had quite a lot of French so I could talk with them. They were grizzled looking and one of them had one eye. They had guns. But they couldn't have been nicer.

I managed to make them understand what had happened and pointed to the footsteps and up to where the accident was, and they did understand. They went tearing down to get sleeping bags and make up some kind of stretcher. They took their dogs and with the two men up there worked all night. They got him down to a shepherd's hut and there he stayed. It took about a week before they could get him out.

In the meantime I had to find my way back to White Pass. I knew I'd gone wrong, but I had a pretty good sense of direction, so I kept working my way to the setting sun. I was too tired to get back the elevation I had lost, so I was beating through brush. I was rather foolish. I finally got to White Pass and just about collapsed. Then Clarence, who had stayed behind, just about ran down that trail and got the ranger at Lake Wenatchee and that ranger organized the party. All he could get then were CCC boys who were from New York and had never even seen a mountain before, let alone gone up one. My mother and I kept a vigil but were running out of food, hoping for the best, and it was getting kind of scary again.

That evening, along the skyline, there came the funniest looking sight. There was a horse. The ranger was riding it. He had a lot of stuff with him. Behind the horse, actually hanging on to the tail, were these CCC boys. One hanging on to the tail. I should have taken a picture. They were just dead tired. The whole rescue took about a week, then the weather broke and it rained. And mom and I had to cook for all these folks. What a vacation! But we finally got him down. That's about the only accident. Fitz never walked right after that. They got him to Leavenworth—not the Leavenworth you see today, pretty drab little place—and put him in traction but it never healed properly.

He had to walk with a cane. But he never complained.

I really preferred rock climbs to snow and ice. I think that gets awfully boring, like Rainier. When I climbed St. Helens, it was early enough we could glissade. I didn't like the Gibraltar route on Rainier because you had to hurry. You had to be back down under Gibraltar by, at least one o'clock. So fast, you couldn't stay on top long enough. I made all the majors on the first try except for Adams, which was the third try.

Did you have a sense that what you were doing in the mountains was in any way pioneering?

In those day we were considered oddballs, really and truly. But we were very unusual. One night a group of us were caught out after a climb of Hibox. When we got out, we had to get back to our cars at Mount Margaret, and nobody would pick us up. We looked terrible, just tramps. I know Fauntleroy thought I was crazy. They still do (She laughs).

*H*arland Eastwood played football in high school and college. His regular position was quarterback, in the days when quarterbacks were blockers, although he occasionally got to handle the ball. "We had a couple of plays where I'd pass," he says, "just for fun, if we were ahead. One of the halfbacks would get the ball and he'd hand it to me. The first couple of times I threw the thing, everybody on the other side stood there with their mouths open. I could sling that damn ball almost forty yards, like nothing." Eastwood was tall, strong, agile—he was a champion high hurdler in high school. He was also one-armed.

« I did quite well going up, and I carried a piton hammer and a couple of pitons, and 150 feet of rope and I used the rope for letting myself down. If I could I'd just pull

one end or else I'd just leave the piton there. I was fairly good going up, but going down was horrible. »
—*Harland Eastwood*

Eastwood lost his arm in a hunting accident when he was a teenager, but he refused to accept it as a handicap, and it has rarely kept him from doing what he wanted to do, whether it was football, climbing mountains, downhill skiing, fire-fighting, piloting boats, building homes, or driving a stick-shift truck. Harland also developed an aversion to the word no, and often the people who said it to him. Eastwood has always been two parts abrasive, one part roguish charm, and several parts bulldog determination.

Shortly after arriving in Seattle, Eastwood distinguished himself on the epic search, in 1936, for the body of Delmar Fadden on Mount Rainier in the dead of winter. Although still a relative novice in the mountains, he spent several days in frigid temperatures high on the mountain searching for the lost climber. Eastwood later worked for the National Park and Forest services. While working for the Forest Service, he spent his honeymoon with his first wife, Catherine, manning the remote and airy Three Fingers Lookout.

During the winters he and Catherine started a mountaineering equipment company which until World War II made a variety of tents, parkas, packs, ice axes and freeze-dried food which sold all over the country. They retired to Lopez Island in the San Juan Islands. Catherine died in the late 1970s, and several years later Harland married Esther Carhart, a teacher and world traveler. One of her teaching assignments had been in Bulgaria. For their honeymoon Harland customized a VW van and toured Europe. They have visited my wife and me in Helena on a couple of occasions and have refused our offers of beds each time. Eastwood is presently at work on a memoir of his days with the Forest Service.

▲

When you moved to Seattle did you get involved with any mountaineering clubs?

Harland Eastwood: No, Eddie Bauer and I got to be real good friends, and I was down seeing him one day when the word came that Delmar Fadden had tried to climb Mount Rainier in January.

On the Delmar Fadden rescue, you weren't part of any organized group.

When the word came in that they wanted volunteers, I went home to get my stuff. In the meantime the rescue team all came into Eddie Bauer's and we talked, and took our cars. In those days we had to park our cars out on the highway that runs from Enumclaw and Chinook, out there by the billboard that said Mather Memorial. That's as far as you could go. We had to ski in the rest of it to White River Campground. Fadden had probably been missing for three to four days.

How long were you out on the mountain?

It was the seven or eight days that I was above Steamboat Prow which is around 11,000 feet. It was the middle of January. Nighttime, anywhere we could, we'd put an ice piton in and tie it to our sleeping bags and get down inside of it. I had an eider down bag. The down came from Hudson Bay. In those days the Eskimos could take the nests of the eider down and sell it. I can't remember all the names of the people with me. Wendell Trosper was in the back. There was a man from the Park Service who did the telephone work. I had come down after that long time of looking to White River, and a plane flew over and saw the body. The reason was that there was such a wind and it took the new snow from out around the body. His feet was sticking up in the air. So then I was delegated to go up and bring the body down.

How long did it take you to get the body out?

Well, he was about 1,500 feet above the Prow. It took us a little while to chop the body out of the ice. He was buried about up to his shoulders.

Were you able to ascertain at that point how he had died?

No, we didn't pay any attention to that. We had a piece of canvas and I wrapped him in it. And in places where we could, we just let the body free ride. It was real steep, and real hard. Of course, it was about minus 40. Instead of trying to toboggan him, we just let him go. There was no place for him to go anyway. The crevasses were all covered up.

What sort of clothing did you wear to survive in those frigid temperatures?

I was getting ready to do some climbing. I had silk underwear that was made in China and silk socks. My mother knitted a hat that went over my head with just a mouth and a nose in it and eyes. I had some woolen underwear, and a windproof parka. That was about all. The thing we worried about most was eating. The Park Service was supposed to be right up there giving us help, but they never showed up. We had one little Primus stove made in Sweden. I still have it.

You didn't have tents. Did you have any insulation under your bags?

No. With the freezing temperatures, it was just hard. It didn't melt any. One thing that I've always felt bad about this whole thing was I told the boys to get themselves some food and stuff to bring with them. Nobody brought anything. Well, I had made some pemmican up, and I had some nuts and raisins, some cheese and stuff. And at night I ate it in my sleeping bag, because with the five of us it wouldn't have lasted any. I decided that being that high up, in that kind of temperature, I was going to take care of myself. The Park Service was down at the campground doing the publicity work.

The weather was bad, with high winds. Sometimes I'd look back down the rope and Wendy Trosper would be knocked flat. He was quite a heavy boy. During those bad days we just kept on the best we could. We kept roped up. We had two-hundred feet of rope.

After the rescue were you still interested in climbing?

Oh yeah, we went on and climbed Mount Baker, Glacier Peak, Rainier of course, Adams and St. Helens. I climbed mostly with a fellow by the name of Bart Gagnon from Yakima. He was with the Cascadians. I hadn't gotten into college yet. I didn't get into college until 1935.

Did you join the Mountaineers?

I never joined any club. Everybody asked me if I wanted to go, so I just went. There was never a problem finding people to climb with. I never went on any of those big outings with fifty or a hundred people.

When you had to belay someone, did you have a special technique for stopping them if they fell?

Well, falling on the ice axe or laying the pick down and squishing your body on it. Sometime the ice was so hard the crampons just slid on it like skates.

Did you have to develop a special self arrest technique?

Yes. I carried a couple of ice pitons. I think it was late 1929, I took a two-week course with Hans and Heinz Fuhrer who were the Swiss guides on Mount Rainier at the time. My ice axe came from Mount Blanc, which I still have. That's why I still wear my little black hat. They said, "You bear da little hat on da head and you keep varm all da time." They gave me instruction more just because they knew me, and got a kick out of a one-armed fella. They never charged me anything, but I just went with them to Camp Muir and things like that.

Did you go out on any other rescues while you were working for the Park Service?

Oh, nothing. When I was there it was mostly Saturday and Sunday nights out looking for lost kids, people with broken legs, climbing along Sourdough Ridge, Mount Fremont, just local stuff. I made a few trips up to the summit looking for people who were supposed to have been lost, but we never found. They had came out and went down the other side.

Did you get involved with the Silver Skis race?

Yes, I was with the ski patrol, just under McClure's Rock, when Sig Hall died. He hit a rock at full speed and he crashed into this rock and killed himself right in front of me. The weather was so bad later on, that we put the body under-neath some trees and even the mountain goats came in and lay down alongside of us, and the next morning we brought the body down. They had gotten the race finished, but I was by myself and by the time they got somebody up to help me with the body the weather had gone bad. When he hadn't showed up at Edith Creek, they knew he was somewhere along the way. He was on full bore and it was steep there. I'm sure he died instantly.

When you joined the ski patrol, what sort of test did you have to take to qualify?

Nothing, they just said, "Do you want Snoqualmie Pass for the winter?" So I went up there. Some of us up there got together and called ourselves the Snow Owl Ski Patrol. And that's what was the first group there for a couple of years. That's all they did.

In the beginning the ski area was a little bit larger at the bottom than it was at the top and straight down, one tow. Now trees are gone everywhere. It was first run by the Seattle Park Board, then something happened and the Forest Service took it over and called it Government Hill for a while. I would go up Thursday evening and come back Sunday night. Most of the time I just stayed up there at the station. And I got in a little skiing myself.

When did you start your outdoor equipment company?

You know, I don't know. I started it one winter after I was married, so I would guess about 1937. I started making little back packs and some belt packs and we sold a bunch of them to Sun Valley and then I made ski waxes and then we'd go into the Forest Service about the first of May and then get back in September and sometimes Catherine would go down and start the stuff, making packs and mitts and all that kind of stuff. And we made tents and dried food.

Did you make everything that you sold?

Yes, just about. We made our own ice axes, crampons. I had the crampons forged. I had a forge in the back yard, and my dad would hold them while I hammered, knocked 'em over and got them all evened up.

Did you have a storefront?

No, I had a salesman in California and one in New Hampshire and they sold the stuff for me.

Was it ever something you thought about doing full-time?

Probably. If the war hadn't come along I would have. Yeah, I started with a sewing machine and about $50. We made some little packs that went around the waist. We bought several skins of harbor seal and slit em up and made little diagrams on 'em, make em look nice. And Sun Valley would buy them by the gross.

Nobody else had these like mitts and little packs, one-day packs. Then we made a thing for the ski patrols, they fit around the waist and pockets for all the different things. And we sold those things like hot cakes.

I named the packs I made K-2 packs. Gee, I sold a lot of that dried food. I had it made specially for me down in California. I'd get it in five-gallon cans, and we'd package it. It was all pretty good stuff.

It lasted about four years. Some of those days in there, we were so busy I didn't keep much records. But it was a full-time job, boy. It was called the Harland Eastwood Company. I made alpenstocks, too. The Mountaineers bought a lot of those. I had special braided rope that I had made up—four strand. It was made by a company in Vermont. They made it for me in hundred-foot and two-hundred-foot lengths. At the fifty-foot mark I wound thread around it and on each end it was a different color so you'd know where you were on the rope. The only thing I didn't make was carabiners. I got them from Switzerland from a company named Fritsch. I bought some tricouni nails from them too.

Were your prices competitive with the other outdoor stores in Seattle, like The Outdoor Store and Eddie Bauer?

Well, they bought from me. Most of the ice axes I gave to the Outdoor Store; they were hand-forged. There was a big forging outfit down there underneath the viaduct, down in the south end near Sears and Roebuck that did the breaking of them into little pieces. I drilled the hole to put the handle in and give them the arch and polish them.

What did you do with your inventory?

It wasn't too much, easy to get rid of, because the war was starting. Everybody in the ski business was clamoring to get stuff. No, I had no problem. We sold everything.

Now you said that the Army wanted you to make a thousand sleeping bags.

Well, that was a figure of speech, but he talked about taking over production and everything and doing this and that. We'd have to do what he said. He was going to take us over lock, stock and barrel, and I didn't go for it. I don't know how I was going to get paid. I didn't get into all that. I said, "Sir, it's closed." And that was the end of it.

Were you ever able to do any sort of rock climbing?

I did quite well going up, and I carried a piton hammer and a couple of pitons, and one-hundred-fifty feet of rope and I used the rope for letting myself down. If I could I'd just pull one end or else I'd just leave the piton there. I was fairly good going up, but going down was horrible.

You must have had to rely a great deal on balance.

Yes, that's right.

That probably made you a better climber than most.

Well, as Esther says, "You're still here."

CHAPTER

10

RAY CLOUGH

In the summer of 1938 four teenage boys, Calder Bressler, Tom Myers, Bill Cox and Ray Clough, left their car at Sulphur Creek and headed for Dome Peak and points north along the trailless crest of the Cascades. Two weeks later they were back at the car having completed an alpine traverse from Miner's Ridge to Cascade Pass. They hadn't eaten anything but Jello for the past two days, their tricouni nails were worn away, dust clouds kicked up by their boots choked them the last 20 miles, but they had reason for exhilaration. Along the way they had made first ascents of LeConte, Spider, Formidable, Magic, Johannesburg, Boston, and the first summit traverse of Dome, plus early ascents of Spire, Sentinal, Old Guard, Sahale, and Buckner. The young men bestowed upon the traverse the name of their climbing club, Ptarmigan. The Ptarmigan has since become the classic alpine traverse in the Cascades, attracting climbers from all over the United States.

The Ptarmigan Climbing Club existed for only about ten years, but in that decade the loosely-organized group of young men and women explored the most remote areas of the Cascades with little attendant fanfare: the north side of Glacier Peak, the Northern and Southern Pickets, the Redoubt area, as well as the Ptarmigan Traverse.

Ray Clough says of the Ptarmigan trip, "We didn't tell anyone where we had been. It wasn't until later that people pieced together the record that was left on the peaks."

World War II and college graduation eventually brought an end to the Ptarmigans, although the mystique surrounding the club continued to grow with each passing year. Clough, who got his doctoral degree in structural engineering from MIT, taught at the University of California for 38 years. A few years ago he and his older brother, Ralph, a founding member of the Ptarmigans, spent time hiking out of Stehekin. They met many people who were familiar with the Ptarmigan Traverse and excited to meet real Ptarmigans.

I spoke to Ray Clough on the phone. He makes his home in Sun River, Oregon.

« It's interesting that the Ptarmigans turned out to be a pioneering group because there was no set intention of becoming a pioneering group. We just got ideas about

places to go, and typically we wanted to go places nobody had been before. Of course the end result of that is pioneering. »
—Ray Clough

Did you learn about climbing through the Boy Scouts?

Most of the Ptarmigans were in Boy Scout Troop 150 in Seattle. My brother was one of the older ones in that group. He's four years older than I am. It was that group that really started the Ptarmigan Climbing Club. As that Boy Scout group got older, Boy Scout activities began not to be as attractive. What we liked about scouting was being outdoors. Before quitting altogether, the George Vancouver Rover Crew was organized. As I recall Ome Daiber was one of the leaders. I was really too young to be brought into it when it was first organized. I became a member at age fifteen or sixteen. The George Vancouver Rover Crew had as its objective just going out and being out in the mountains. We became more and more interested in serious climbing. Eventually the same group decided that the Boy Scout affiliation wasn't useful anymore, so they just quit and changed the name from the George Vancouver Rover Crew to the Ptarmigan Climbing Club.

How organized was the Ptarmigan Climbing Club?

It was not organized in terms of having lots of activities other than climbs, but it did organize a sequence of climbing trips. Typically the individuals of the Ptarmigans would get together and go out in groups of three and four. Sometimes there would be a consolidated group of three or four cars on a trip.

We were continually thinking of new places to go. The one most outstanding trip that I participated in was the Ptarmigan Traverse from Sulphur Creek up along the crest to Cascade Pass and back down again on the back side.

People come from all over the country to do the Ptarmigan Traverse today. How did you choose it?

I wish I could say I was the one who did. The ones who went on the trip were Calder Bressler, Bill Cox, Tom Myers and myself. I would guess that Bill Cox and Calder Bressler were the two who had gotten the basic idea of where to go.

A trip like that in the Cascades is virtually impossible today, but you were going places no other climbers had ever been.

No question we were early in the business, and we were pretty aware of that. Of course, in those days, if somebody had been up a peak before, there would be a record, some sort of a marker or a tin can with some writing in it. If you didn't find

something like that you were pretty sure it hadn't been climbed, or if it had you could at least claim you were the first.

We followed Mountaineers journals to some extent just to see what others were doing, so we knew something about climbs being made. But we were not at all interested in becoming part of the Mountaineers. We could do what we wanted without getting tangled up in that big organization.

That set you apart from the vast majority of climbers in Washington.

In that organization we would have relatively little opportunity to choose trips, so from the time we were Boy Scouts we just decided where we wanted to go, did what we could do, and if we didn't succeed we didn't let it bother us much. One thing we were proud of was that we didn't get anyone killed (laughs).

We knew our limitations and were not willing to push our luck too far.

On the Ptarmigan Traverse did you have any problems with route finding or was the trip pretty straightforward?

Oh it was fairly straightforward in the sense that from the topog maps we knew where we wanted to go, but of course from a topog map you can't tell whether you can do it or not. So we had to just start out, see what we could see and find out if we could do it or not. In general we found it was possible to go what seemed like the appropriate route on the traverse.

When I did the traverse in 1975, I found that once you got off the glaciers, there was a footpath created by the great numbers of climbers who had done the traverse by then.

(Laughs) It's hard to imagine, but I guess it could well be.

When we were climbing there just weren't that many people in the mountains. We didn't see a soul from the time we left our car until we dropped from Cascade Pass down the drainage towards Lake Chelan at the confluence of several trails.

How did you get back to your car?

We had to make a loop. We hiked down the backside of Cascade Pass (the east side) to Agnes Creek, then from Agnes Creek to Suiattle Pass and back down to Sulphur Creek. It was a large effort. We camped one night down at Agnes

47

Creek and then hiked up over Suiattle Pass and down to the cars in one day. We were blistered by that time, and it was an uncomfortable trip to say the least. We were running out of food too.

You must have been carrying gigantic packs?

Well, we had planned on a pound of food per man per day for our rations. I forgot what we estimated our time out to be, but I think we took the exact number of days we planned on. On that trip there was not a cloud in the sky.

I don't know why we chose to go south to north. People had been up in the Dome Peak area, but from that point onward it was uncertain what we were going to find. I guess we figured if we got past that point, if we got close to Cascade Pass, we could finish the route.

What kind of equipment were you using?

We had nothing but Trapper-Nelson packs and big old wool-type sleeping bags. I don't think any of us had any idea of getting down bags in those days. We had this great big tent that we carried along, one that we made ourselves sewing together muslin and some sort of waterproofing compound. I carried that in my pack, and of course we never unrolled it. It was a heavy weight but I was glad that we never had to use it.

On the Ptarmigan you had to find campsites off the glaciers each night.

Basically we camped at the edge of the glaciers, just along the edges. At that time the glaciers made awfully good traveling. My recollection is that we didn't have much trouble choosing a path that would get us from one side to another without too much difficulty. We did have some climbing that was as hard as we cared to push it carrying packs. We had a three-quarter-inch hemp rope.

When you returned was there much of a fuss in the climbing community over what you had done.

None at all. We didn't tell anybody where we had been. It wasn't until later that people pieced together the record that was left on the peaks. I'm sure we told people we had made the trip, but I don't think we ever advertised it as an adventure.

Did the Ptarmigans have any rules or rituals?

I would say no. We didn't, as far as I can recall, have any rules at all. It was just one-hundred-percent democracy. We did have meetings occasionally which were more than planning

a trip, but I can't recall exactly what we did at those meetings. Anyway, we just decided we were going to do things, like going on ski trips. We climbed St. Helens and skied down once. There were about five or six women in the group who were active. One of them was my sister.

What were some of the other really good trips you went on?

One that I think of was one that I made with my brother, Chuck Kirshner and Mitzi Metzger up in the Picket Range. We climbed Terror, and I can't remember all the names. That was definitely one of the most interesting climbs. We went in from the south. We met the Beckey Brothers up on Challenger on another trip. We also climbed Luna and Fury on that one. The Pickets was an area we hadn't heard of until rather late in our climbing careers and when we did, we all got excited about going up into that area.

I did all of these trips while I was still in college. I think all of us were still in college. As soon as I got out of the university, I was a candidate for service, so I was in the army for the next four years.

Did any of your children become climbers?

Yeah, I have one daughter who became distinctly interested in climbing. She got to the point of climbing El Capitan and a couple of the major climbs in Yosemite.

She must have found the Ptarmigans to be a fascinating group.

She has known about the Ptarmigans. She tried to talk me into making a repeat of the Ptarmigan Traverse on the fiftieth anniversary. It was something that would have been interesting to do, but I was tangled in some sort of project I had to take care of that summer.

I would imagine it would have been interesting to see the Ptarmigan fifty years later.

It certainly would have. I would guess that some of those really major glaciers up there along the traverse are dramatically smaller.

Did the Ptarmigans end as casually as they had begun?

They really stopped because everybody got involved in some type of wartime activity, a large percentage of us overseas. It's interesting that the Ptarmigans turned out to be a pioneering group because there was no set intention of becoming a pioneering group. We just got ideas about places to go, and typically we wanted to go places nobody had been before. Of course the end result of that is pioneering.

My brother and I went up to Stehekin Valley Ranch about four summers ago and spent four or five days just hiking out of the ranch, but we met several people up there who were aware of the Ptarmigan Traverse, and when they found out we were amongst the original group it did impress a few people. I was a little surprised that it made such an impression on people. There were in fact people taking pictures of us on the boat up the lake to Stehekin Valley Ranch.

I still recall talking to Bill Cox and Calder Bressler when they were describing what we were going to do. I never had any thoughts about going on that specific trip, but the more they said, the more it seemed like a great idea. We did talk to a ranger somewhere, trying to get his ideas about whether such a trip was feasible. He had very negative thoughts about it. He just didn't think there was any way we could do what we had in mind. The rangers typically walked on trails, and if it wasn't trail, it wasn't possible.

*T*he rain has been torrential, the traffic bumper-to-bumper, Cliff and I have been doing interviews since 7 a.m. Trying to find Will Thompson's Bothell home in the rainy dark is difficult. My shoulders and neck ache from tension, my ears hum from the white noise of freeway traffic. Cliff is falling asleep as I find the Thompson driveway.

Despite the fact that we are late and dripping water on their floor, Will and Helen Thompson are cordial. Helen asks if we want coffee. I will definitely need a strong cup. As she goes into the kitchen to make a pot, Will ushers us into his study to show

« *Every time I ever went out with Ome someone was in trouble. If it wasn't a rescue, something*

happened to approximate a rescue situation. It never failed. **»**
—*Will Thompson*

us the project he has been working on for several years, a scholarly paper on climate-related landscapes in world mountains that is going to be published by a Swiss magazine. Thompson is a retired geographer. He spent 18 years working as a civilian physical geographer with the Army Materiel Command. His area of interest has always been world mountain environments, something he says the army has very little interest in.

For the next hour I sit next to him while he shows me a pile of black-and-white photos of mountains all over the world. The photos are beautiful and his thesis fascinating, but I'm going cross-eyed from exhaustion. Cliff is sitting next to me, and suddenly I feel a head on my shoulder. Cliff has dozed off, and we haven't begun to talk about the Ptarmigans.

Will Thompson was one of the founders of the Ptarmigans, a group of young climbers in the late 1930s who made some of the first explorations into the farthest reaches of the North Cascades. He made first ascents of Fury, Luna, Bear and Blue (Gunsight). The Ptarmigans were mavericks, bucking the Mountaineers tradition. Thompson today is still a bit of a maverick.

When the talk gets around to his experiences in the Cascades, we realize that it is very late. Helen mentions that Ome Daiber's wife, Matie, lives next door and suggests that another conversation, including Matie, would be in order. We agree.

The evening sun is blazing on the horizon the next time Cliff and I pull into the Thompson driveway. Thompson's paper has been published. He is pleased with it but interested to see what response it will elicit among geographers. He seems a bit more relaxed, having the paper behind him.

For a half-century Ome Daiber was one of the most ubiquitous figures on the Northwest climbing scene. At any given gathering of mountaineers, there was a good chance you'd find Ome. Daiber had made a name for himself with his first ascent of Mount Rainier's Liberty Ridge in 1934. He also was in the outdoor equipment business. Daiber was the creator of SnowSeal, the melted, waxy goo that climbers have been slathering on boots for years. In 1948 he co-founded the Northwest Mountain Rescue Council. He had also led the George Vancouver Rover Boy Scout troop that later became the Ptarmigans—he was named an honorary Ptarmigan as a result. Matie deflects attention from herself towards Ome, but it was Matie who often coordinated rescues from the Daiber home. She seems to share the ebullience that was a Daiber hallmark.

▲

Mrs. Daiber, are you a native Northwesterner?
Matie Daiber: Yes, I was born near Spokane. I always liked the outdoors. I did a little hiking around Eastern Washington. I belonged to the Spokane Mountaineers. We did rocks mostly.

What brought you to the west side?
Matie: Marrying Ome.
Will Thompson: They met in the Tetons.
Matie: I joined a Seattle Mountaineers' summer outing and met Ome.

Was it a whirlwind courtship?
Matie: I don't know, let's see. We met . . .
Will: Ome claimed to have spent a lot of time on the road between here and Spokane.
Matie: We met in '39 in that summer and were married in December of 1940. We did a fair amount of climbing before we had kids. After that it dropped off, although we did some after that. We climbed quite a bit around here. I did all the majors except Olympus. I think now I could climb St. Helens again. I'd like to. Wouldn't you like to go up there, Will?
Will: I'm not terribly interested in volcanos as such. Volcanos don't last long enough to respond the way a proper mountain should to climate.

Do you find that your interest in the mountains is related to your interest in climate?
Will: My dad was a fisheries biologist. He

did quite a bit of research, particularly the outstanding work on the halibut. I did take a bachelors in that field, but at about that time the war came along and it also became obvious to me that it was a small field and was going to stay small. My dad was pretty dominant in it, and there were quite a number of people in the field who were not interested in having two Thompsons in the field. I was very much interested in the mountains, and after I had gotten into the Army's 10th Mountain Division, why it seemed to me that we had a massive ignorance of mountain and landscapes systems. I knew that mountains were very different in different areas.

So I went into geography with the idea of pursuing that theme. I was told I would have to go in different directions for professional reasons, and I have gone in different directions at different times. I ended up with the army for almost twenty years. They don't like mountains. I was stubborn enough to keep the mountain thing going most of the eighteen-plus years I worked for the army. In the process I managed to accumulate the material for the paper. It has pretty much been my life's interest.

How did you get interested in the mountains?
Will: The first significant hike I made was a two- or three-day hike out at Camp Parsons in 1929. The mountaineers of my age group and before very often got started out there. The Boy

Scouts, when I joined, were run by a man by the name of Stuart Walsh. He was very unusual among professional scouters and executives in that he placed no serious restrictions on what the kids did in the mountains. Kids, especially the older boys at Parsons, who had been through the mill, were allowed to go out in groups without taking a counselor. They took maps and simply went out criss-crossing the range in all directions. A truck would take them to their takeoff point and they would be met on a certain date at another point. They never had any problems.

In about 1934 a request came out here to all the councils around the country from national headquarters, that they form groups of older boys, an organization that would hold boys through their later teens into college. These were called Rover Clans. Wolf Bauer was put in charge of it.

Wolf set up a series of these clans that were the forerunners of Explorers. They set up a mountaineering clan built around a troop where the older boys were already active in climbing. This troop was taken over by Ome Daiber, and we did fine. But about that time one of the kids in that clan who we always thought was pretty wild—he did a lot of hiking and climbing by himself and was enthusiastic about motorcycles—shut himself in his car and asphyxiated himself. We were shocked and didn't understand it at all until the national headquarters sent a team out. And it appears that he had been involved in homosexual activities at Scout headquarters. It was a more serious matter than it would be now. The council organization was shaken up very thoroughly.

The impact on our clan was that these people from national headquarters discovered that this council had been heavily involved in mountaineering. All they could see was violent headlines in the papers. In those days when you fell off a mountain you got big headlines. They said either you guys quit mountaineering or else get out of the Scouts. So we changed our name to Ptarmigan and brought the girl friends into the outfit and forgot about the Boy Scouts.

The Ptarmigans were responsible for some of the most adventuresome traverses and climbs in the North Cascades. You were perhaps the first person to travel into the Luna Cirque from Ross Lake.

Will: One year I sat down with a Forest Service planimetric map and followed the trail system from Ruth Creek to Hannegan Pass, Whatcom Pass, Beaver Pass (Ross Dam didn't exist then) down to Diablo where I persuaded people there to give me some groceries and went up Thunder Creek to Park Creek pass, up the Agnes over Agnes Pass and down to the Suiattle in ten days. I got fairly excited about the Pickets.

The following year Bill Cox and I plotted another ten-day trip. We went up to Redoubt, up Redoubt Creek, which led into a horrendously rocky, dirty canyon. We backed off that and packed over the divide to the head of Ruth Creek and took a look at what we called the Twin Spires, Mox Peaks. We tried to get to Silver Lake and those peaks over there but we had a storm. We had enough food for our future plans, but we had to forget about the Silver Lake area. We went down Redoubt Creek and up over Beaver Pass and beat our way up to the Luna Cirque.

We did Fury and Luna in one day. We came out Challenger Glacier, over Perfect Pass and out Easy Ridge. We were cooking in a big honey tin. We were using that as all our cooking gear. Nobody carried stoves in those days. The last day we had been hung up trying to get down to Perfect Pass because it was cloudy. We got down there and had just enough oatmeal to fill that bucket, probably about a gallon bucket and ate all the oatmeal and went out light from there. There were no tents in those days because the summers were dry.

Tell me about your experience with the Tenth Mountain Division.

Will: The Russian invasion of Finland focused a great deal of publicity on ski troops, and so everybody always thought in terms of ski troops. Well, the fact that Finland happens to be flat escaped most of, not only the public, but the Army as well. So ski troops we were, whether we should have been or not. The army never developed tactics suitable for mountains primarily because they wanted to march people around in large groups. They put us up at Camp Hale, in the Colorado Rockies, because they had a big, flat valley where they could build rows and rows of barracks and march people up and down, march out to the ski slope and march back again. But once we got into the rougher country—and it wasn't very rough— our large units were essentially immobilized. But the army never accepted that fact.

As far as people, we had a very strange mix of volunteer skiers primarily, some mountaineers, but dominantly skiers. And that has been the backbone of the 10th Mountain Alumni Association; all of them still skiers. They think skiing, and you can't talk anything but skiing to any of them.

With those skiers we had a great many draftees. Those who were doing the assigning had very little concept of what the 10th was doing or what the 10th needed. The 10th itself didn't know. I was with the medic unit and we got a bunch of fellows from Boston because they were presumably used to the New England climate. But they had grown up in the Boston slums and were not exactly high class outdoor material. The classic instance was when they assigned us a bunch of Indians from the Rio Grande Valley, who had never seen snow. They put them on the train, shipped them up there, unloaded them in a blizzard and these guys went straight from the troop train to the hospital. It didn't help that the Rio Grande Railroad was running enormous coal-burning locomotives up and down the grade all day long everyday. I've seen places where the snow was feet deep in cinders.

Our hospital was constantly full of people with severe hacks, upper respiratory diseases. Camp Hale Hack was the nickname for the disease. Had the army not been so dictated by altitude and chosen a climate and location more prudently . . .

If you had been the commander and had the choice where would you have stationed the 10th Mountain Division?

Will: I suppose I would have tried to get them into the Cascades. If I had done that, well, the Army would have given over the experiment immediately because obviously their formations would not have worked there. Our army doctrine was one of forward movement, so they tried to train us to be mobile in the mountains. But basically it's not practical. Now we did make a landing on Kiska in the Aleutians, which went pretty much as planned primarily because the Japanese had evacuated three weeks before. And we had some success in Italy while operating in division strength at that time. Actually the 10th Division, as a unit, was educated, had initiative and was extremely effective.

Matie: The 10th Mountain Division had a lot of good men from the Northwest, because I remember Ome writing some letters of recommendation.

Will: I guess the army has assigned PR people to put out publicity on the 10th Mountain

Division, and it's just a little hard to convince anyone of the reality of what the 10th Division was because it has been hyped so much.

Ome was the creator of SnowSeal.
Matie: Yes, he put it together.

Cliff Leight: There's some funny graffiti up on the outhouses on the Juneau Icefield that reads, "Ome Daiber wears rubber boats."

Matie: L.L. Bean sent me, with my last order, a couple of packets of SnowSeal. I thought that the next time I order something I might write a little note and thank them.

What were some of Ome's other creations?

Matie: Well, he worked on suntan lotions that were good. He came up with the Penguin sleeping bag, which had legs. Ome liked the mountains and he couldn't afford in the beginning to go out and buy all this stuff. Economically he needed to make much of his equipment. So he got into the business because friends wanted what he was making. He worked through the Boy Scouts then started the Hike Shack and finally Ome Daiber, Inc.

Tell me about Ome's role in the creation of the first mountain rescue unit.

Will: Before Mountain Rescue, if there was an emergency people called Ome.

Matie: The press really got ahold of Ome's name after the Fadden rescue on Rainier. And I think they just picked up the name and they would call him in those situations.

Will: Well, I think everyone was aware that was the number to call if they had a mountain rescue on. Whenever an airplane was down in the mountain, Ome was the one you called.

Matie: And he just called all his friends. I remember one time we had just gotten back from a day of skiing. I can remember Ome's wet ski pants being just dropped to the floor as he climbed into a pair of climbing pants and went off on a rescue.

Will: Every time I ever went out with Ome someone was in trouble. If it wasn't a rescue, something happened to approximate a rescue situation. It never failed.

Matie: It didn't necessarily have anything to do with your party.

Will: No, it was never our party. It was partly a situation that if a party knew Ome was in

2

(1) Ome Daiber drives in a piton on Castle Rock while on practice maneuver of Mountain Rescue Council.

(2) Climbers on the west ridge of Forbidden Peak during first ascent June 1, 1940. (3) Lloyd Anderson, Lyman Boyer, Tom Campbell and Helmy Beckey after completing first ascent of south tower of Howser Spire in the Bugaboos.

3

— Lloyd Anderson Photo

1

— Lloyd Anderson Photo

2

3

(1) Triumph Peak, first climbed July 31, 1938 by Lloyd Anderson, Lyman Boyer, Louis Smith and Dave Lind. (2) Wolf Bauer in the North Cascades. (3) Wolf Bauer, 1934.

(4) First ascent party on summit of Mount Goode, July 5, 1936. Left to right: Jack Hossack, Joe Halwax, Wolf Bauer, and George MacGowan.

— Phillip Dickert Photo

1 — Lloyd Anderson Photo

2 — Lloyd Anderson Photo

(1) Mountaineers party on Mount Rainier, July 20, 1930. (2) Rescuers gather around Ray Riggs, who had fallen into a crevasse on Mount St. Helens, August 3, 1930.

(3) The Andersons on backpack to Dewey Lake in Mount Rainier National Park, July 21, 1945. Left to right: Lloyd, Mary, Ruth, Sue. (4) Gunsight Peak (Blue Mountain), first climbed July 3, 1938, by Lloyd Anderson, Lyman Boyer, and Agnes Dickert.

3

4

— Lloyd Anderson Photo

the area and they got into trouble, they could run to him.

Matie: Now, this guy up in Glacier Basin didn't crash down on his head just because he knew Ome was in the area.

Will: I don't know about that (much laughter). We were climbing in the area when the accident occurred and within a very few minutes we had a full-scale rescue going.

In those instances you had to improvise the rescue.

Matie: Well, those guys went equipped so they could improvise.

Will: I learned in the army, though, that the first aid stuff they sent you out with was never quite what you wanted or needed, and practically everything you might ever want to do could be improvised.

Matie: We never went out without our ski tips bored, so that we could make a toboggan if necessary. We had to do that on Mount Rainier with a man who had broken his leg. Ome fixed the leg, and we put him on our skis. I had several bandannas to tie things together with.

Will: All the years I've climbed I've had no accidents myself and nobody in my party has ever had an accident of consequence. The Ptarmigans were very competent people and we did keep an eye on each other's techniques. We contributed to all of the decisions. There was always a consensus. Nobody led anyone else around by the nose. I've been safer than I would have otherwise because my primary interest was not necessarily the summit, but what I was seeing along the way and keeping track of what was happening on the mountain, which of course affects one's safety. And the remarkable fact is that the farther it is to the car the less accidents happen.

Although that may change as more and more people go out into the mountains, or the remote places become more accessible.

Will: I really think that the social health of a community like the Puget Sound area will benefit enormously if we can keep our mountains accessible, not just to a few people, but to large numbers. People have got to have a sense that there is more back of our social structures, that there is more required of our social structures than to proclaim authority.

Kids tend, even here, to band together in gangs to defy authority, defining their identities in that way. Whereas if you have been out in the mountains and have a sense of the scope of the natural forces that you encounter and that those are the same forces that civilization is holding off your back, literally, then you've got to have somewhat more respect for authority. You may also be able to evaluate the functioning and non-functioning of authority, better able to cope with authority, have a sense of what they are supposed to be doing besides pestering you. So I have a sense that the more thousands and thousands get into our mountains, the healthier the community will be in the long run.

Helen Thompson: How are you going to do that for people in Nebraska?

Will: Sorry about them.

1946 1960

*H*arvey Manning met the enemy at Cascade Pass in the mid-1950s and it could have been my family. "We were camping right at the pass, as we all did in those days," he remembers. "I saw a party coming up the trail, and I went out to greet them because they were bound to be friends. And they were strangers, total strangers! What the hell were they doing in my mountains?"

At the end of World War II, many of those damn strangers were born—myself included. But it would be another twenty years before we baby boomers would flood the Cascades, call them our own and moan about those "damn Californians."

Overcrowding wasn't really a worry to the post-war climbers. They could set out for almost any Cascade peak, decked out in Army surplus Brumani boots, wool pants, parka and sunglasses, and still have the mountains to themselves. But for those climbers, many who had served overseas, the Cascades just weren't enough. On a cloudless day, from the summit of Rainier, Stuart or El Dorado the best climbers in Washington imagined a horizon arcing far beyond the Cascades. During the late 1940s and the decade of the '50s these young climbers transformed not only Northwest climbing, but the international scene as well.

Although the Cascades and Olympics were a few decades away from trailhead gridlock, there were strong indications that mountaineering would not be a passing fad. By 1948 the membership rolls of both Mountaineers and Co-op had swelled to almost 2,500, more than four times pre-war numbers.

The 1950s ushered in a new age of climbing pluralism as well, with Boy Scout troops, University of Washington and others—using the Mountaineers course as a model—offering

their own climbing courses. The Co-op grew apace but also saw its preeminence in the climbing market challenged.

The Co-op remained a labor of love for Lloyd and Mary Anderson, but it began to outgrow its quarters in a downtown accountant's office. By the end of the '50s, the expanded Co-op catalog reflected the growing interest in downhill skiing and the desire for "luxury" items once found only at Eddie Bauer's. Its membership numbered over 20,000. Co-op disappeared from the logo; the word "incorporated" was added to Recreational Equipment (REI). The Andersons finally got paid for running the place, and they were assisted by Big Jim Whittaker.

Although most of the major Cascade peaks had been climbed by World War II, many of the hardest faces and ridges remained untouched. Mount Rainier's north side had not seen repeats of the historic climbs of Liberty and Ptarmigan ridges, but a group of Ellensburg climbers calling themselves, somewhat facetiously, the Sherpas, swarmed over every difficult and un-climbed northside route in the mid- to late '50s. At the core of the group were Gene and Bill Prater, and Dave Mahre.

Climbers also discovered the Cashmere Crags, in the Enchantments, as well as Castle Rock and Peshastin Pinnacles. Weighted down with an arsenal of pitons, carabiners, slings (and sometimes even wood blocks and nails), these "rock specialists," including Fred Beckey, Pete Schoening, Ralph Widrig, Don (Claunch) Gordon, and Jack Schwabland, pounded their way up some of the impressive granite walls and sandstone spires around the then sleepy logging town of Leavenworth, giving them names like Trigger Finger, Jello Tower, Cat Burglar, and Canary. In the process they advanced the rock climbing standards in the Pacific Northwest a notch or two.

With the proliferation of new routes in the Cascades, the need for a comprehensive guide book became more pressing. Fred Beckey, recently graduated from the University of Washington, took on the task unofficially begun by the Mountaineers climbing class in the 1930s; that was to put together a guide book for the Cascades and Olympics. His first effort served as the prototype for what has become the standard in American climbing guides. At times the route descriptions seemed to grab you by the hand and walk you step-by-step to the top of any mountain in the Cascades and Olympics:

". . . Climb ca. 30 ft. up a rock basin and cut sharply right (N.) around the skyline via some loose rock outcrops and ledges. Continue to traverse across an exposed slap with a 15-ft. section of fingertip holds to the base of a steep, brushy gully."

The guide also featured Dee Molenaar's exquisite pen and ink drawings of many of the peaks. I would trace the dashed lines with my eyes and fingers from woods to summit again and again, slowly gaining the courage to try those peaks for real.

The Mountaineers also determined a need to update the climbing course booklet. That small 160-page book, which in 1960 would metamorphose into the classic mountaineering text, *Mountaineering, Freedom of the Hills*, was published in 1948. It contained tips already made quaint and anachronistic by a new climbing order and emerging wilderness ethic. Much of the equipment described in the book would be obsolete by the mid-1950s. Nailed boots were described in great detail, while no mention was given to the new Brumani lug sole which would soon make the tricouni a museum piece. It could not anticipate kernmantle climbing ropes, 12-point crampons or the Kelty aluminum frame pack.

Under the heading of Mountain Etiquette, the booklet stated, "Therefore hide, burn

or bury all waste, including orange peels, candy wrappers, lunch sacks, cigarette butts, and film packs . . . If you must cut trees for firewood or get boughs for mattresses, do it so as to minimize the scars; thin a dense thicket or take a whole tree cleanly, so that the stump is not noticeable."

In the section on route finding, the book described the best way to signal for help in foggy conditions. "When the vision is restricted, vocal signals such as a high-pitched cry 'Coo Coo' carry very well and serve to keep the party together." Fred Beckey, Harvey Manning, or Dave Mahre yelling "Coo Coo?" I don't think so. The best mountaineers did spend a great deal of time looking for climbers who were lost in the fog and maybe even screaming, "Coo Coo." In 1948 the loose-knit group of mountain rescuers became an official mountain rescue unit, the first in the Northwest, led by Wolf Bauer, Ome Daiber and Dr. Otto Trott.

For many of this new generation of climbers, and a few of the not-so-new, the Cascades could no longer contain their ambitions. Fred Beckey, Dee and K Molenaar, Pete Schoening, Dave Harrah, Tom Miller, Dick McGowan, and many other Washington climbers made first ascents in Alaska and South America during the late 1940's and early '50s. And there were the Himalayas. The mystical mountains of these climber's childhoods, described in stuffy books by stuffy British climbers—Everest, K-2, Lhotse, Gasherbrum and Masherbrum— became real goals for Molenaar, McGowan, Schoening, Beckey, Tom Hornbein, and Willi Unsoeld. Most of those expeditions of the '50s were glorious failures or modest successes, although in 1958 Pete Schoening became the first American to make a first ascent of an 8,000-meter peak, Gasherbrum I (Hidden Peak). A few years later that ascent would be cast in the shadows of the first American ascent of Mount Everest.

CHAPTER

12

DEE MOLENAAR

*A*sk Dee Molenaar to recall the famous fall on K-2, and he will recount the accident in great detail. He has sketched the fall, talked to all the members of that 1953 expedition—just to get it straight in his mind. There is very little that escapes his attention, a good trait for a cartographer, one of Molenaar's many talents.

"From the time I started having adventures, in my teens, I started keeping diaries of everything. Every trip I took, I'd write it down and type it on an old manual typewriter. I didn't think it would ever amount to anything. But I just liked to document these things. Now, I have finally put my K-2 diary into a MacIntosh computer and have a book with photos and sketches I did. I hope to eventually add the St. Elias trip, Kennedy, the Juneau Icefield, the Alps trip."

Molenaar's attention to detail is evident in his pen and ink sketches of mountain scenes and his elegant full-color wall maps of the North Cascades, Rainier, the Olympics and St. Helens. It is also apparent in his classic account of climbing on Mount Rainier, *The Challenge of Rainier*. Dee, who grew up in Los Angeles, says, "It always surprised me that it took an outsider to write a book on Mount Rainier."

Dee Molenaar wants to remember every step, every belay, self-arrest, and summit, to remember it correctly, unvarnished by nostalgia. His time is not spent in mere recollection, though. He continues to climb with friends like Pete Schoening and in 1990 trekked to the Everest base camp.

Molenaar and his wife, Colleen, give Cliff and me a complete tour of their home, their garden and the trail that leads to the wooded stream which borders their property. We have lunch in one of their favorite restaurants, a tavern that overlooks the water in Gig Harbor.

Returning to his home, Molenaar shows us his basement/ work room/study which is filled with mountaineering memorabilia, maps, and works-in-progress. From a shelf he takes a copy of his Rainier book. It is covered with signatures. "For years and years I took my Rainier book, the first one off the press, to every mountaineering meeting, and that thing is just loaded with

«It's only been in the last 20 years that you began to have a stigma on you if you weren't a rock climber, and just a snow bump climber. Now it doesn't have to have a

summit, just a slab with trees on top of it.»

—*Dee Molenaar*

autographs from guys like Ed Hillary, Tenzing. I've even got Noel O'Dell and Eric Shipton in there. I've got Walter Bonatti and all the top mountaineers." He pauses momentarily, then adds with an affectionate laugh, "Ome Daiber probably signed the thing twenty times."

▲

Dee Molenaar: When I first started climbing, first started guiding on Rainier, I did the Kautz Route which involved quite a bit of ice climbing. Back in those days you went over the ice cliff. It wasn't the wall like it is now, but a bunch of terraces, ten to fifteen foot vertical sections. You worked from terrace to terrace. Now the glacier is advancing and is just a wall. I never hear of anyone climbing the Kautz icecliff route. But back in the '40s you went up over the cliff or up the chute.

In those days we considered it technical climbing. You chopped steps up this first stretch of thirty-five feet of ice and then got into the pinnacles. Yet when the Soviets visited in 1975, they climbed the Kautz Route, and they just front-pointed up that thing and walked right down it. We were always belaying. Normally we had "scissorbills," you know, clients, with us. Before the war it was considered too dangerous for inexperienced people to use an ice axe. So only the guides used ice axes, and we gave our clients these big alpenstocks. They were climbing this technical stuff with an alpenstock. So we had to belay them down. We really thought we were the top ice climbers in the country because we could lead up the Kautz route. But back in New England they were winter climbing in Tuckerman Ravine.

Most of your climbing then had been around Mount Rainier. You hadn't really explored the Cascades much.

Oh, a little with the Coast Guard during the war. I had joined the Mountaineers by then and went on a couple of their trips. That's when I first met Fred Beckey. I also climbed with Helmy Beckey, Fred's younger brother.

Had Fred developed his reputation at that time?

Well, he was just starting. I met him in the Mountaineers club room when it was somewhere on First or Second Avenue. I remember Clark Schurman introduced me or pointed him out. Fred was in there browsing around in the books. The summer before he and Helmy had done the second ascent of Mount Waddington, and they were just teenagers, which was really something

after so many attempts on the mountain. It took Fritz Wiessner and Bill House to finally do it. Here the Beckey brothers come along and knock it off, amazing.

Fred, Helmy, Maynard Miller, my brother "K" and I, after World War II, went skiing in the Sierra briefly. We got together with the Beckeys down in Los Angeles. We were driving to the Sierra and the Beckey boys were sitting in the back. Maynard and I were sitting in the front. We were jammed together. God, those two Beckey brothers were jabbering back and forth, talking about climbs, and we couldn't get a word in sideways, and I finally turned around and said, "Goddammit, shut up!" They didn't say anything for the next two-hundred miles.

Helmy had a bad knee. I think he got it banged up on Waddington and eventually he gave it up because of the knee. He didn't have the driving interest, I guess, that Fred did.

Few people do.

No, Fred's something else. I don't think there's anyone who has as many routes anywhere in the world as Fred. Although he's counting all these little splinters and things in the Cashmere Crags as new mountains. Most of my climbing was on the glaciers, and the rock climbers weren't the leading figures in the club. Lloyd Anderson and some of those guys did some new rock routes. It's only been in the last twenty years that you began to have a stigma on you if you weren't a rock climber, and just a snow bump climber. Now it doesn't have to have a summit, just a slab with trees on top of it. Now they have these indoor gyms, like the Vertical Club.

I went down there a couple of weeks ago just to see what it was like. I saw some friends in there working out. I always enjoyed rock climbing, but not with the bandoliers of pitons. I just hated carrying all the gear. In fact I don't enjoy glacier climbing anymore. Everyone has to have the harness and all that crap. But any time I've climbed a mountain in the last twenty years, leading beginners up, I've had to harness 'em in, put their crampons on, make sure they fit. I really enjoy the rock scrambling, the class three and four stuff. In fact K-2 was just class three, mostly scrambling with a couple of ten-foot vertical things, no harness, no stirrups or anything. That's all stuff that's come out since.

When we talked to Pete Schoening, he said the guy to talk to about K-2 was Dee.

That's because I don't have any other expeditions to raise the memories like these guys. They go on one every few years. You know if we hadn't had that tragedy, it would have been just another failed expedition. It wouldn't have made the news at all.

Do you think that had it not been for Art Gilkey's death, you might have tried for the summit.

I've looked through my diary, and the weather had started to get us down, and you know, we had the wrong philosophy. They've learned since that the big thing when the weather sours is to come back to base. But we thought by going up that we were saving our acclimatization, and so we were actually getting weaker and not thinking as clearly as we should. I know that Gilkey and Schoening were still eager to reach the summit, but Charlie Houston and I were the only ones with children, and we started thinking about wife and kids more than the summit after a few days of storm. I was ready to head down, or at least be support rather than climb the mountain. We had all eight climbers up there, and we should have had more back-up below. We had everything ready up there, but we were also eating it all up during that ten-day storm. Then Gilkey got that blood clot.

Do you remember "The Fall" with much clarity?

Oh yeah. I typed that up several times. You know it's amazing, but every book that's been written about K-2, including our own written by Bob Bates and Charlie Houston, gives completely different descriptions of how we were all on the slope, how we were roped up than the way I remember it. Everyone seems to have a different version. I typed up the thing the way I remembered it. In fact I drew a sketch of it on the way back. I made a little watercolor of the expedition after we got back to Rawalpindi. I had these guys check it, and they seemed to agree with the way I had everyone positioned and roped up, before and after the fall.

When you were jerked off your feet, did you have a sense that "this was it"?

I remember looking up at the slope. Pete Schoening was up there in the fog somewhere, belaying at the top of a band of ice, and there was a boulder apparently embedded in the ice, and he had his axe above. He was facing up the hill. Bell was coming down from below the cliff toward Art Gilkey, and Gilkey was down at the end of the rope Schoening was anchoring. Then I had a rope tied across the slope pulling—we were trying to get Art across the slope to our Camp 7, which was just a little notch in the slope. We knew we weren't going to get to Camp 6 that night. Tony Streather, who was tied to George Bell, was standing next to me pulling in the rope from Gilkey, while I was taking it in around my axe. Houston and Bates, I thought, were doing the same thing, pulling in a rope from Gilkey. I remember, distinctly, the fact the one that was pulling in the rope was behind the guy with the axe. At least that's what it looked like to me. But later they told me they weren't even taking in rope. They were trying to find a decent place to jab the axe in. I was about to make a remark when all of a sudden I saw George, above, slip down the slope, and I said, "Goddamm, there goes Bell." I saw Bell sliding down on his back; I couldn't see he was making any effort to turn over. And he shot down on the opposite side of Gilkey.

He was tied to Streather, so the rope doubled around . . . it must have slipped underneath the rope that went from Gilkey to Schoening. It doubled around the two ropes coming from Gilkey and pulled us all off our feet. We just went down. That's the way I remembered it. As soon as I got jerked off I was going down the slope headfirst, and I felt no pain, just an exhilaration of movement. I sort of thought, "I'm going to get knocked out soon and that's it." They were the only thoughts I had, but then I got pulled up with Bob Bates on top of me. At first we assumed that the ropes had got tangled and that's what happened.

Were you able to take in this tableau of bodies strewn across the slope?

I remember Streather was up above on the ice a ways. Houston was down below us about twenty-five feet, kind of leaning into the rock groggily, and Bell was way below climbing out of an ice gully. He'd gone the farthest. Bob Craig wasn't involved. He was over at the tent chopping out a platform. I don't think he even knew it had happened.

There are a lot of ifs in a situation like this, but had you all fallen to your deaths, he would have been alone.

Well, Schoening has given me two versions. He says he wasn't actually tied to the rope, that he could have let it go. Then later he said he was tied to it. I believe he probably was tied to it. Then recently, he said he was below that rock cliff, rather than above it. That's not the way we remembered it all these years. I've given so many lectures on it, pretty soon, the way you describe it is the way you remember it. Whether my version is right, I don't know.

You were a pretty sorry bunch at that point with the odds certainly stacked against you all making it down.

When we started down with Gilkey that morning, we sure didn't know how that day was going to end. We knew it was going to be a tough thing. We were all really weak, dehydrated. But we had that focus. We just worked from moment to moment doing what had to be done.

But your senses must be so dulled. Are you at all sharp?

Compared to what? I suppose if there is a guy sitting in a chair with an oxygen mask just observing it all, he most likely thinks, "God, those guys are crazy. What are they doing that for?"

In hindsight, with Schoening the only anchor, I probably should have driven in an ice piton. We didn't have any ice pitons, but a big rock piton. Because my ice axe, the tip was just barely into the ice. It wouldn't have held anything. But if you could have driven in a long angle rock piton, put a snaplink and the rope through there, you might have had an extra holding point for Gilkey.

That night in the tent must have been pretty harrowing.

There were four of us in a very narrow two-man tent, kind of sitting side-by-side. Houston, Bell and I were in the one tent. I was kind of laying on my back, half out of the tent. I had cracked ribs. I remember Houston kept passing out and then he'd come to. And when he'd come to, he'd have a hard time breathing. He wanted to go. He said, "We're suffocating." He was going to cut a hole in the tent so we could breath. He wanted to

go out and look for Art Gilkey in the middle of the night. So he was half in and half out. He'd been real sharp up until then, but he had a concussion.

Even when we got back to Camp Two and were reading our mail, he had to put his hand over one eye, because his eyes were focusing differently. Houston was the last one down the House Chimney, and he describes that vividly in the book. It was in the dark. There were different ropes, and he didn't know which one was the new rope or the one left by Wiessner in 1939. He thought at one point, "Ah hell, I'll just jump off the cliff and end it all," but then he thought of his family.

K-2 was one of those experiences that changes you forever.

When I was on K-2 I was married to a woman who didn't really want me to go, and at the last minute I was about to withdraw from the expedition, then she insisted that I go. All the time I was on the mountain, I thought, "Gee I shouldn't be here." I was worrying about my wife and daughter. That was an inhibiting factor. So I decided I was going to enjoy myself and do my part to help the guys get up, but as far as sticking my own neck out, I just couldn't do that. Things can happen when you don't expect them, where you don't have any control over them. And I've got too many other things to live for. I've got maps to make, things to write, friends and family to love.

That's a decision that a lot of mountaineers make.

I'm also a geologist. My reason for climbing was not to climb vertical walls just to see how I could do. I enjoyed scrambles to see what's on the other side or up above, but just the act of climbing itself wasn't my whole reason for climbing.

Unlike most of your climbing contemporaries, you have managed, with your illustrations and maps, to stay closer to mountaineering. When did you start making maps?

My first one was the Rainier map in 1965. It's been revised—as a matter of fact I've got to revise it again. I want to put stuff on the back, more information, extract more stuff from my book.

I used to spend hours looking at Beckey's guide, still do for that matter, and I was really drawn to your illustrations, not so much for what they actually showed but what they suggested. There was so much about climbs I could imagine through your sketches.

I like sketches and artwork better than photos to show routes. Most of Fred's, the North Cascades—the third one—I think that the thing is lousy as far as illustrating routes. The shadows on the peaks leave whole sides dark. Sketches, especially the three-dimensional kind, delineate the ravines and crevices much better.

How has your climbing changed?

You know, it's really funny, but the last time I climbed Mount Rainier was in 1979. I was sixty-one then. I tried it again in '86. Pete Schoening used to climb it on his birthday weekend at the end of July. He'd invite me along with my kids. Last time I did it was with him and a group, going up the Emmons route. Then in '84, we went up and had beautiful conditions. There were hardly any crevasses, just an easy route. I had all my kids along. We got up to Steamboat Prow and camped up on a little row above there.

There was a full moon and I remember getting up at one in the morning, leading off, plodding along, with my shadows on the snow. I thought, "Four more hours of this drudgery." Then my daughter says, "Dad, I don't feel so good." That was just like music to me. I right away converted that into, "We can unrope and go back down and let these guys climb it." But I went through the normal motions of slowing down and telling her to breath deep. We plodded another hundred yards or so, and she said, "I don't feel so good". I said, "Okay, I'll take you back down." We went back down, laid in the sun and really enjoyed it. My two sons went on up with Pete and his crew, made the summit and had a good time. My daughter still felt guilty about making me turn back. She said she had felt okay, she just didn't want to climb it. I said, "Well, that's the way I felt."

Two weeks later I went down with a nephew and did a lot of climbing in the Oregon Cascades, like the Sisters. Then we ended up on Mount Shasta, and my nephew wasn't feeling so good, so I said I'm going to climb Shasta anyway. Shasta is now a two-day climb. You used to climb it in one day. I still thought it was a one-day climb. So I started way down around 7,000 feet. I plodded my way up to the top of that thing, and I did it in the same time it took me when I was twenty-one years old. Here I was sixty-six. I was doing it all alone. I really dragged my butt up to the top. I hadn't remembered so many false summits before. I just touched the top and turned around and came back down. I really felt good that I could take 14,000 feet without dying. And I enjoyed it.

CHAPTER

13

FRED BECKEY

*F*red Beckey's climbing career spans six decades. During that time he has stemmed, front-pointed, jumared, and occasionally lassoed his way to the summits of thousands of peaks. Hundreds were first ascents— a record perhaps unparalleled in North American climbing history.

A multitude of Cascade peaks, spires and rock walls, many named by Beckey as well: Despair, Forbidden, Phantom, Outer Space, Cat Burglar, Crooked Thumb, Cruel Finger, Flagpole, Big Kangaroo, Mushroom Tower, Burgundy, Chablis, Pernod, Prusik, Tomahawk, The Hook, Bear's Breast, and Ostrich Head.

That is just a sampling from his Cascade climbing log. There are climbs in Idaho, Oregon, California, Utah, Arizona, British Columbia, Alaska and Nepal. First ascents, second ascents, winter ascents, free ascents.

For almost every climb, another "Beckey Story" is added to local climbing lore. The myriad anecdotes paint a complex and confusing picture: demented rock technician, safety-conscious, self-absorbed, meticulous, obsessed, Don Juan, practical joker. Aware of the his public personna, Beckey posed for a magazine ad a few years ago in a T-shirt that read "Beware of Beckey."

The peripatetic Beckey has always been difficult to pin down. His home has often been his car as he has criss-crossed the country in search of climbs and climbing partners. Friends often get phone calls in the middle of the night, Beckey's urgent voice outlining a climb, no time to lose. The amount of his phone bills has been the subject of spirited conjecture over the years, but Fred isn't telling.

Fred Beckey pioneered a lifestyle that revolved around climbing. The older generation of climbers didn't understand him, thought him irresponsible, although many privately envied him. The majority of Beckey's contemporaries couldn't maintain his manic pace or chose not to, but younger generations of climbers, several decades removed from the Depression, eagerly embraced his nomadic lifestyle.

Perhaps no one else was better suited to the task of

《 I'm not as competitive for getting first ascents as I used to be. In a way I kind of look at it as something meaningless. What does it matter whether it's a first ascent except to yourself or a few people? And I'm not climbing for other people. 》

—*Fred Beckey*

compiling Cascade climbing guides than Fred Beckey. He began in the late 1940s while attending the University of Washington. Working from the piles of mimeographed route descriptions collected by the Mountaineers, he wrote *The Climber's Guide to the Cascades and Olympics*. Over the years it became known as Beckey's Bible. His crowning achievement was the three-volume *Cascade Alpine Guide*. Containing over 1,000 pages of detailed route descriptions (although Beckey has said he purposely left out some routes so that climbers could discover them on their own), the guides are also source books on geology, climate, natural as well as climbing history of the Cascades. Nothing compares with their scope and depth. Beckey has also written guides to rock climbing in Leavenworth. He is currently working on a comprehensive history of climbing in the Cascades.

This interview was conducted by Cliff Leight in Beckey's car as they drove to the Selkirk Range in British Columbia. Beckey, in his late 60s, continues to climb at an exhaustive pace and enviable standard. After the Selkirk climb he was off to India to attempt a first ascent. Leight reports that during the interview Beckey constantly referred to his box of note cards with names, addresses and phone numbers of climbers all over the world, stopped a number of times to make calls and blithely drove through a few stop signs as he told "Beckey Stories."

▲

What makes a good guidebook? What is the process of putting one of your guidebooks together?

There was need for a guide book, and it seemed like no one was working on one, or planning one. It was just a matter of doing something during the winter and fall months when it was rainy and cool, between ski trips, whenever I could do some work on it. I started compiling all the information I could on different routes. I pulled all that together, got all the reports from the Mountaineers climbing committee, plus from other people; there was an outfit called the Ptarmigan Climbing Club and they had compiled some stuff.

I don't think I had any feeling, particularly, about what was a good guidebook at the time. I approached the Mountaineers about publishing it, because I obviously couldn't publish it. And I really wasn't that interested in making any money on it. The Mountaineers—I don't know how many meetings they had, or how far the discussion went—decided not to do it. It shows what I've said about them for a long time, that they are extremely conservative, narrow-minded. Some of that has changed, of course. Later on they did get into publishing, but at that time, there were a lot of things they could have, or should have done to help get mountaineering off the ground, and they didn't do it.

So I got the American Alpine Club to publish it. They were glad to have it, glad to do it. After I got the whole thing ready with pictures,

they published it. I think Ira Spring had a few photos, maybe Tom Miller. But there was never any money made on the thing. That was the first one. It was actually called *Guidebook to the Cascade and Olympic Mountains*. That guidebook came out in, I think, 1949. The first book was kind of a skeleton that showed the mountain scope of the Cascades from a hiking and climbing standpoint, and also from a geographic standpoint. In that book there were probably only five pages that covered Rainier.

Later on the guidebook was revised by a committee of the Alpine Club, the Seattle chapter. It's a big job, revising and expanding. A number of people, George Sainsbury, Pete Schoening, worked on it and I did too.

Eventually that edition went out of print. I don't think they printed more than 2,000 on the first edition, and maybe not much more on the second edition.

In 1943 you made the second ascent of Waddington with your brother Helmy. That climb kind of opened up people's eyes. What kind of climb was that for you? You were both teenagers.

We went up there just to climb Waddington and to do some other climbs; hopefully make some ascents of unclimbed peaks. It was kind of a milestone as far as I was concerned. It was a major trip. I didn't look it at it in terms of what other people would think of us, but as something we were interested in doing. It looked like a great place to go.

Did you realize at the time that climbing was going to be the most important thing in your life?

Oh, I don't know whether I realized that. I just thought it was important. It was something that appealed to me. Anything further away than Waddington would have been financially impossible, like Alaska. I wanted to go some place other than the Cascades.

What was your most memorable climb?

It's hard to say. Waddington was a memorable climb, at that time for me. The Devil's Thumb/Katchina Needles trip that we did later was a real epic. It was isolated and unknown; the first serious climbing that had ever been done in the Alaska Panhandle; I should say serious mountaineering.

People we've talked to say you have a great sense of humor. Do you remember some of your best practical jokes?

We locked a guy in the john of the boat going up Lake Chelan for the entire trip up there. It was kind of funny. We were getting pretty bored on that lake steamer, or motored vessel, and we saw this guy going into the john. I don't know who got the idea, there were several of us, but we thought locking him in the john might be kind of funny. I think we may have taken a fire axe, which isn't too smart really, and put it cross-ways across a narrow passageway.

Once you're in the john and doing your duty, you can only get out by pushing the door out. He did have a port hole, but the port hole was only so wide. You couldn't get out of it, I don't think. And for some reason, I don't know why, nobody had to go to the john that afternoon, or maybe people thought it was something official. I remember hearing the guy pounding on the door and yelling, "Let me out." We were pretty nonchalant about it, pretending we didn't know anything about it.

Pete Schoening mentioned the logging you guys did on Castle Rock at Logger's Ledge and that somebody had to go down to the road and stop traffic.

We didn't do that, no. We didn't stop any traffic. There were three or four of us cutting. We had a cross-cut saw. One tree, or part of a tree fell over the road, actually slid across the road. We were hoping someone would drive through there, not get hit, of course. But we thought it would be kind of funny if somebody had to stop and move the log out of the way.

Have you had any close calls?

Yeah, we had a pretty bad avalanche out on the Coast Range, a trip I did with the Harvard bunch. We had an avalanche and four of us slid well over 1,000 feet down the south face of Sarah.

How did that accident affect you?

It definitely resulted in some soul searching. But we were on an expedition and we kept climbing. One guy was killed. A bunch of us were hurt to one extent or other. Snow—it must have been a wind slab that we didn't recognize—broke.

You've probably done the most first ascents of anyone . . .

Just in this area. I'm sure more people have done more first ascents in rock climbing and in certain places in Europe, like Saxony, Czechoslovakia and also Australia. It's a question of what's a first ascent. I would say in the Northwest you would be accurate.

You climbed with your brother Helmy a lot and then . . .

He kind of lost interest in climbing, pretty much after the Waddington trip, maybe a few years afterward. He didn't keep up with climbing much. He just didn't have the enthusiasm for it. Then I got involved climbing with people like Ralph Widrig, Schoening, and we did a lot of climbing in the Stuart Range and other places in the Cascades. Then I went to Alaska with Bob Craig and Cliff Schmidke on the Devil's Thumb.

Has your enjoyment or approach to climbing changed much over the years?

I'm not as competitive for getting first ascents as I used to be. In a way I kind of look at it as sort of meaningless. What does it matter whether it's a first ascent except to yourself or a few people. And I'm not climbing for other people. Nowadays it seems like a lot more people are interested in sport climbing, doing routes the fastest, the hardest routes, rather than who makes the first ascent of an alpine route or any kind of route for that matter. The first ascent thing only matters, it did matter to me and still does, but only if I think it's a pretty good route, a classic line and is attractive from a climber's standpoint. If your only objective is to make first ascents, you'd find all kind of climbs that have never been done in some very unattractive areas. If that's all you want to do, but that's kind of meaningless. Who are you doing it for?

Was there a real race or competition to do some of the unclimbed peaks in the Cascades?

A few people cared about first ascents; not many people that I knew of. Maybe only a dozen people at any particular time.

And there was also a little bit of a competition for Bonanza Peak, although I don't know whether anybody from Seattle had ever made a serious try at it. It's kind of amazing, actually, that Portland climbers like Everett Darr came up in the mid-1930s and explored the Bonanza area, and nobody from the Seattle area even seriously looked at Bonanza from the standpoint of climbing.

The only one I knew of that even looked at it was Hermann Ulrichs. He was certainly capable of climbing it and probably would have climbed it, or at least tried it, because he had climbed both Maude and Fernow and spent some time around Holden. But he thought it had already been climbed. There was a problem because the map showed a triangulation mark on the summit of Bonanza, and that was a topographic mapping error, or I should say, not in the mapping but in the preparation of the maps. They had inadvertently placed the mark on top of Bonanza and it should have been on top of North Star.

So he got the idea that Bonanza had been climbed, but he had no idea by whom. You'd think he would have been curious enough to have gone and climbed it or tried to climb it and find what it was really about. For some reason he didn't and apparently the Mazamas didn't let that deter them. They seemed pretty sure it hadn't been climbed or at least were ready to take a chance on it. Besides, it would have been a worthwhile climb anyway.

Yours has really been a pioneering lifestyle. Did you get much criticism from family or peers about the fact that all you wanted to do was climb?

No, not really. That's not the only thing I wanted to do. I think I kept up the average social life of people I knew. I went to college, took jobs that were serious to me. It was just that I spent my free time climbing instead of engaging in other sports. I probably took off more time for my sport than other people would take for theirs. But I knew people who took an equal amount of time to travel to Europe or wherever they went. As far as the criticism, I don't particularly remember any criticism. There were always a number of people who didn't understand why I climbed, but there still is

that; maybe not as much as there used to be.

So it was relatively easy for you to live the lifestyle you chose.

I wouldn't say it was relatively easy. I had to work at it. I had to try to focus my activity into jobs that I could maybe get a little more than the usual two weeks vacation, try to plan it a little bit. My business career gave me a chance to do some of those things. I sometimes made job changes or took a year off so that I could do some climbing, go to Alaska. With other jobs I wouldn't have been able to do it.

So lectures and guidebooks never . . .

No, there's not that much money in it. I made more money off the Sierra Club book than any of the guidebooks. The new guidebook, which didn't come out until the late '60s, I got a royalty on. It's selling better than it used to, but I never did that just to make money, although I probably would not have done it at that time if I had known there was no money in it.

Do you plan on writing another autobiography, finish where you left off in **Challenge of the North Cascades***?*

I have no plans to, not right now. I have this history project that I have to work on, and another project I'm supposed to work on. I don't even see that I have the time for it.

What do you think of the changes that have taken place in mountaineering over the years? What do you think of climbing competitions and artificial walls?

I've never really been for it. It's a totally new dimension. I think it's kind of a strange concept. I'm not against doing difficult climbs. Artificial walls are fine for practice. The Vertical Club is fine. I like the University rock. There are quite a few places like that around the country, Canada and probably Europe. But I think using them to make climbing competitions is a gymnastic sport. And I'm not against someone doing that, but I don't see any relation between that and mountaineering or even rock climbing because you're not doing any leads. Essentially you're just top-roping or limiting the amount of your fall, taking the risk factor out of it. I realize it's extremely acrobatic and takes specialized abilities to do some of these things.

Some of the guys who do well in these things are amazing gymnasts. I just can't get very enthused about it.

CHAPTER

14

HARVEY MANNING

« The American standard of living has been declining since 1960. Some might say since John Kennedy died. I attribute it to the

Space Needle. I think that was the beginning of the end, some arcane power to generate evil. »
—Harvey Manning

No writer is more closely linked with Northwest hiking and mountaineering than Harvey Manning. He chaired the editorial committee which produced The Mountaineers' seminal instructional text, *Freedom of the Hills.* He wrote the last word on hiking, *Backpacking: One Step At a Time,* which has gone through three editions since it first appeared in 1972. In 1986 Manning wrote *Walking the Beach to Bellingham,* an evocative memoir intertwined with a foot journey along the shores of Puget Sound from Seattle to Bellingham.

Manning possesses a wry, sometimes lacerating wit, peppered with curmudgeonly irreverence. No one is spared whether it is a perpetrator of eco-outrage, a manufacturer who has abandoned the A-framed tent for the sexy geodesic dome, or Manning himself.

It is in Harvey Manning's dining room that this interview takes place. The Manning home sits in the middle of a three-acre forest amidst the angular neatness of Bellevue, Washington suburbia. Harvey and his wife, Betty, have lived there since 1952. Manning has been at the forefront of the fight to preserve neighboring forestland on Cougar, Squak and Tiger mountains, dubbed, by him, the Issaquah Alps. Several thousand acres of lowland forest have been saved from development, preserved as county and state parks, and state forest, thanks in large part to his efforts. Manning's latest passion is a proposed greenbelt, following Interstate 90 on both sides from the crest of the Cascades to Puget Sound. A press release issued by the Issaquah Alps Trails Club (Manning is in charge of publicity) describes the corridor as a patchwork of "linked greeneries within a framework of urbanization, preserving for the future the experience of a trip from Snoqualmie Pass to Puget Sound—by foot or wheel—that is a satisfying denouement to a westward crossing of the continent."

Manning's house is simple, rustic and a bit rumpled. Piles of things, at one time destined for other locations, have become permanent fixtures in dusty corners of the dining and living rooms, including stacks of Harvey's books. On the living room walls there are black-and-white photos of the North Cascades, their frames slightly tilted, and in the dining room a poster advertising Sir Edmund Hillary's lecture in Seattle shortly after his ascent of Everest. Manning is quick to point out that Hillary's name is misspelled.

Harvey Manning, too, is in a friendly state of disarray. A stout man with a wild beard, his gray-black hair is an unkempt mass of curls left to their own devices. The hair hides a face that looks younger than its 60-plus years. He is wearing an old pair of black work pants, an antiquated paisley shirt with the sleeves rolled to the elbows and a Harley-Davidson t-shirt that reads "Party Til You Puke."

▲

When you first became interested in mountaineering and took the Mountaineers' basic climbing course, did you have dreams of becoming a great mountaineer?

Oh, no, no! I just wanted to stay alive. After leaving the Scouts, I had followed a typical Scout pattern of becoming a scrambler, a daring scrambler, and got in some pretty stiff fixes. I took a few falls, and it got so that if I got off a trail onto a snowfield, I was scared shitless. You know you can't travel in the Cascades if you can't handle yourself, know the basics of balance climbing, handling an ice axe. So in 1948 my wife, Betty, and I took the Mountaineers basic mountaineering course. I expected to be in it three months, and then I'd know how to use an ice axe, handle myself on rock and carry and use a rope for emergencies, but I just got sucked in.

Where did you go from there?

I would say that I became noted as one of the leading "third rate" climbers in the Northwest. I can hear my friends yelling, "Fourth rate!" I had a lively sense of my limitations, and so I never had any ambitions to make first ascents. A lot of my ambitious friends would say, "Well, I want to do first ascents." But I never on purpose made a first ascent in my life. In the fog I sometimes made first ascents, but that wasn't what I was aiming at.

I was what you would call an active explorer. I wanted to get into interesting places. I would stand on Mount Shuksan and look over at the Pickets and think, "My God, I've got to get into places like that." And in the course of climbing in some of the remote areas of the North Cascades, peaks which are really quite easy, in those days you made third and fourth ascents. It was kind of unusual to find any peak in the North Cascades which had been climbed more than five or six times.

Who were your partners on these explorations?

The people I started with in the climbing course: Tom Miller, Bob Grant, Eric Karlson, Paul Brikoff, Vic Josendal, Doc Spickard ... I realize now how many of those people are dead. They were killed in the mountains. Spick was killed on the Twin Spire, Franz Mohling was killed on McKinley, Mike Hane on some peak in Peru.

1952 shocked the hell out of our group, because up until that point, the drive home had been the most dangerous part of the climb, that's for sure. But in '52 three of our group were killed. Paul Brikoff was killed by lightning on top of Mount Stuart. Art Jesset fell into a crevasse on St. Helens. He was carrying the party's rope. In July Dick Berge was killed when he fell off the north side of Baring. May, July and August, they came in quick succession. It was a lost climbing season. We weren't climbing. We were going out on rescues. Most of us came back to climbing; I had more climbing seasons, but after that, the great days were over. After that summer I was quite ready to back down.

What was your worst night in the mountains?

I think the most memorable, and there have been a lot of bad nights, was an evening we spent up the North Fork of Bridge Creek underneath Mount Goode. The lightning began at 6 p.m. and went on until 10 o'clock the next morning. We were lying under a tarp looking up at the face of Mount Goode and lightning would light up the entire north face. There was no count; the lightning flash and thunder were almost simultaneous.

The storm would move down the valley, and just about the time you began to feel a lull, another would move in.

There was torrential rain all the time, great sparks coming down the face of Goode caused by falling boulders, whole sections of the mountain seemed to be falling off creating these tremendously large sparks.

We were camped under a waterfall at Many Waterfalls Camp. During the day they had been these nice, white, lacy ribbons, but now they were swollen to enormous size, brown and thundering. There was the thunder of water, thunder in the sky, and sparks coming down Goode all night long.

The weather improved, but four days later, as we were leaving, we felt real fear. We had been camped in a huge, open meadow. A quarter-mile down the trail had been an identical meadow. When we hiked out we found that the landscape at that second meadow had changed. Where was the meadow? Where was the trail? Where did this big pile of rocks, mud and trees come from? A blowout had come down in the middle of the storm and obliterated that huge meadow. It just as easily could have been our meadow. Talk about objective dangers, and we were just hiking. If you have been in the mountains in a storm, you know there is no safety anywhere. You may be in the woods during a wind storm, and the trees will rock back and forth. You can see them pulling themselves out by their roots. Where do you go?

Well, a tarp wouldn't inspire much confidence. Speaking of tarps, what was the equipment like when you started climbing?

Well, with ice axes, you had about three choices, really whatever Lloyd Anderson, at REI, was importing. The ice axe stayed essentially the same until about ten years ago when they began coming out with metal models with all the little ratchets, scoops and god-knows-what on them. Ninety percent of the use of the ice axe has always been as a walking stick. You can't use those little things for walking sticks now. I don't know how people stay upright, because when I started climbing, if you took a climber's ice axe away he'd fall down in the trail.

How about packs?

The Trapper Nelson was standard for a long time. I can remember when a friend bought a Kelty in 1953. We jeered at him. You couldn't buy a Kelty in Seattle in those days due to franchise agreements. REI couldn't carry them. The Co-op eventually made their less expensive model, the Cruiser. It's been interesting to follow the Trapper-Nelson through the ages and watch it gradually disappear from the REI catalog. My kids all had Trappers, but Betty got a Kelty and when my Trapper busted, I borrowed hers. It was a revelation. You can't go back to a Trapper after you've carried a Kelty.

Had REI begun to expand when you started climbing?

It was a closet. Lloyd and Mary Anderson were virtually the whole staff for years. It wasn't until the early '60s that it started to become a national institution. We were climbing in the Selkirks in the 1950s, and I remember staying at Wheeler Hut. There was this one snotty group of Harvard Mountaineers, off in a corner. They were snotty until they found out we were from Seattle. Then they came over and said, "You're from Seattle. You must shop at the Co-op in person." Back in Boston, they'd spend their winters pouring over the Co-op catalog envisioning this huge treasure house, but we got to go to that closet in person!

Lloyd was a Depression mountaineer. He was a cheapskate. We were all cheapskates. We all liked war surplus, cheap stuff, and Lloyd served that purpose. He always used to sneer at all that expensive crap. I still tend to myself.

Well, along came the more affluent climbers of the '60s who weren't all poor like we had been before. They wanted the top, flossy stuff and Lloyd wouldn't carry it. Eventually REI, under Jim Whittaker, began to go into top-of-the-line gear.

When I was doing the second edition to *Backpacking: One Step At a Time*, there was this freaky little thing, internal frame packs, which we had barely mentioned in the previous edition. The backpacking department at REI said that was all they sold now. I keep trying to tell people that as beginners they need a Kelty, an external frame pack, and they say, "Oh, no, we want this thing that's as sleek as a Ferrari." The internal frame pack has its place, but for the average hiker, the external frame is what he should have. People in their backpacking gear, like everything else, want to get with the action. They're looking at what's neat. That happened with tents.

Tents were so bad when I first started climbing; well, there weren't any tents worth carrying except in polar conditions. We used seven-by-eleven-foot life raft sail. It was the first waterproof shelter you could carry, the universal tarp. Through World War II you only heard about nylon in women's stockings. Suddenly, after the war, we get this marvelous nylon dumped on us. You could get a tarp for five dollars. They started making single-walled tents, which of course was a disaster. We bought these army mountain tents. You'd crawl into them and spend the night bailing sweat off the floor.

After years they finally perfected the two-walled tent. The A-frame, my god, they were beautiful tents! But I go to do the next edition of the backpacking book, and they don't even carry them at the Co-op. Nobody will buy them. Everyone wants the bubble tent. You can sit up in them, play cards, but they're heavier, less dependable and more expensive. Equipment reached what I consider to be perfection at several levels, and then everything went style crazy.

What was a typical dinner in the mountains for you?

Just what it is now, Krap Dinners (aka Kraft). I've gone through freeze dried and out the other end. I've gotten fed up with freeze dried, although some good came from it, instant potatoes. Before the war you had to do it yourself, fool around at home, cooking the potatoes and drying them yourself in the oven. It was a mess. But instant potatoes were great. It became a staple of my dinners along with quick cooking spaghetti, another wonderful thing. Minute Rice became another staple and still is. There were a few freeze dried items, like peas and carrots, which at the time were air dried. I think the freeze-dried dinners wouldn't be bad for an emergency.

When I was on assignment for National Geographic for a month and on an expense account, I went down to the Co-op with my kids and loaded up with literally hundreds of dollars worth of freeze-dried food—and that's easy to do. I did it mostly for the kids because they would always look at what the other people on trips were cooking while we were having Krap dinners. After a month in the Sierra though, the kids were saying, "Oh, lasagna, again? When are we going to have Krap dinners?"

Did you cook over stoves or open fires?

The Primus 71L was the standard in those days. I just bought myself a Whisperlite last year, and man, that's the end product as far as I'm concerned. Basically we were wood fire people, and it's been very hard for my generation of hikers to get away from wood fires.

Was there any sense of environmental awareness among mountaineers back in the 1940s and '50s?

I think we were very good about garbage. We always followed the rule of "Burn, Bash and Bury." Pack it out didn't really get started in the Northwest. I remember when the Mountaineers brought out the first edition of *Freedom of the Hills* in 1960, we gave the rules of "Burn, Bash and Bury" and received anguished cries from Californians that they were going out on excavations to dig up tin cans in the mountain meadows of the Sierra. Environmentalism early on meant leave a clean camp and a dead fire.

I remember a friend, Dick Brooks, moaning about the logging that was going on in the Sauk Valley in 1948 when we were hiking up to climb Glacier Peak. I didn't think there was anything you could do about it, and, so what, logging happens. There was always going to be enough wilderness behind the ranges. But that encroachment hit me in 1960. I recall being above White Rock Lakes along the Ptarmigan Traverse, sitting above the lakes and looking in all directions; wilderness as far as the eye could see. Then through the lowland haze down Downey Creek, the forest seemed a different color. I suddenly realized I was looking at a clear-cut. I was in the middle of the roaring wilderness and I could see a clear-cut! That was when I began to get active in the environmental movement.

Did you envision the enthusiastic reception **100 Hikes** *would receive, and that it would spawn this whole sub-culture of* **100 Hikes** *fanatics?*

We had worked from a European hiking guide that Tom Miller had picked up, *100 Hikes in the Alps*, and it had the whole format: concise text, the little map and photo, a cookbook design. Instead of being an area guide where the hiker had to take the ingredients and make his own recipe, here were the recipes. We knew that it would be big. We didn't know how big. We printed 5,000 copies and they sold out in the first week.

We heard later about people trying to hike all 100 hikes, but we weren't too surprised. The

Mountaineers had their pin peaks. But we frustrated the hell out of them by bringing out 101 and 102.

It seems that **100 Hikes** *has sort of set the standard for guide books.*

Let's be honest about it. It did set the standard. Other organizations got into the act, and they pretty much followed our pattern. But none has done it as well.

100 Hikes *brought hordes of people into the Cascades. Did you ever think about the impact the book would have on those areas?*

That's always been on our minds, because as soon as the book came out, we called it, among ourselves, "100 places not to go hiking on the weekend." But better one-thousand boots than one chain saw, and that's been our philosophy from the beginning. That's why we went on from 100 to 101 and 102, and now to a whole string of "100s," to distribute the impact. In those days we were in combat with the Forest Service. Many of our hikes were in areas where they had timber sales going, and we were fighting that. Today we work together with the park and forest services. We'll ask what are the impacts on certain areas, and they will tell us and suggest that maybe we drop those areas from the next edition. But we have to play fair with the hikers. You can't just leave out everything that's in a wilderness area or park because it's saved. But we try to distribute the load.

What major changes have you seen in the mountains since you first started going into them?

People! When I went out on Boy Scout hikes in the Olympics in the late '30s it was exceptional to meet anyone in the mountains. It wasn't until the '50s that you became less than startled to see other people in the Cascades. I remember in the mid-50s camping right at Cascade Pass—as we all did in those days—and seeing a party coming up the trail. I went out to greet them because they were bound to be friends. There never was anyone at Cascade Pass except people I knew. And they were strangers, total strangers! What the hell were they doing in my mountains? I've since gotten use to it. But I still know places to get away. We all have our little spots, and we preserve them for our solitude.

Are you optimistic about the future?

Fundamentally I'm a pessimist. I think the world is getting worse and worse, but it's a ques-

tion of keeping it as good as we can within limits. To make the United States a livable nation you'd have to go back to a population of 120,000,000. You get above that number, and there simply aren't the resources to support the lifestyle we've become accustomed to. The American standard of living has been declining since 1960. Some might say since John Kennedy died. I attribute it to the Space Needle. I think that was the beginning of the end, some arcane power to generate evil. The changes that have occurred in the Puget Sound area have definitely been for the worse.

On the other hand there are things that can be done. For example, when the development began on Cougar Mountain there was never any thought given to open space. Our lot is the largest open space, three acres, until you get over to the regional park. But when that park is completed with access corridors, and associated green belts, it will be five to six thousand acres of open space; one of the largest urban parks in the country. And it is next to state forest, a working forest, but cut in small chunks evenly spaced over a sixty-year cycle.

Do you see the Cascades as someday becoming just a park in a sea of civilization?

What I see is that the timber industry, as we have known it, is coming to the end of the line. There is going to be a timber industry but based on the model designed by the Washington State Department of Natural Resources for Tiger Mountain. It's going to be low-level based, even flow based. Right now it's market based. Prices are high so let's cut it all out. But that doesn't provide an even flow of raw material, doesn't provide a stable job base.

I think by the middle of the next century there won't be a Weyerhaeuser; there won't be private timber land. You'll go back to Gifford Pinchot's foundation that the forests are too important to be run by private enterprise. Meanwhile we'll have lost an awful lot of trees. Weyerhauser is cutting in the West Cascades up to elevations of 5,000 feet. There won't be another forest there for another five hundred years, because they don't even think of tree planting at those elevations. They're just tree mining. But if you look back to what the prospects were in 1960, there's an awful lot of good country that's been saved. I used to believe that wilderness was inexhaustible. I'd be sorry to see this or that wilderness go, but there was plenty more. Then I saw that there might not be anymore, and I realized we'd have to stand up and fight.

In Footloose in 1970, the Footsore series that followed, and your book, Walking the Beach to Bellingham, you departed the mountains for the lowlands. It was a wonderful celebration of the obscure, small places in our lives that are too often ignored. Yet they have so much value.

That's what I think it was about. Unfortunately it got too obscure, because my publisher went broke. If you want a good buy, go to the basement of the University of Washington Book Store. It's been remaindered for about five dollars.

I haven't lost my interest in the high wilderness, but I find I get just as much pleasure poking along a Puget Sound beach where there are different combinations of sights. There's his-

tory where the wildness comes within the home of civilization.

I like to go to the mountains to get completely away from mankind. But I'm not such a misanthrope that I don't like to be among people, meet the people who live on the beach. You know the people who live on the beach are frequently very interesting folks. They have a sense of place, whereas you could tour the whole of Bellevue and not find a hundred people who knew where the hell they were.

Do you still get the same things out of the mountains you got in the 1940s?

It's the same range of things. It's been a long time since I looked at a really tough mountain and thought I really wanted to be there. I find that the best views of a mountain are from the bottom anyway, looking up at it.

*P*ete Schoening has been defined forever in the minds of mountaineers by one belay, a standing ice axe belay that miraculously stopped the falls of five companions on the blizzard-swept upper slopes of K-2 in 1953. At the end of Schoening's rope was the dying Art Gilkey in a makeshift litter. Establishing the best belay in a bad position on the 45-degree ice slope, Schoening watched George Bell slip. Bell pulled Tony Streather off his feet, they caught the rope of Houston and Bates and they began to fall, and those two took Dee Molenaar—who had tied into Gilkey's litter—with them. From that web of ropes, one strand led to Schoening, and when the full weight of the five falling climbers dug the rope deep into Schoening's back and gloved brake hand, he held them. When the rope went pencil thin from the force of the falls, he held them, and until they could stagger to their feet, Pete Schoening held them.

That belay has assumed an almost mythical place in mountaineering lore; quite a load to hoist on one's back, but Schoening has never seen it as burden or badge of honor. To him the belay was a mixture of skill and luck.

If Pete Schoening is aware of his place in 20th Century mountaineering, he hides it well. He is open, engaging and looks more comfortable in a wool shirt and work pants than a suit. He also possesses a raucous, infectious laugh. Yet there are moments when his voice drops to a contemplative whisper as he talks of tragedy or the philosophical side of mountaineering. Schoening is a truly modest man who takes pride in his considerable mountaineering skills and accomplishments but values even more the freedom and friends he has found in the mountains.

Despite a hip replacement operation a few years ago, Schoening, in his mid-60s, still marches up trail and peaks at a pace that leaves climbing companions half his age gasping for breath.

《You know as well as I do that people will come up and ask, "Why do you do that crazy stuff? Why do you risk your life?" I don't feel like I'm risking my life. I wouldn't do it if it were. I mean, people think golf is a great activity. Why isn't climbing a great activity? But talking about climbing as a positive thing doesn't sell newspapers. But portraying some poor guy falling down a 500-foot cliff and splatting out with a big pile of blood at the bottom; boy that sells stuff. 》

—Pete Schoening

It is certainly not competition that drives Pete Schoening, but rather a desire to do all that a human body can do in a lifetime, with little help from extraneous technological gizmos.

The interview takes place at Schoening's office at American Chemgrate, where he is president. As he shows us to the car, Pete points out his bicycle, a fat red Schwinn Typhoon with one speed, balloon tires and coaster brakes. Schoening has owned the bike for almost 35 years and often rides it the eight miles to work. There is no trace of irony in his voice when he says, "I've always preferred this bike because, frankly, I could never get used to hand brakes."

For the past several years Schoening has taken part in the 200-mile Seattle to Portland (STP) bike race. Although he has never finished the ride in one day, he has come close and is confident that he will do it one of these years. I leave with a vision of Pete Schoening, knapsack on his back, smiling broadly, as he peddles past hordes of high-tech lycra-clad bikers.

▲

There were still a lot of unclimbed peaks and crags in the Cascades when you graduated from the basic climbing course in the late '40s.

After World War II, I got in with a crowd that liked to get out and explore. Obviously the local guy who was the driving force behind the climbing was Fred Beckey. Every time you went out with Fred, his primary interest was to do something that someone else hadn't done. These kinds of interest became contagious. At that time there were very few people climbing. I would venture to say no more than a hundred people in the Northwest. It seems to me that climbers were looked on as oddballs, in the same class with motorcycle drivers.

Did you have a sense during that period that you were pushing the limits of climbing?

I don't know whether there was an intent to push the limits. At that time people in California were doing some pretty spectacular rock climbing. Fred Beckey and I got involved in what was going on down there. To go down to climb in California was like going to the North Pole today. That was a big deal.

There was a little communcation between us and the California climbers; about pitons and bolts. I remember these guys in California would drill a bolt hole and they'd have dirt in the hole. I think Al Steck sent up this little spoon that somebody designed to get the dirt out. At that time I was working in a laboratory and was blowing some stuff with a little hose and all of a sudden I thought, "That's how you do it. You don't need that damn spoon." Trying to figure out new ways of doing things was kind of fun and exciting.

You made your own pitons?

Well, we were making some angles. Joe Hieb's dad had a place in Seattle. He made radio-electric ovens for bakeries. We made some bolt hangers at his dad's shop; this was before people were using bolts. We were just experimenting with them. We would sit down, figure out how to do something and then, usually, find something available commercially that was much better, much simpler and sometimes cheaper.

One of the reasons we made a lot of our stuff was that we couldn't afford the commercially made stuff. Fred brought in an angle piton, and we went down to Joe's shop and made them. It didn't cost us a thing. The metal we used was stuff that had been thrown away, stuff we found in the garbage can, little end pieces.

We even tried wood blocks on some little towers between Chinook Pass and Yakima—really crappy, terrible, crumbly, dangerous rock. We'd take an axe, whittle off the end and drive them into big, wide cracks. Some of the rock was very soft and you almost had to use nails. In fact I did use nails on Chumstick Snag, which is sandstone.

Cliff Leight: I think the bolts are still hanging there with nails in them.

You were in that group that did the first climbs in Leavenworth at Peshastin and Castle Rock.

Yeah. I don't remember the names of the routes we climbed. Fred started naming them. Fred was big for that. We'd go out and do different things; two guys climbing here and two over there. What was neat about that area was that you could climb earlier in the year when you couldn't get higher in the mountains. That was the primary reason for doing it.

You know, there's a ledge part way up Castle.

I don't know what people call it now, but we called it Logger's Ledge. There used to be trees, fairly good-sized trees on that ledge. You could climb for an hour in this garbage and and fifteen feet away would be this tree. That bothered Fred. He'd say, "We've got to get these damn trees out of here. You can't take any decent pictures with all these damn trees around."

Well, a few of us—I had worked at a sawmill—went over there one weekend and started cutting those trees down. They fell clear to the road. They brought a lot of rocks down to the road as well. Fred would go down to the road and stop the cars. People would ask what was wrong and Fred would tell them, "There's some logging going on up the road." Fred could come up with some incredible reasons for things. That guy was really something, innovative. I really didn't want to cut down the trees and was kind of embarrassed. I refused to go down to the road and stop cars.

I remember we had been climbing at Peshastin and were coming back between Peshastin and Leavenworth. I was driving. Up ahead of us was a jeep, a guy and his wife or girl friend. We'd stopped somewhere and gotten a quart of milk. Fred told me, "When we go by this guy pull in close." So as we went by, I pulled fairly close to the jeep, and Fred opened the door and stuck this bottle of milk in the guy's lap and we drove on by.

Just past Leavenworth a big red light and siren turned on behind us. Evidently this guy had called in, or maybe the policeman had seen us. He pulled us over and took us back to Leavenworth to the judge's house. It was really embarrassing. You could look in the window and see the whole family having Sunday dinner. The judge came to the door, the officer told him what happened and the judge mentioned a fine. Fred starts arguing, "Where's the law? What law is there to prevent us from putting a bottle of milk in a guy's car." Why the judge did not throw us in jail, I'll never know. Fred is really something. He just takes it right to the limit.

Did you get up into the North Cascades during the early '50s?

A little bit, if you call the Southern Pickets the North Cascades. It was a bit difficult to get into, probably still is. To do much climbing on the weekend you had to hustle. A lot of time we'd drive up Friday night, kind of get on the trail so that at daybreak you'd be near the difficult cross-country terrain.

So most of your trips were epic weekenders?

Oh, yeah, you had to work. Sometimes you'd come back from a climb and go straight to work on Monday morning. It was all right if your job was physical, but I remember going from a climb to a dentist appointment. The dentist said it was the first time anyone ever fell asleep in his chair while he was drilling.

What was your first climb outside of the Cascades?

A trip to the Alaska Coast Range in 1951-52. I think we were one of the first groups to leave the area.

After that trip did you feel that you were ready for a big expedition?

I do think that as a result of the trip to the Coast Range, that I was invited on the K-2 trip in 1953. I had been invited to show slides of our Coast Range trip at the annual AAC meeting and Bob Bates and Charlie Houston, who were organizing the trip, were there.

In reading the book, K-2, the Savage Mountain, I was impressed by what seemed to be a real camaraderie among your group.

Yes, I think there probably was. I suppose to a certain extent that was because of Charlie and Bob, who were very sensitive people, really fine individuals. I think that was true of everybody on that trip, even though everyone was different. I really do think there was a little tighter bond there with our group, and I don't think that's changed. This past year we were going to get together, but it fell apart. It could be that it won't be many years before somebody will come to the end of the road. Bob and Charlie must be in their late 70s.

When I interviewed Harvey Manning, he was talking about putting together the first edition of Freedom of the Hills, and he said, "There was a hell of a lot of controversy over the boot-axe belay. What really screwed it up was that we had tested the ice axe belays and found that the only one that could be depended upon was the one using the boot. This hip-axe belay is totally unrealistic, so what is the most famous ice-axe belay in the history of mountaineering, the one on K-2 by Pete Schoening, and that was a hip-axe belay!"

Harvey has got a very good memory and an eloquent way of expressing things, too. We used to do things with Harvey, and he's a real fun guy. We'd do stupid, really stupid things. But Harvey was a guy who was not interested in this high angle rock climbing. He had no interest in it. So I knew that if we went out with Harvey, we were probably going to do some stupid crawl through the mud someplace.

Tell me about that famous belay. At the time it happened did you realize what you were holding?

No, that was a very confusing time, you have to appreciate that. I was the guy who had the belay on Art Gilkey who was sick. That was my job and that the ropes all interconnected was happenstance. I knew it had to be a pretty good belay, and it was a bad place. It was pretty steep, about forty-five degrees and there was a little rock, about a foot across, stuck in the ice, held by a little ice finger. Actually there was no way you could get a belay in the ice very effectively. But it was cold, the wind was blowing, and we had to get a guy down who couldn't help himself. I could have been taking off the belay, just as easily been climbing, and had that been the case, looking back, we could have lost some people. It was just a very fortunate thing.

I think George Bell was just below me when he slipped, but I don't recall. I'd have to read the book (laughs). Dee Molenaar has tried to have a clear picture of exactly what happened. I think everyone has a little different impression. But I kind of recall George sliding by out of the corner of my eye, so I knew there was the possibility of something happening.

As I recall the rope went around the ice axe and around my back because I was facing in. I saw George slip, but I don't recall saying much. But I knew there was the possibility of something bad happening if he didn't stop. I don't recall anything else other than, obviously the force of the rope. I do recall that I knew there was something else on that rope.

Even though every one was stopped, things were still pretty desperate.

It was not an easy situation. Charley was in pretty tough shape. He was talking, but he wasn't making a great deal of sense. And that was sort of scary. I hadn't had that much experience with someone getting knocked unconscious. Now I would watch like a hawk. Even though the person might be mobile, he doesn't know what's going on. The next day I went down with Charlie. I recall vividly that here was Charlie, the older guy

and me the young, punk kid, and at that time you had respect for older people. Charlie and Bob were kind of like your dad. You don't argue with Dad. But coming down with Charlie I almost had to tell him what to do at times. "Charlie do this, do that. Put your foot here."

It's amazing that you all got off the mountain all right after that.

I'm sure there are events in people's lives that are difficult. Everyone has difficult times.

You returned to K-2.

A few years later, Nick Clinch organized a trip to Gasherbrum I. Nick had originally thought that this would be the last chance for an American group to make a first ascent of an oct-thousander. We went over and fortunately we climbed the peak, Andy Kauffman and myself. Coming back we got to Concordia and I said I'd love to go back up to the K-2 base camp. So Nick and I hiked up there and spent a day. We saw Gilkey's little memorial. The little memorial rock had been scavenged to some extent. That was in 1958. An interesting thing about that side trip was that some of what we had left behind was now down the glacier about a mile and a half. Now there are so many people going into those places. I like to go to places that aren't inundated with humanity. I suppose that sounds isolationist.

The expedition to the Pamirs in 1974 must have been different than any of your other expeditions?

I think it got along reasonably well, but if I were to choose, I would not do it again. There was the language barrier, but you can expect that. But, within our group there were stresses. No one was shaking a fist at one another. You see that was an official expedition, and we were charged with getting a cross section of American climbers: young and old, ice climbers, rock climbers, male and female. I hadn't had that kind of experience before. From that aspect it was a difficult trip. I think it worked out reasonably well, but I will not go on a trip like that again.

Bob Craig's book, Storm and Sorrow, is one of the best expedition accounts I've read.

I don't like Bob's book. I shouldn't say that. I don't mean it that way. The book, to me, puts more emphasis on the negative aspects of climbing, in my opinion. I think if you read Nick Clinch's book on Hidden Peak, that much more reflects my feeling about climbing, as being a fun thing, something that stimulates, something you plan together.

The trip to the Pamirs was a tragic trip. It really was, and the events that were given the greatest emphasis in the book were the tragic events: the Russian women, the Swiss, Gary Ullin. But there was a lot of positive, neat things about the trip too. You don't get that out of the book, and that bothers me.

I don't know how you write a book that gives you that good balance. In some respects our K-2 book gives a better balance. I think that somebody reads that and says, "A tragic event happened but that wasn't the focus of the whole trip." When I read Bob's book, I say that the tragic events are the focus. As a climber that bothers me. I think Bob knows that. I have a great deal of respect for Bob, but that's the way I feel.

I think Craig was sensitive to the victims of the tragedy. He writes eloquently about those events. I don't think of it as a sensationalized account.

Absolutely not. What is here is Bob. I don't think there's any question about that. Bob is sensitive to those kinds of things. But I also think those things can give the wrong impression of climbing. You know as well as I do that people will come up and ask, "Why do you do that crazy stuff? Why do you risk your life?" I don't feel like I'm risking my life. I wouldn't do it if it were. I mean, people think golf is a great activity. Why isn't climbing a great activity? But talking about climbing as a positive thing doesn't sell newspapers. But portraying some poor guy falling down a five-hundred-foot cliff and splatting out with a big pile of blood at the bottom; boy that sells stuff.

Have you been injured climbing?

No, not really. I got frost-bitten on Mount McKinley and lost some fingers. But I've really been very fortunate, well not fortunate. You don't go out there to get in accidents.

So you would consider yourself a pretty cautious climber?

I would hope that's the case. I've heard talk about Fred Beckey. People say, "Wow, he really does scary things." Fred's the most cautious climber I've ever climbed with. Fred must be pushing seventy, and you don't get to be seventy years old unless you're super safe. Fred doesn't make mistakes.

Have you seen any of the sport climbing competitions?

No, I've heard about it. I hear some people saying it's great and others saying it's stupid. I kind of doubt I would have participated. I recall having a conversation with Willi Unsoeld about this, and we didn't see anything wrong with it. We also talked about solo climbing. Willi would take greater risks than I would. I'm not sure that he wasn't more capable of doing them than I was. We both agreed there was nothing wrong with solo climbing as long as you didn't climb past your capabilities.

Willi always had a way of expressing himself that was absolutely fascinating. I heard that he had this presentation that he gave that was "Around The World on $50." As I recall he and another guy left Oregon and they left with $250 in their pockets. They spent a year bumming around the world and when they got back they had $200. So Willi put on this little program and they didn't have a camera. He had no pictures and it was just him getting up there and telling the story. He was able to tell that story different for different evenings. He totally improvised the thing. His was a totally different style but I would compare him to this Garrison Keillor.

Willi and I never went on an expedition together. Willi was one of these people like Fred: super capable, really knew what he was doing. I certainly agreed with his feelings on some things. I'm not so sure I lived all of them. But I think to a certain extent, Willi's philosophy was that to get any value out of this thing you've got to keep it lively. I can, in some respects, say that Willi died because of the attitude, because coming off of Rainier, it seems to me that they did have the option of going around another way that—I won't say an avalanche couldn't have happened—the probability was much less. I can only imagine that Willi recognized the possibility of something sliding if they went that way.

I think to some extent Willi would weigh risks and decide whether it was worth it or not. On the climb of the West Ridge on Everest, he and Tom Hornbein took a heck of a chance, no doubt about it. I guess you'd have to put yourself in the position and decide whether you would be willing to take the risk.

Willi was a fellow with a great deal of faith, and when I say faith I mean a great deal of capability too. Sometimes a person goes on faith and we overlook that that person is doggone capable. You can really make the judgement, but I would bet that if Fred was with that group up on Mount Rainier, he would look at it, and say we can get down fast going here or it might be longer and windier going down here, and I think he would have opted for the safer way and I think I would have too. I don't want to say that either decision is good or bad, they're just decisions. And maybe I'm overemphasizing that Willi believed in not sterilizing the activity. He believed in making everything lively, get the juices flowing.

I think to some extent my interest in climbing came from the freedom I sensed in the mountains that you don't have in town. You have a certain structure in town that you don't have in the mountains. If you want to scream and yell, you can scream and yell. If you want to piss on the ground, you can piss on the ground. There's a freedom, because there's no one around. For me I'd rather go out in the mountains where there aren't a whole lot of people where I can build a fire and camp without some little ranger coming in and telling you, "You can't do that." But at the same time, if everyone camped where they wanted then you would, and do, have a mess. It's a difficult question.

Did it ever bother you that you didn't get up Everest?

I don't think you think about that. I believe that when the American expedition was being organized, I won't say specifically, but I think that I was invited to go on it. But with a job and kids, you can't go on all the trips, so you have to make some sacrifices. It would have been a good trip to go on. I think that the possibility of going to Everest now, I don't think I would have the drive or capability. But you know, Tom Hornbein and Nick Clinch went on this trip to China a while back. I had some things come up and couldn't go. There's the possibility of going back next year.

So you don't think your hip would be a problem?

Oh, it's different. There's no question that anything like that changes what you can or can't do. But if you sit and put restrictions on yourself, I don't see that it does any good.

I went to several doctors before the hip operation, not for advice, but to find the very best doctor. When I set up the appointment, the doctor told me that I wouldn't be able to do a whole bunch of things. I knew it was a serious operation, but I told him, "Please don't give me any more of this, 'You can't do this or that.'" And you know, I think that I've done a lot more than was on his allowable list. I suppose I could pop or break something and he would tell me, "Pete, if you hadn't done that, what I told you not to do . . ." But to not do it is to, again, sterilize your life. I have to say, and I don't want to dwell on religion, but I think there are powers significantly beyond our imagination. I say, why fear them? You've got to do what what you can. And when you can't do it anymore, you can at least say, "I gave it my best shot."

*I*ra Spring is on the phone, and I have a moment to stare out his picture window which overlooks Puget Sound and the Olympic Peninsula. Beyond the tall firs in his back yard, sunlight cracks the gray clouds and plays on the choppy waters of the sound. A ferry boat cuts through the waves on its way to the peninsula, and in the background snow-covered summits of Constance and the Brothers appear and disappear amidst the slow flow of clouds. It is a scene that makes up for a lifetime of rain. It is an Ira Spring photo.

So many of my impressions of favorite hikes in the Cascades were formed by black-and-white Ira Spring photos: Meadow Mountain, Spray Park, Gothic Basin, Lake Ann, and especially Cascade Pass, which appeared in *100 Hikes in Western Washington*, became familiar places long before I hiked to them. I imagined myself diving into Copper Lake with the happy bunch of swimmers in the photo, fishing off the rock at Deep Lake, or leading the line of backpackers up to Dutch Miller Gap. Where there weren't people, my tent would be just behind the camera. I rarely considered the photographer, and perhaps that was the strength of those photos, the absence of artsy intention and ego.

Ira Spring admits to being a traditionalist in the mold of the late Ray Atkeson. His pictures are classically composed—mountain balanced by lake, meadow, hiker. In his early seventies, Spring is the dean of Northwest outdoor photographers. He and twin brother, Bob, first gained prominence in the early 1950s with their series of *High Adventure* books. Ira continues to run his free-lance photography business and now is teamed with his daughter, Vicki, and her husband, Tom Kirkendal. Spring still focuses almost entirely on outdoor shots.

After finishing his phone call, Spring returns to the living room and sits down at the table. I haven't even asked my first question when he tells me, "You know, of course, that I have never really done much in the way of real climbing. I photographed the good climbers—Fred Beckey, Pete Schoening, Jim and Louie Whittaker—when they were teenagers. But I am not a good climber. I just took pictures of the good climbers. I think

« I'm old-fashioned in that I like the grand scenes; the mountain,

not dead center, just a little off to the side, not arty. »

—Ira Spring

Fred lists me on one or two of his rock ascents, but he drug me up, literally. He wanted a picture up there on top."

▲

When did you get started in photography?

In 1930 Kodak celebrated its fiftieth birthday by giving every twelve-year-old child in the country a box Brownie camera. My brother and I went into the one and only camera store in Shelton and picked up our cameras. At about that time we became interested in hiking and the two just went together. I knew when I was a teenager what I wanted to do. Figuring out how I was going to do it was another matter. We piddled with photography in high school, but at that time there was one college that was giving instruction in photography. Over at Central Washington College there was a professor who taught the whole rigamarole, taking pictures, developing. That's where we really learned how to do it.

Both Bob and I were sort of into photography during the war, and after the war we went into business. Bob was in the medics and I was in the Air Force, ground photography; in the Air Force! We were supposed to be doing engineering in the South Pacific. I was using four-by-five cameras at that time.

You must have carried a lot of extra weight into the mountains.

Yeah, when we did take color, there was a limit on how many film holders you could take. Film holders and film add up to quite a pile.

Where did you set up operations after the war?

In Seattle. After all that's where our market was. We had sold a little bit of our work before the war. You know, mountaineering and mountain scenery probably never paid for itself, but it did give us exposure. Right after the war there were mountaineering stories appearing in Saturday Evening Post, Geographic, Life; trips on McKinley and some early expeditions into the Himalayas. But no one was doing anything on U.S. climbing. So we appeared in all the popular magazines of the era with our mountain stories and they led to a lot of other things. It paid and I think that a person who stuck to it now, people like Galen Rowell, could probably do really well. We couldn't. We considered going to the Himalayas when we were young and had the energy to do those things. The cost of getting there and the time spent wasn't going to pay our way.

Our books, with black-and-white photography, wouldn't go anywhere now. Color's the thing. And that's too bad because black-and-white has a lot to offer. In our first book, the black-and-whites were done beautifully, but then the publisher got cheaper with each edition and as a result, they didn't sell as well. But we were lucky to get things published.

How did you choose where you would go to take pictures?

I went to places that were photogenic. Several times I would go up on Mount Rainier, either on the Ingraham or Cowlitz glaciers and set up camp with a crew for a week. I used high school or college-age kids; they didn't have summer jobs and this was great for them, great training. Gary Rose and Dave Nicholson were favorites and the two Marsten sisters. I had a whale of a time.

A couple of the teenagers I took out on photographic trips were Jim and Louie Whittaker. Both of them said that the stories they appeared in and the publicity helped them get their international start. The climbing was actually pretty simple. They give more credit than I actually deserve.

Fred Beckey was probably twenty when I started working with him. Pete Schoening was a teenager. I've run into almost all the climbers of that time when they were teenagers and look what happened to them. Of course I spent a lot of time with Ome. He appears in many of my books. So do Wolf Bauer and Otto Trott.

Did you have the luxury of asking climbers to redo a climbing sequence so you could retake the shot?

Sure. You see, these were trips I planned. The young ones, before they got to be gungho, were happy just to go out and have some fun. Of course we climbed. We just didn't go to the top.

If you go out with some gungho climbers you're not going to have time to take pictures. If you go out with the idea that you're going to stop along the way and take pictures, you'll get to the top all right, but it will take a lot longer. That's the only way you can do it, especially with a four-by-five. Our Ptarmigan Traverse in the early '50s was three weeks. In fact we went all the way from

Cascade Pass to Image Lake, climbing around Dome Peak and across.

That area is beautiful.

You'll have to tell me. In two weeks, we only had three days of sunshine. It made me sick in such beautiful country. We wandered across from Dome to Image Lake in a dense fog. We didn't have a USGS topographic map then. All we had was an old, old Forest Service map and it wasn't accurate. We were getting pretty discouraged. We'd been walking through fields of wet lupine and our feet were squishing. We sat down to lunch, didn't know where we were. There was a little break in the fog and we suddenly saw the trail that led from Totem Pass to Image Lake. We didn't know that. It wasn't on our map, but there it was!

I heard so many stories of how the traverse had disintegrated that Pat and I went back just to see in 1980. We only went as far as White Rock Lakes and then went out the South Cascade Trail. The trail was beat in, but I didn't see any huge damage to campsites. And there was no garbage.

When did you first go up into the Cascade Pass area? There are plenty of photo opportunities there.

We went up with my daughter when she was five months old and she's thirty-six now. At that time the road was all the way up to where the parking lot is now. The trail took off right from there and you could go straight up and intersect the trail. It was the only way to go, not this zig-zag they have now. When they put in the new trail I complained to the district ranger, but he wouldn't listen because at that time it was the way to go. He told me that the biggest complaint was that the old trail was too steep. As time has proved he was wrong.

Is most of your work outdoors nowadays?

Mine is all outdoor photography. I'm still taking pictures and we're working hard to sell them. Stock pictures are our market, a few calendars, a few pictures for textbooks around the world, and guidebooks. My daughter and her husband are into the same thing, and I've been trying to pawn the whole thing off on them, but they're more oriented to bicycling. They did a bicycling guide from Tijuana to the north end of Vancouver Island. They've done a couple of guides on cross-country skiing, mountain biking. They do the text and photos together. I work with Harvey Manning.

What does one need to start a photography business such as yours?

Our initial investment wouldn't last more than a month or two now, but then you didn't need much.

How did you pack your equipment into the mountains?

I just wrapped it up in clothes. Nowadays I put my cameras in plastic bags. With a four-by-five you needed a tripod.

Did you use a Trapper-Nelson pack?

Oh yes! I don't have it anymore. It would be a museum piece now. It was certainly the "in" packboard back when. I used to replace my pack every couple of years. The Trapper-Nelson firm was located in Seattle. Instead of fixing them, they'd just give me a new pack.

Now that's the way to treat a good customer.

I don't know how good a customer I was, but the packs sure showed up in a lot of pictures.

Did you write your own texts?

Not really. I've always had help. That's why I teamed up with Harvey because he can write. I write but my text would never sell. Harvey throws my words around and it ends up I recognize my own writing, but he's made it sing. Some people think he's a wonderful writer but others don't like him, because he's got his own English. Our guide books would be dull if he didn't make them sing like he does.

I did a flower book for Mount Rainier, working with a naturalist at the park, and Harvey did the text. When the book was finished the naturalist wrote a nice letter. He'd said it was the first time he'd ever read a flower book and got some chuckles out of it.

*I think that the **100 Hikes** series is the best in almost every respect.*

I did the research on probably ninety percent of the trails for those books. Harvey did wonders with what I gave him. You can always tell the ones he did himself because they're all two pages long. I try to write with my pictures. Harvey does it with his pen.

How did you go about gathering the information?

I have used a camper ever since I did the first book. I'd drive the camper to the trailhead, spend the night there, wake up early and be on the trail when it was light enough to walk. I'd get to my destination by eight or nine o'clock in the morning, take my picture and head down. That's the way we went, early in morning when we were fresh; no bugs to bother us. We'd see a lot of game.

Back at the camper I'd spend some time to write the hike description and then head to the next trailhead. If there was an overnight, or a three-day hike, I'd still do it in one day. Without a heavy pack, you can do a lot. Sometimes we'd do twenty-mile round trips in a day. I was still using the four-by-five, but it got to the point that I realized that I had to use something else. I just couldn't carry that many camera holders. I took all those pictures especially for the book, except for the hikes that Harvey wrote up. And his pictures looked darned good. He was using an old Rollei, pre-war.

Which photographers do you admire?

Ray Atkeson is one I always admired. When Bob and I first started out, he came to our place several times and gave us valuable advice. He was a competitor but he was just a very nice person. He takes the kind of pictures that I admire. I'm old-fashioned in that I like the grand scenes; the mountain, not dead center, just a little off to the side, not arty.

Cliff Leight: You used to see the classic picture of the mountain in the background with a tent in the foreground pitched in a field of heather, next to a pond. You can't publish a scene like that much anymore, for environmental reasons. I suppose you could have a person getting a drink of water.

Ira: You can't even do that. We took all the pictures out of the guide book that showed people drinking from streams because of the giardia problem. My personal view, it took all the fun out of it. We used to drink out of every stream. I think you can drink out of ninety-nine percent of them, but which ones? They aren't numbered. I use a filter on overnight trips, but I think you're probably just fooling yourself. I now carry water from home, and I never did before. If I'm camping with a stove, I boil it.

What's your favorite area to photograph?

You get up into the mountains and every place has something to offer. From a spectacular point, I suppose Mount Shuksan and Rainier. I can't really say I had any favorites. I just liked getting up in the mountains.

C liff and I are lost and a little bit late for our interview with Tom Miller. I am driving slowly peering at house numbers, but Cliff isn't looking. He is fidgeting with his camera and wondering aloud how he will ever find a copy of *The North Cascades*. This book was published in 1964 to publicize the fight to create the North Cascades Park. Miller's distinctive black-and-white photos of the North Cascades were the centerpiece of the book which has become a Northwest classic, and hard to find. Cliff is attempting to lure me into an elaborate book heist when I pull into Miller's driveway.

Unlike color photos which tend to soften the North Cascades, Miller's black-and-white photos get to the essence of the rugged range: rock and snow, jagged ridgelines against billowing clouds, cold, wild and off the map.

Black-and-white photography remained a passion but never became a profession for Miller as it did for Bob and Ira Spring. The same was true for his climbing. Miller jokingly refers to himself as a second-rate regional climber, but despite his protestations, he has some fine climbs to his credit: a first ascent of Mount Cook in Alaska, the second Ptarmigan Traverse and new routes on Formidable, Johannesburg and Torment. Miller was invited on the 1956 International Everest Expedition, but he reluctantly turned down the invitation. "At the time, I had real mixed feelings about going. I wasn't confident about what I wanted to be, an engineer or climber." A vice president in Boeing's aerospace and electronics division, Miller decided to confine his climbing to the Northwest.

Miller was a member of the committee which created *Mountaineering, Freedom of the Hills*. His future wife, Nancy, was also on that committee. She had grown up in a mountaineering family. Her father was Burge Bickford, a past president of the Mountaineers. Nancy, a lawyer, was the first woman to climb

« When I first went to California, the people in the Stanford Alpine Club were so unused to climbing on snow, and I remember we'd go to Tuolumne Meadows sometimes. I think it was Mount Lyle that supposedly had a glacier. And we saw this glacier and it was not a glacier. It was this little piece of ice. They just were not used to snow at all. »

—Nancy Miller

the north peak of Index, Forbidden, and Formidable. The Millers still climb, although they refer to it more as scrambling.

Tom and Nancy live in North Seattle along the shores of Lake Washington. The interview takes place in their living room. Tom is friendly, a bit reserved, but possesses a self-deprecating sense of humor. He speaks quickly in clipped sentences. Nancy is a bit more relaxed, her pleasant voice has an almost girlish quality to it. As afternoon shadows begin to darken the room, Cliff gets Tom to show us some of his black-and-white photos. I notice a copy of *The North Cascades* on the bookshelf across the room. So does Cliff. He gives me a conspiratorial smile, but when we leave the Millers, the book is still on the shelf and Cliff is still looking.

▲

Did you have any real ambitions as a mountaineer? Were you interested in expeditions?

Tom Miller: I spent three months in the St. Elias Range trying to do the east ridge of Logan, which at that time had never been done. There were four of us, much too small a group for that kind of climb. The members were Dick Mc-Gowan, Dick Long, Tim Kelley, myself, and Franz Mohling, who was killed in an avalanche on Logan many years later.

Dick Long had to be flown out, because of appendicitis, as we were trying to climb MacArthur, a satellite of Logan that had never been climbed. We were at our second camp, eighty-eight walking miles from the Malaspina Glacier across from Yakutat. We had to carry him about 4,700 feet down to the glacier where he was flown out.

You were able to radio for assistance?

Tom: We had a radio, but it didn't work. We had bought our own plane for $1,000 to do our own drops. It was much cheaper to do our own drops than hire someone to do it for us. One of the members of our expedition had decided to not go on the actual climb. He stayed in Yakutat and would fly over every five or six days when the weather was clear and drop mail.

When we got Dick to the glacier, we stomped out an SOS in the snow and requested a message drop as well. He flew back over the next morning at 2:30 and we made a successful message snatch— a loop of string between tent poles was snatched by a hook trailed by the plane during a low fly-by. He contacted the Coast Guard in Anchorage which had a big Grumman Albatross. It should have had no problems landing on the glacier, but it was a very expensive airplane. The top of the Logan Glacier was only 7,000 feet, and the son-of-a-bitch wouldn't land. He dropped us a radio and told us he had a doctor on board who listened to Dick's

symptons and agreed that we had to get him out right away. We said, "So land," but the pilot said he wasn't about to get his airplane stuck on the glacier.

They flew back, talked to a bush pilot in Yakutat who flew to the edge of the Malaspina and changed to skis for the landing on the Logan Glacier. The guy flew in in really bad weather. It was real hairy trying to fly through small saddles at 9,000 feet with an airplane which had a maximum altitude of 10,000 feet. He landed in snow so soft he couldn't taxi at full power, so we had to snow-shoe-pack a 20 x 4,000-foot runway. The runway started to freeze about 2 a.m., and Dick and the pilot were just able to take off using all 4,000 feet of the runway. He had to land in Yakutat on his skis, in the tall grass alongside the old runway.

It turned out later that it probably hadn't been necessary to get Dick out after all. Years later he came back and climbed the Hummingbird Ridge on Logan. We did climb Mount Cook on that trip, a first ascent.

Did the Logan expeditions whet your desire for more?

Tom: After Logan, I finished college at the University of Washington, started work, and was invited on Dyhrenfurth's International Everest expedition. McGowan and Fred Beckey went. I had real mixed feelings about going. I wasn't that confident about what I wanted to be; an engineer or climber. And I wasn't super strong carrying loads. I was OK, but I wasn't a giant.

You did the second Ptarmigan Traverse which has become a classic.

Tom: Yeah, it's a neat trip. It's very different now than it was in 1953. I've been back, not to do the whole thing. We went back in 1971 from Cascade Pass to just beyond the Red Ledge and scattered Mike Hane's ashes. He was on the 1953 traverse with us. He had been killed on the south face of Chacraraju, the wildest peak in the Cordillera Blanca of Peru.

Did any of your gang specifically train for climbing?

Tom: Nobody ran. Nobody trained. Fred climbed all the time, and the others of us climbed almost all the time. We would climb buildings, along the water tower at Volunteer Park, trying to traverse all the way around it. We climbed in Tumwater Canyon, and at Peshastin in the winter, but as far as training, that's all we needed to do.

I guess the top-level climbs didn't demand the sort of rigorous training you see today.

Tom: There were still a lot of things to climb, places you hadn't been, and the techniques we had were getting us up.

Were there many women climbing in the '50s?

Nancy Miller: When I was at Stanford, there were women in the alpine club. Irene Miller was there. When my father was a climber, there were few women climbing, Agnes Dickert and others.

When did you two meet?

Tom: Through climbing, through the Mountaineers. I knew Nancy's father, Burge Bickford, before I knew her. She had been at Stanford. She actually hadn't started climbing any earlier than I had even though Burge Bickford was a long-time Mountaineer. He didn't want her to climb when she was young, although she certainly hiked.

Nancy, did you learn to climb at Stanford?

Nancy: I took the Mountaineers climbing course. I had gone camping with my parents on the Mountaineers summer outings when I was very young—five or so—and I don't ever remember being turned off. I saw kids of some Mountaineers turned off. Their parents were too compulsive. It was doing something in the mountains every weekend.

There was this group called the Campcrafters. All these people would go up and all the women and children stayed in camp while the men went out and climbed. I knew kids who got tired of it. But our family didn't do that so much that I felt oppressed. My father was worried, because at that time there was a theory that children should not go high too young, eight or ten thousand feet,

until you were an adult. Therefore, he was not too hot for me to start. I suspect they had mixed feelings about climbing at all.

I belonged to the Stanford Alpine Club which had a hundred people, max, and I think somebody was killed three out of the four years I was there.

When I first went to California, the people in the Stanford Alpine Club were so unused to climbing on snow, and I remember we'd go to Tuolumne Meadows sometimes. I think it was Mount Lyle that supposedly had a glacier. And we saw this glacier and it was *not* a glacier. It was this little piece of ice. They just weren't used to snow at all. That was one reason a club member was killed climbing Mount Shasta. He couldn't believe that he'd get hurt on snow and ice and refused to take off his skis.

Tom and I certainly didn't push our kids into climbing. My parents didn't push me either and I thought, therefore, it might be fun to try. I started when I was sixteen. I don't think Tom's parents realized what mountaineering involved as much as my parents.

Here is something you love to do, and yet there is that apprehension about passing on that love to your children.

Tom: There doesn't have to be as high a mortality rate as there was in our generation. We lost a lot of people. Our kids climbed a little, but mostly we hike. We didn't push climbing one way or another. We've had direct experiences with climbers who lost their children climbing, and it's crushing. Dick Emerson lost his son on Castle Rock. You're never really whole after something like that.

You were, for many years, active with Mountaineer publications.

Tom: I became involved with the first *Freedom of the Hills.* The original group was Harvey Manning, Rowland Tabor, Carl Henrikson, Franz Mohling, Jock Hazle, Lesley Stork Tabor and Nancy. This was before we were married. We were doing it for fun. We were all volunteers.

Nancy: There was a committee, and then they went out and solicited people to write chapters.

Tom: It all started out fairly modestly. I'm sure Harvey told you that our fund subscription drive turned out to be a big success, and we got all money that had been put into the book back. At that time *Freedom* was very useful to people, as there was a lot less general mountaineering knowledge in print. There was not much out there in print.

In the early years nobody got any money out of the book program. The first book where anyone got paid for their efforts was *100 Hikes in Western Washington*. We paid Ira Spring royalties for pictures and Louise Marshall royalties, although Harvey did a great amount of rewriting. Louise did all the research. She was the energy behind the first *100 Hikes* book. Then the book operation grew so big; that's one of the reasons I got out. We were running a big business. You don't need that day and night. I was more interested in the artistic side; design and photography.

What was the genesis of your book on the North Cascades?

Tom: That was a political book dealing with the National Park issue. We were trying to do, as quick as we could, a Sierra Club format book. We had the money from *Freedom of the Hills* that we could use for the project, and it snowballed from there. That was the first of the North Cascades books, which gave us a little bit of leverage, got the place known; all the things you've got to do to get the land redesignated.

Cliff Leight: What do you think you could accomplish with another book? In the first book you said, "There's a lot more."

Tom: You'd like to push to get those unprotected areas protected. I think Bacon and Hagen are still unprotected as are the valleys that go into the Buckindy area.

You were involved in the production of Fred Beckey's climbing guides.

Tom: I worked on the first one of the new series. I did the general design, format and layouts, and helped in selecting pictures, working with the printer and so forth.

There's nothing like his guides, nothing as comprehensive.

Tom: That's right, for a range this complicated. You can find guidebooks for smaller areas, like the Tetons, that are equally as good. It was Leigh Ortenburger's Teton guide that we used for a model.

Beckey must bring the same meticulous care to books that he brings to his climbing.

Tom: Yes, when he was working on the

guide, he had his files in the back of his car. You never knew where he was. You'd call him in L.A. and occasionally you'd get him, but he disappeared a fair bit of the time on climbs.

Nancy: The amazing thing about Fred is that he is still alive; for a person to climb that long and well.

Tom: I was sure I saw him dead one day. We were going to climb Cruel Finger. It was in the spring, and we were climbing out of the Ingall's Creek Valley, just about to cross into this gully. Fred was up ahead, when this roaring, giant wet snow avalanche came down, filling the gully, wall-to-wall, knocking down the trees. And I thought, well, Fred finally got it. There wasn't any doubt in my mind he was gone. The noise went by, and I could smell the rock dust in the breeze. I said, "We may as well go and look, just in case." I yelled, "Fred", and he screamed, "What?" And he was hanging on a bush. The avalanche had gone right by him.

You mentioned others of your generation who weren't as lucky.

Tom: I was with Fred and Dick Berge in 1952 descending the north face of Baring in the dark when Berge took a wrong step onto a loose slab and fell some two-hundred feet to his death. Our good friend Paul Brikoff was killed by lightning on Mount Stuart and Bob Grant survived on the other end of the rope. They were right on top. They had climbed the west ridge. A storm blew in from the east and they couldn't see it coming. The lightning hit Paul and the charge went down the rope to Bob. You could see the burns on him and on the bowline-on-the-coil that had been wrapped around his waist. The charge went down his leg and out through the heels. The electrical charge was so severe that he became immediately dehydrated, and a doctor, Otto Trott, said he lost forty pounds water weight.

Bob was more or less paralyzed, so he kind of skidded on his butt down the gully and got partway down that day and into the meadows by himself the next day. I was a member of Mountain Rescue and was called out. We found him on the third day, and Otto said he wouldn't have lasted another day.

Do you continue to climb?

Tom: I really hike. I really don't climb. Nancy and I still get out on some alpine traverses where we're camping very high, sometimes on snow, where you have to use the rope a bit here and there to get across schrunds and get inexperienced people across little rock pitches. I guess an example would be the Bailey Traverse in the Olympics. We did that a couple of years ago. It was more of a hike, but a trip where the old climbing skills made everything go a lot better.

Was there a point when you decided that you weren't going to devote as much time to hard climbing? Was it a conscious decision?

Tom: Given that my little body holds together, I'd like to think I can go climbing any time, and I have, on and off, for a long time. But I never made a conscious decision to stop. There are still a lot of places I want to go. I have a long, long list of neat places to be.

I've never been to Tank Lakes, for example, or Dutch Miller Gap. There are neat places around Lake Chelan; Fourth of July Basin, and up around Tupshin.

Are there any moments in the mountains that,

despite the intervening years, remain crystal clear in your memory?

Tom: I can clearly remember, years later, specific holds on rock climbs. I can tell you exactly what combination of holds I used to get up the slabs on the north peak of Index. I can see it. It's immediate. I certainly remember the night Mike Hane and I spent on the north ridge of Forbidden. We'd been trying to climb the northwest face, an early attempt. We had gotten a third of the way up, couldn't turn the nose and got discouraged. We decided to give it up. We had no bivouac gear—too smug I guess. We anchored in on a sloping slab and went right to sleep. Of course we'd wake up whenever we'd slide down and the rope would go tight. By about 2 a.m. it got too cold to sleep so I amused myself by singing and banging the rock hammer on the rocks for accompaniment. I can't sing worth a damn, and because of the awful sounds, Mike said it was his worst bivouac ever.

Gene Prater traces his interest in climbing to his mother. "When she came out to Washington from Colorado and married my father," he says, "she had already done some mountain hiking and scrambling. My father had no interest in walking. If he could get there on his horse, he'd be glad to go. He didn't want any part of mountaineering, but my mother thought it would be nice if her boys climbed mountains."

From his father, Prater gained a love for farming, and it has been a farmer's sensitivity to the vagaries of nature, coupled with common sense, that has guided his mountaineering philosophy, even as he was making first ascents of the most challenging ridges and faces on Mount Rainier in the 1950s. Prater was a founding member of the Sherpa Climbing Club, which included his brother, Bill Prater, Dave Mahre, Fred Dunham, Fred Stanley and Jim Wickwire. That group was responsible for most of the important northside ascents on Rainier as well as first ascents on Mount Stuart and other peaks in the Enchantments.

In all Prater has climbed Rainier 28 times by 19 different routes. Six of his climbs were first ascents on the mountain including Curtis Ridge in 1957 and second ascents of Ptarmigan and Liberty ridges. Despite tackling virtually every ridge and face on the mountain, Prater claims to have never been caught out in a storm. There is a little luck involved, but not much.

"You see these mountaineering epics where they got stormed in here or there, they didn't have a problem until the storm hit, and then problems were all they had. The Oregon Episcopal School calamity on Mount Hood was an example. All they had to do was turn around and go back. That's the one thing they didn't do and nine people died on the mountain."

Farming determined the course of much of Prater's mountaineering. More and more the best time, the only time, for trips

« These mountains are alive and changing. That's what I liked about the alpine snow and ice climbing. You couldn't give it a decimal grade, because it was different each time. Numbers leave out the human element in climbing, the emotional part. »
—*Gene Prater*

to the mountains was winter. Prater became one of the acknowledged experts on winter mountaineering, especially snowshoeing. He has written a number of books on snowshoeing and traveled across the country giving talks on the subject. He has also been at the forefront of snowshoe design for several years. His brother Bill was creator of the Sherpa snowshoe which revolutionized the sport. Some of the modifications were Gene's. A few years ago REI considered buying Gene Prater's model, but when they didn't it didn't bother him much. "They did me a favor really. All I needed was one more demanding job. It would have been intolerable."

Prater makes customized snowshoes in a workroom off his barn. Snowshoes of all types and sizes, many of them museum pieces, line the wall. Prater puts the finishing touches on a pair while we talk. He answers questions and makes snowshoes with equal facility.

▲

With your interest in winter mountaineering, you must have run into more than your share of avalanches.

Only two, although one was too much. Knowing that there is a hazard isn't too critical. It's whether you can act on what you know. And since that last avalanche in 1960 my advice has always been the only sure way to avoid an avalanche is don't go into an area that could avalanche. But the direct personal experience communicates in a way nothing else on earth can.

When I was caught in that second avalanche, I knew a great deal about them. And just the instant it began I was thinking, "Here I am in the lee slope, but I don't think there's much hazard here. It's such a small gully." But on the other hand, it was on the lee side, deep powder snow in it, just where it ought to be for an avalanche, and the gully fanned out, not a tree in it.

The first thing I did when it hit was nothing. My brain locked. This swimming motion, I don't think many people do that because things happen so quickly, unless they're a lot sharper than I am. I just stood there and my feet got caught by the non-sliding layer and the snow pushed me over so I was going down headfirst on hands and knees. Both times my injuries were due to running into solid objects. I hit a tree with my quadriceps and it flipped me over. My brother hit one tree with an ankle, twisted it a little bit and hit the next one with his ribs, and a lot of the weight of the snow hit him in his diaphragm and knocked the wind out of him. It left him spasming, and he thought he was going to die. I had a tremendous bruise on my thigh, but I snowshoed out five miles for help, while two others in the party stayed with him. We made a bough bed, got a tarp over him, got a fire going and melted water. Twenty-one people came in and brought him out.

When did you start the Sherpa Climbing Club?

In 1949 we started the first annual climb of Mount Stuart. People were reading about the Sherpas in Nepal for the first time, and we started calling each other Sherpa. Very shortly it became the Sherpa Climbing Club out of Ellensburg. It's really more of an attitude than an institution. When we first got started, the decision was that we would not have a constitution. We would not have dues. We would not have officers. We would not have minutes. We'd just go climbing. That's as serious as the group ever got about setting up club traditions. It was strictly oral, no records, except word of mouth. My brother and myself were two of the originals. Ev Lasher, Vic Josendahl, and four guys from Ellensburg.

We still have meetings once or twice a year to show slides. It's more for encouragement than anything else. Since my brother and I are past our sixties—so is Dave Mahre—about all the business we've conducted over the past twenty years is to raise the age of youth a bit. We can still be members.

It's a tradition around here, at least it's become one, whether we intended it to, that you complain a lot about being old, but you do everything you can to stay as active as you can, egg the young people on. It's been a great motivator over the years.

So, when did you really become committed to climbing? When did you attempt your first ambitious ascents?

In 1955. This German immigrant, Marcel Schuster, had settled in Yakima. He was a good technical climber. He was one tough cookie. He taught Dave and me the twelve-point technique.

We went up Liberty Ridge with him, the second ascent of that in 1955. That was all that Dave and I needed to get us going. I had been up the mountain a couple of times before, and I thought that was ice climbing. That was what it was regarded as back in those days, cramponing up the glacier.

When you climbed Liberty Ridge, did you feel that you were ready for that sort of climb?

By the time it was over we were ready. It was a whole new experience, opening up a whole new world. There was a lot of rockfall. Marcel wasn't too concerned. He had climbed in the Alps on poor rock. He said, "Oh, I've been on climbs I did not think I would come back alive." That's what we thought we were on. It was the days before hard hats, but I had a hard hat by the next season. We probably had the first rock helmets in the Northwest. For a while it really put the Mountaineers, the westsiders, to the test. They had an awful time with us doing that sort of thing. They hadn't gotten into it, but each generation upped the standards a bit, so now they're way beyond where Dave and I left off.

After that you spent a lot of time on Rainier.

Well our ascent of Liberty was the second. Then Schuster and I climbed Curtis Ridge which was the first ascent of that one. Three years later my brother and I climbed Ptarmigan which was the second ascent.

Were you particularly attracted to Rainier?

Oh, no question about it. It was the hardest and toughest mountain in the Northwest, and being a farmer here, it was difficult to get away in the summer when the climbing was good. And raising young kids, it was definitely a handicap. It was a totally different experience than the young climbers who are getting publicity now. They're professionals, full-time climbers. They have a sponsor, I think. We didn't have sponsors, and in 1959 when Dave and I climbed the north side of Little Tahoma, I think by then he had four kids. I had two and both of us were farming. In spite of those kinds of handicaps, we were just given the strength to do it, I guess. Dave was one of the strongest climbers I've ever climbed with. I don't think he's slowed down an awful lot. He once said, "You know, when we were doing those early climbs, we just didn't think there wasn't anything we couldn't climb." And that's true.

You can't imagine how poverty stricken we

were compared to what you see now. The affluence is just absolutely unbelievable. There are so many aids to climbing that have been invented. There were no ice tools when we were climbing on Rainier. We were climbing around on verglass on Liberty Ridge with ice axes and a blade ice piton; that was an ice dagger. There was no such thing as a grooved pick; ice axe or hammer. They were all straight. The ice screw hadn't been invented. Lug soles were fairly new. I climbed Rainier with a sort of nailed boot, some old Eckenstein twelve-point crampons.

It would be interesting to try that now.

Oh yeah. It would be fun to put them on some of the young tigers. They would definitely get a new understanding of what a tremendous help it is for climbing right now. It is absolutely fantastic.

Your occupation has made you a winter mountaineer.

Yeah, because my brother left the farm in 1966. Then it was nineteen years before I had more than one night off in summer. So going on expeditions to bigger mountains was totally out. But I've had a good time. I didn't lose anything. I don't have any problem explaining why I never went on an expedition. I didn't have the time. I was invited, but with small kids and a farm, if I'd gone in the summer, it would have lost us a year's income. With the modest pay scale of farming, I couldn't have given it up. Now I really don't mind. I've seen some of the relics that have come back from expeditions, and I'm not sure I would have wanted to pay the price. I've had enough honors for many people, and I've never lacked for attention.

In one of your guide books, you talked about companionship in the mountains, and the importance of that. With expeditions, often, that doesn't seem to be a primary concern. You often climb with strangers . . .

And they end up hating each other, wanting to kill each other. I've concluded, as I wrote, that the mountain experience is about half of it, just being out there in that setting. But the people that you go with are at least equal to the mountain. And if they're not, there are some around who would be well worth that. It's been long-term friendships. I helped get Wickwire and Dunham twisted into the mode at a tender age. And Barry Prather—his mother credits me with getting him

90

started climbing. And I think many people were just as significant as the mountains around.

I can't really ever recall being in the Cascades and having the sorts of disagreements that you see on expeditions. And that had to do with the fact that at the root of the climb was the companionship. If the weather came in, there was the sense that you could try it again. With an expedition, it's harder to do it again.

I think getting caught in those two avalanches made a certain impression—that when you discover early that you can do something that may get you killed, you may get over the ego-centered idea that you need to make a name for yourself. I try to forget all that nonsense. I'm just out there to have a good time.

Were there any women in the Sherpas?

Wives, up until now. We started including women because we started running across a few that are extremely strong. That's about it. I never met Marty Hoey, but I met Catherine Freer; she was living in Ellensburg for awhile before she got into real world-class climbing. If a woman has that kind of strength, why not? My daughter was a Sherpa—I forgot about her. One time she went back to New England with me, and women back there, well, they are in trouble. They're repressed so much more than out here. Then again, that's not so bad, because so are the men. Most of them are women anyway, compared to the guys you run into out here.

They were having a little talk one evening on how these women ought to act around men out in the backcountry, not let the men help them so much, and not do everything for them, how women should be stronger. My daughter climbed a lot with me, and her favorite trip was a one-day trip up Stuart in the spring. We wouldn't camp, just leave here early in the morning, do the whole thing and come out the same day. It's a 7,500-foot elevation gain in all. So these guys asked her, "Well, Connie, you're from out west. How do you handle it? You climb with men a lot."

"Oh yes, all men. There's hardly another woman out there."

"Well how do you do it?"

"Well, I just like to get into good condition and stomp the men into the ground."

They'd never thought of that. That's all they needed to do.

With women in particular and lots of guys,

I think my role in a lot of ways has been to break the shackles, the emotional ones; to free them up and let them know that all they need to do is get out there and do it. I just went out and did it, and that's all I probably needed to know. The mountain will teach the rest. I was lucky to get two more breaks.

When did you start making snowshoes?

I actually began making them in the late '70s, but I made an unbelievable discovery in 1958. The biggest drawback to climbing up steep slopes was a long toe. The snowshoes were designed for flatland travel, for putting the weight right in the middle of the snowshoes so that neither toe nor tail could sink in. When I moved the front cross-piece forward it became an unbelievable snowshoe for mountains. My brother had trouble figuring it out because it was such a total change. I made some other modifications just after that, a whole lot simpler design. But I wasn't too good at doing that, so I called the guy who ran Tubbs snowshoes and asked him if they would do it at the factory. They moved it forward, and REI sold these snowshoes to hunters as a Cascade model snowshoe. It was *the* climbing snowshoe until the advent of the aluminum Sherpa. It was almost ten years between development.

Tubbs just went under trying to compete with Sherpa. The market for wood snowshoes just dried up and Tubbs just couldn't part with tradition. All he would have had to do was do just like Sherpa and sell it, and he would have still been in business. His pride was such that he had to make something different.

My brother is the creator of the Sherpa, and if it hadn't been for these things, finding out where you ought to put the bindings to climb well, he would have never been able to proceed on and add the step or two and create the Sherpa.

How long does it take you to make a pair of snowshoes?

Well, I can make more than one pair a day, with my methods and handcrafting, if I really wanted to get in there and do it every day. But I priced it high enough so that I don't have to. I put out advertising a few years back, but I decided— I was sixty-one last month—how much security do I need?

That's the thing about the mountains, you acquire an appreciation for the simple things.

The rest of it is just cosmetic business. And

I've had two boys in wheel chairs with muscular dystrophy. The oldest one died in 1979, and the other one has lined up an apartment. So I've seen people who have real physical problems, and I can tell the difference between these hypochondriacs, claiming there is something wrong with them, when all they need is a good kick in the butt. Hey, just go out and work a little bit. The same goes for culture, class and status. I can see through that.

The mountains eliminate, at least for a while, class and those other social distinctions.

It is a neutral ground where you don't have the political, religious, emotional, cultural, sexual differences that you would like to dispute if you were in a bar somewhere. The mountains are a great equalizer.

Have you found that your spiritual beliefs are enhanced when you're in the mountains?

Some people claim that they did, but as I analyze myself, I got the best spiritual instruction by sitting in church with the preacher explaining parts of the Bible about what one's role as a Christian needs to be. I did get renewed tremendously, physically and emotionally by the mountains. There are a lot of needy people and the Bible is concerned a whole lot with mankind and its needs individually, for one-on-one experiences, so going out in the mountains is a means of renewal. You're all worn out from too much evangelizing, too much working, too much something-or-other. Renew yourself out there, but don't forget there's a responsibility as a Christian on the face of the earth too. I would like to say, "Oh yeah, that's my church out there, but I'd be a liar.

You haven't had a lot of spare time, but I get the sense that you are not the sort of person who likes to sit around and relax.

I think having two boys in wheelchairs has kept me from enjoying fully sitting around in front of the T.V. and that. I realized what a gift I was given with physical strength. I see people who were better athletes than I was in high school and college who have pretty much given up and went for old age instead of continuing the athletic and physical stuff.

These mountains are alive and changing. That's what I liked about the alpine snow and ice climbing. You couldn't give it a decimal grade, because it was different each time. This static decimal thing, 5.7 or 5.9, I really kind of felt was dumb. Trying to give it that kind of grade is like saying that this climber is this quality and this grade.

Numbers leave out the human element in climbing, the emotional part. When you're dealing with emotions, you can't find words to express what you would really like to convey. So any attempt you would make would be gilding the lily. You'd just make an ass of yourself. Someone is supposed to have asked Louie Armstrong, "You play good jazz don't you. What's the different between good and poor jazz." And Louie said, "Friend, if you've got to ask, you'll never know." That's true with mountaineering. You can't convey emotions with words.

That's the thing I can't understand about life, you know. You look out from inside your body through your eyes or whatever, and to me the world is still no different through my eyes to me, and what I

feel, and what I like to do than when I was 20 years old. And yet you look in the mirror and know that a lot of water went under the bridge, but as long as the old body keeps doing it, I don't care what I look like.

—Dave Mahre

For the past 25 years Dave Mahre has been the mountain manager of the White Pass Ski Area. It is the sort of job that most ski bums yearn for, and Mahre wouldn't disagree. But when asked if he had to choose between skiing and climbing, he answers surprisingly, "I never had to make a decision between skiing and climbing. Climbing is number one. Next would be flying. This is a job I have fun at. I get paid for playing, in a way. There was no planning, believe me. I don't believe there's been much planning in our life. We just let it happen. That's what really happens to most people. You can make the best plans in life and then have to kiss them off."

Mahre's belief in kismet is a bit at odds with his origins in Eastern Washington fruit ranching. "It wasn't a fruit ranch at first, but that's where it headed. My grandfather, father and uncles grew anything they could. It was just grubbed out of sagebrush. The first crops were probably alfalfa and grain. Eventually they planted orchards. While the orchards were growing they planted crops in between the trees."

From the ranch Mahre had a great view of Mount Adams. "In the back of my mind I just knew I was going to climb it someday." He first climbed the mountain with his brother-in-law. They made a few sandwiches, filled a canteen with water, and headed up. It was several years before he began to acquire real mountaineering equipment. Mahre eventually hooked up with the Prater brothers, became a founding member of the Sherpas, and made several first ascents on Mount Rainier and peaks in the Stuart Range. Mahre epitomizes the belief among many of the Sherpas that there really wasn't any peak they couldn't climb if they decided to try.

At 64 Mahre certainly hasn't lost his zest for climbing. He was on two Everest expeditions while in his 50s and would certainly welcome the chance to try again. He still has an eye on a couple of new routes on Mount Stuart.

None of Mahre's children inherited his love for climbing, although they still occasionally accompany him on climbs. The twins, Steve and Phil, did become two of America's greatest alpine skiers. When I ask Dave if any of his children can keep up with him on a climb, he laughs and says, "I'd wouldn't say that, but they always said I can go uphill better than downhill."

The conversation with Mahre was done by phone. In this day of deregulation getting a call through to White Pass is a bit of an electronic expedition. Mahre is personable, a self-described sentimental fool whose voice occasionally chokes with emotion when talking about the mountains, climbing companions, and family.

▲

When did you first meet the Praters?

I bought a ranch in Ellensburg and tried to grow pears and apples after I got out of the Merchant Marines after World War II. When I came home I worked for my father and uncle for a few years. I got married in '47. I probably met the Praters along about 1955. I don't pay much attention to dates. I was on the National Ski Patrol at that time and worked on mountain rescue which wasn't really mountain rescue. That was just being formed. I met the Praters at one of these mountain rescue practices.

So you learned mountaineering through the mountain rescue practices.

That's right, probably the biggest part of it, other than what you gleaned from the people you climbed with. Probably one of the most prominent people in our circle was a German, who had been a prisoner of war, and had been allowed to teach skiing at Garmisch. His name is Marcel Schuster. He had been decorated by Hitler for making a first ascent of a 3,000-meter peak in the winter. He'd skied in the '36 Winter Olympics. He knew quite a bit about climbing that people around here didn't know. Around here people frowned on twelve-point crampons.

It was a pretty cautious type of climbing that we were doing in the U.S. We were probably forty years behind the Germans in the 1950s, maybe more than that, maybe a hundred years. He taught the Praters, myself and the young guys: Prather, Dunham and Stanley and Wickwire. He had quite a bit of influence on what all of us learned about technique, just a different attitude. He brought this alpine style of climbing to our area in Central Washington. And in a few years basically we were the leaders. I'm not one to brag, but people looked to us as such.

It seemed that in the 1950s you guys owned Mount Rainier.

We kind of owned anything we went to, really. At the time I tried to raise fruit on the ranch, but it didn't pan out. Prices weren't too good during those years—prices during the war had been high. But there were two or three frosty years where it didn't set good crops, and I couldn't make the payments. So I ended up back on my skiing experience to make a living. For a couple of winters to hang on to the dream of farming, I worked on weekends as a professional ski patrolman and on the weeks I would go home with the family on the farm. After a couple of years they asked me if I wanted to be their mountain manager. I wasn't making any money farming so I ended up doing that instead.

Gene Prater said that you did the first ascent of the Ice Cliff Glacier on Mount Stuart and it was the only climb you did all year. I guess if you're going to do one climb a year, you may as well make it a dandy.

That was the attitude. When you went out you didn't read the guide book. We looked at something that intrigued us and did it, whether it was a first ascent or not. When you were farming, you were geared to the work. If you got two or three climbs during the summer that would be a busy one, but we always went on good ones.

What was the Willis Wall like?

That's one I don't like to talk about much, because there's been a lot of controversy over that thing. And I'm not the guy who said it. The Willis Wall, in Schuster's opinion, was tougher than the Eiger because of the potential hazard of rockfall and that the big ice cliff hangs over it, and ice falls wherever and when, and you didn't know when.

Actually the first time I climbed Rainier was

in 1955. We went and climbed Liberty Ridge which hadn't been climbed for twenty years or so. Liberty is a classic, a real nifty climb. If conditions are good, it's not too bad, but I've met a lot of people who had a lot of adversity on it the last few years. They try to go on it the wrong time, too early in the year or too late. Do your homework and you can have a real good time.

I did some big mountains in Tibet but nothing that's more awesome than the Willis Wall when it's active, believe me. That's an emotional statement. The wall doesn't have any granite or great rock climbing. It's just a bunch of crud. It's got some awfully hard polished avalanche paths. You talk about black ice and that's exactly what it is. You can't hardly even stand up on it with crampons when it's exposed. It's not all that difficult but it can be that dangerous. It's a type of climb that you better be prepared to take pressure and hum it. You can't take two or three days on it. You've got to do it in a matter of hours if you want to do it safe.

It seems that one of the advantages that you guys had . . .

We were dumb. We didn't know any better.

Besides that is that you climbed with the same group of people.

I'll grant you that's an important thing, and I've always told young people, "Find someone you like, someone whose style you like and learn one another's styles and climb together and you'll probably climb a long time." But be wary of picking up and going with anybody on a given weekend just to be going climbing because you might just get yourself in a pickle. And I don't mean to be critical but that is a factor in climbing. Once you know one another's abilities, attitudes, strengths, it's a lot more fun than having a lot of anxieties.

I think people have found it amazing that from your neck of the woods so many really fine climbers have emerged.

On the expedition I made to Tibet, the majority of the people on the climb were right from my own backyard. I knew them personally. A lot of them I'd climbed or guided with. It was super. I don't think many expeditions have an experience like that. Both of my expeditions were to Everest.

What sort of luck did you have on Everest?

Well, we killed a good friend on one and got one man on the summit on the second one. Both times we were trying the great couloir on the north face.

You tried Everest both times in your fifties?

Yeah, the first time when I was fifty-five and fifty-nine the second time.

Did you regret that you hadn't tried younger?

I have no regrets. I've known all my life that the best climbers, a lot of them, don't ever get to go on expeditions. That's just a fact of life. There are some whose bootlaces I couldn't even tie who never go on an expedition. So you accept that. I'm just lucky I got to go there a couple of times. I was a good pack horse. I hope that I'm not telling you wrong.

I think that expeditions are made or broken by people at all levels.

Or by the attitude of the team too. If you don't get along or pull together, you're probably not going to get anything done. No, I don't have any regrets. I tried. I packed lots of loads and did whatever anybody asked me to do. I told them when I went that's the way it would be. They wouldn't get no trouble from me. Whatever had to be done, I didn't give a damn, I'd do it.

I think, when you're stateside getting ready, a lot of people have that attitude, but once you get to the mountain, it's hard to maintain.

That's one thing about climbing. Egos can get in the way. We all have egos or we wouldn't be there. Either that or we're damn dumb, like I said before. I don't want to say that I'm a hotshot or anything, but I've always had confidence that I could put one foot in front of the other and go uphill. What I'm trying to say is that you have to have some confidence in yourself or you're not going to jump the crevasse, and that's what it boils down to. And another thing is that other people have to have that confidence or stuff's not going to happen. When people say, "Can you climb it?", I have to say, "I don't know. I really haven't had a chance." Well, I have had a chance, it's just the way the cookie breaks.

Would you like to try Everest again?

I don't want to ask to be taken again. I would like to go again, and I would go in a second. But I know I've been there twice and there are a lot of fellows who will never get the chance if other people keep taking the slots. There's only so many people who are going to climb in each generation because of permits, so why should I be so damn egotistical to squander a lot of spots by begging to be taken? I'd go if I was asked, but I'm not going to ask to be on an expedition and that's the way I've left it. I applied for an expedition when I was forty-seven and I got told they wanted men ten years younger than me and I said I'd never apply again. So that tells you about ego. We all have them get in the way. And frankly when that happened, I've never been as aggressive about climbing since then. Only on Everest. The rest of it's pretty laid back.

Did your sons ever develop an interest in climbing?

They climbed with me occasionally. In fact all of the children have climbed with me. We used to go to Mount Adams when they were growing up. They used to have a thing called the Sun Fair climb on Adams. On one of the climbs we took five-hundred people to the summit. What it amounted to was that the little town of Yakima wanted to have some type of a festival. I was one of the guys who was on the committee when it was formed. One of the things they got on the calendar was a Sun Fair climb of Mount Adams. That went on for thirteen years until the Sierra Club and the Lloyd family shut us down. We were ruining the perpetual snow fields on the mountains.

Basically the guys who did the guiding on that were mountain rescue people or friends. It was kind of like a reunion. All these jocks I knew climbing, we'd go down there and spend a week. Put in a fixed rope for safety if we had to. We'd get radio gear packed up to the mountain. I'd take my family down there for a week or ten days every year. And they'd take their skis to the top and ski down. I'd get a lot of flak because I'd let my six- or seven-year-old kids ski from the summit to the bottom without being with them. But on skis they were more proficient than their old man. There were a set of basalt cliffs where I used to live, and we'd go over there nearly every evening rock climbing, from the time they could walk. So they've all climbed. The twins climbed Rainier when they were thirteen years old. They climbed Mount Stuart before that.

Do they have time for that sort of thing anymore?

Steven wants to go up Rainier again this year. I didn't get to take them last year. They were too busy racing cars last year. But he'll get out and do 'er again this year. The daughters have probably been a little more active than the men who've been busy being breadwinners. And of course they have their own likes and dislikes. They do a lot of water skiing and sailboarding.

Do you notice any differences in the sort of climber you were twenty years ago?

I went over to Liberty Ridge here again this last spring, and it's a little tougher to be with the young guys, to go for ten-twelve hours nonstop, but I can still stay with them. I'm sixty-four, but I'm nineteen really. That's the thing I can't understand about life, you know. You look out from inside your body through your eyes or whatever, and to me the world is still no different through my eyes to me, and what I feel, and what I like to do than when I was twenty years old. And yet you look in the mirror and know that a lot of water went under the bridge, but as long as the old body keeps doing it, I don't care what I look like.

In all the people I've talked to, that attitude has really been apparent.

Well, I think that with people who climb, maybe there's a lot to what the poet, Robert Bly, says about male bonding. It was that way with my father. My father, when he was an older man, had a circle of younger men around him all the time, and they kept him young. My life has been the same way. Most of my intimate climbing friends are forty or younger. I've got almost thirty years on most of them.

On Everest most of them were half my age and yet I had a heck of a great time with these guys. And I think that's the thing that keeps you young. If you give in and play the role model, you're going to be the granddad. I am a granddad, but I don't think I fall into the class that most people think of as granddad.

The toughest years are when you are most mature and rugged, and you'll have the most stamina from the time you're forty until probably fifty-seven or fifty-eight. I'm serious about that. The average guy has been there, and no matter how gungho the young guys are there's something about that experience and the fact that he's been through a lot of these things they are going to have to experience or do experience. And it just makes a world of difference.

It's sounds like I'm talking like Patton, but when I got to base camp on Everest in '82—it's crazy—I got out of the truck and it was like, "Hell,

I've been here before." And I didn't know nothing about expeditions. I know that sounds crazy, and I'm a sentimental old fool but that's exactly how I felt. No big deal. They're not going to climb it in a day or anything like that, but everything's relative. Everest is no bigger than Mount Stuart here.

If you are going to succeed on a Himalayan peak, you have to bring some perspective to the climb.

You have to realize that here you go alpine style on a weekend, say to Stuart, and you climb it in a day, and you climb close to 7,000 vertical feet after you start from Ingalls Creek. On Everest, you have two months to travel in and you've only got 9,000 feet to go, so it's really relative. It's just that you don't want it to be bigger than life, because it isn't.

— Tom Miller Photo

2

(1) Fred Beckey on Castle Rock's Jello Tower, October 1952. (2) Classic shot of Forbidden Peak from summit of Boston, September 1952. (3) Dee Molenaar, 1946. (4) Dave Mahre, 1968.

3

4

1 — Tom Miller Photo

2 — Tom Miller Photo

(1) Mountaineers climbing class cuts up, April 1950. Left to right: Ron Livingston, Betty Manning, Vic Jøsendal, Harvey Manning. (2) Harvey Manning on crux pitch of Fuller Mountain, 1951. (3) "K" (left) and Dee Molenaar at Paradise Lodge, Mount Rainier, 1941.

3 — Dee Molenaar Photo

1

(1) Dave Mahre (left) and Gene Prater on summit of Mount Adams after second ascent of Klickitat Glacier icefall, 1958. (2) Pete Schoening on K-2, 1953.
(3) Cache at Cache Col. The second party to complete Ptarmigan Traverse.

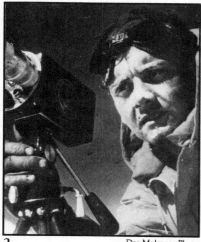

2   — Dee Molenaar Photo   3   — Tom Miller Photo

— Bob & Ira Spring Photo

2 — Dee Molenaar Photo

3 — Tom Miller Photo

(1) Nooksack Tower, North Cascades. First climbed July 5, 1946 by Fred Beckey and Clifford Schmidtke. North Face first climbed by Alex Bertulis and Scott Davis, September 2, 1973. (2) Lloyd Anderson, Jim Whittaker, Harry Papijohn, and Lou Whittaker. (3) Don (Claunch) Gordon exhibits tricouni nails, November 1953. (4) Pete Schoening snowshoeing along Ingalls Creek, December 1952.

4 — Tom Miller Photo

1961 1975

Prior to 1963 most young people living in the Northwest could probably name one famous mountaineer. It wasn't Fred Beckey, Pete Schoening, Edward Whymper or even Sir Edmund Hillary. It was an actor, James MacArthur, best remembered in the TV cop show "Hawaii Five-0" as the recipient of Jack Lord's immortal, "Book 'em Dano." The young actor had starred in "Third Man on the Mountain," the Disney film version of James Ramsey Ullman's novel *Banner in the Sky*. It was a lousy movie—fake mountain, fake snow—but MacArthur looked great in lederhosen, climbed the mountain and won the girl. In the spring of 1963 we found out that real mountaineers were much more fascinating than those Disney alpinists.

On May 1, 1963 Jim Whittaker became the first American to climb Mount Everest. He was followed three weeks later by Lute Jerstad and Barry Prather. On that same expedition Tom Hornbein and Willi Unsoeld made the first ascent of the West Ridge and the first grand traverse of the mountain.

How many teenagers harbored Everest dreams after reading the National Geographic account of the first Americans to climb Everest? One color photo showed Whittaker bundled in down, his face covered by huge goggles and an oxygen mask, standing triumphantly on the summit of Mount Everest, his ice axe pointed skyward, an American flag, attached to the shaft, rippling in the wind. Chris Kopczynski, a Spokane teenager, knew from the moment he read about the Americans on Everest that he would someday stand on the world's highest summit. He told his father, who most likely said, "That's nice son." But almost twenty years later Kopczynski realized his Everest dream.

Nothing seemed impossible in the early 1960s. People were beginning to believe that

a man could be sent to the moon, but short of that, standing on top of Mount Everest wasn't too bad. Jim Whittaker seemed to embody the optimism and glamour of the Kennedy White House. President Kennedy promoted fitness, and those of us who weren't playing touch football were trying 50-mile day hikes around Lake Washington. And the hills were alive with the sound of lug-soled feet tramping along mountain trails, no doubt irritating old-timers who had grown used to having the Cascades all to themselves.

The legions of new hikers had to buy equipment and REI was happy to oblige. The Anderson's attic co-op had finally come of age, with a large store on Seattle's Capitol Hill and a downtown outlet as well.

The membership numbered 20,000 in 1960 and mushroomed to almost 150,000 in 1969. For years my father, number 21,837, had insisted that I use his card when purchasing goods at REI, for purely humanitarian reasons, and for years he got my dividend. In 1970 I finally got my own card, 167,170, an embarrassingly high number which implied that I was one of those newcomers who was ruining the mountain experience for others. In only a few years my number would seem positively ancient.

When Lloyd Anderson left the REI board of directors in 1975, the revolutionary little co-op had become an outdoor recreation giant with membership totaling more than 500,000, a new outlet in Berkeley, California, and a number of local competitors which included the Swallow's Nest, North Face, Early Winters, and Mountain Safety Research.

Where were all these people going? A lot of them were hiking to Cascade Pass, invading what had once been intimate climber's campfires at Eight Mile Campground on the Icicle River, camping tent-to-tent at Image Lake, or scrambling up every pinnacle in the Enchantments. The Cascades had long since ceased to be a place where everyone knew everyone. And it was no longer a dead certainty that you would like everyone you met in the mountains.

Who was to blame for the invasion? Some mountaineers blamed the guidebooks: Harvey Manning, Louise Marshall and Ira Spring's *100 Hike* series, or Fred Beckey's three-volume climbing guide to the Cascades.

Other hiker/climbers recognized that guidebooks were no more culpable than the mountains themselves and pointed out that those books were designed, in part, to divert newcomers from the most crowded areas. Whether or not they were successful, the guidebooks awakened hikers and mountaineers to the fragility of the mountain landscape. And the new hikers and climbers swelled the ranks of organizations seeking to preserve wilderness treasures from the logger's axe, miner's shovel and developer's condos. In 1960, the Glacier Peak Wilderness was created; in 1968 the North Cascades National Park and Pasayten Wilderness were set aside; and in 1976 the Alpine Wilderness Area was created.

By 1960, there were few, if any, major peaks that had not been climbed, but the best climbers were not content to simply make the summit. Every couloir, crack system, face, and buttress had been explored on peaks like Stuart, Shuksan, Forbidden, Johannesburg, Dragontail. Many of the new routes were destined to become classics, while others had no redeeming social, aesthetic, or life-sustaining qualities whatsoever. Rainier's last great problem, Willis Wall, was overcome in 1963 with three new routes, including a solo climb. Many Northwest climbers were making climbing pilgrimages to Yosemite and returning with a thirst for big walls, which they found on Liberty Bell, Slesse, and Bonanza, as well as the faces on Snow Creek, and Squamish in British Columbia. Many of the early ascents were of the siege variety, where the climbers spent

weeks moving up and down fixed ropes, maybe only putting in one new pitch a day. But by the 1970s climbers were leaving the heavy racks of pitons in the garage and climbing with easily removable aluminum chocks. Many of the classic old aid climbs were being freed by gymnastic rock climbers.

I came into climbing halfway through this exciting era and hung around the periphery of what was still a relatively small scene. There didn't seem to be any strangers. In Leavenworth climbers gathered before and after climbs at Sheltons, the only restaurant in town that hadn't had a Bavarian facelift. The comfortable cafe had a register at the entrance where notes were left by climbers heading out and in. Climbing pictures hung on the walls, and climbers hung out in the booths—often slumped, exhausted, in front of a burger and fries or a pile of pancakes. There was big talk, funny stories and tales of near misses. Many of those climbers had already been on climbs in Alaska, Peru or the Himalaya, and many more were on their way. I loved the stories and hoped that soon I might add a few of my own.

Although only a few years older than I, these climbers possessed fearlessness, sometimes recklessness, and committment to setting new standards that seemed to compress a lifetime into the few years that separated me from them. To share a campfire with the likes of Mark Weigelt, Bruce Carson, Chris Chandler, Nils Anderson, Dusan Jagersky and Al Givler was almost enough for me. Carson would make solo ascents of Half Dome and El Cap, Chandler would climb Everest, but they all would die in the mountains. A misstep, a rock, lungs filled with fluid, a broken cornice, and some of the best climbers of a generation were gone. With them went, it seemed, the close-knit community of climbers, replaced with something akin to suburban sprawl.

▲

CHAPTER

20

JIM WHITTAKER

"I think that after reaching the highest point on earth, I was a little less concerned about reaching summits."

— Jim Whittaker

J im Whittaker gave a slide show at the Everett Civic Center after returning from his ascent of Mount Everest in 1963. At 6-5 he towered over Paul Shorrock, a long-time Mountaineer and Rainier park ranger, who had been called on to introduce him. Whittaker good-naturedly endured one of Shorrock's characteristic bear-hugs. After that I remember nothing except that Whittaker, by God, deserved to stand on Everest because he looked like a mountaineer. I figured, with the convoluted logic of a junior high student, that if I could grow to Whittaker-like height, I, too, could scale Everest, or at least play college basketball.

Honored at the White House, he would later take Bobby Kennedy to the top of an unclimbed peak in the Yukon that bore the name of Kennedy's dead brother. A close friendship ensued: Whittaker worked for Kennedy's 1968 presidential campaign and was himself mentioned as a possible candidate for public office. For whatever reasons, Whittaker chose instead to focus his attention on REI which was fast becoming the premier outdoor store in the country. Lloyd Anderson had hired Whittaker when REI was literally a one-room operation. When Whittaker left REI to pursue other interests 25 years later, the store had become an outdoor institution with seven outlets throughout the country.

Jim Whittaker would never stand on another Himalayan summit. He knew he could never top Everest. But he did have a desire to return to the Himalayas, and in the 1970s he organized and led two expeditions to K-2, the second of which saw four men summit. In 1990 he undertook his biggest expeditionary challenge, an American-Russian-Chinese climb of Everest. An extraordinary 20 members of the "Peace Climb" made it to the top, and Whittaker was able to broadcast the news live to President Bush from base camp.

Almost 30 years have passed since Whittaker thought about getting down from the summit of Everest. Now in his early 60s, he still carries with him the Everest aura and has assumed the role of climbing goodwill ambassador, urging people to "climb the mountains and enjoy their good tidings."

▲

There were a lot of climbers who seemed to be living in the Fauntleroy area where you and Lou grew up. One of them was Lloyd Anderson. Did you know him when you were youngsters?

When Louie and I began to climb as Explorer Scouts, we climbed with Lloyd Anderson. We lived in an area that had many vacant lots. We climbed trees, and as we went into scouting and went out on the trails, they pretty much led up into the mountains. Pretty soon we figured out we better learn something about climbing. We did some climbing with the Explorers and then joined the Mountaineers.

Did you realize early on that you enjoyed climbing and this was something you really wanted to pursue?

One of the first difficult mountains we climbed, more difficult than Mount Si, was the Tooth. Three of us—I have another brother, Barney—we were standing on the summit and the three of us said, "God, if we get off this mountain, we'll never climb again." Barney was the only one who kept his promise. A couple of weeks later Louie and I thought, "Well that wasn't so bad." That climb was pretty scary though. We went up the north side. You step across a fairly steep, exposed space. I think we did that one with Lloyd Anderson and Tom Campbell. Tom was from the 10th Mountain Division and had lost his arm. He had a hook. He'd unscrew his hand and screw in his hook for climbing. Before that climb we had been climbing on Monitor Rock. We were almost fifteen years old and it was quite a shock getting up on the Tooth.

You and Lou are really associated with Rainier. What was the attraction for you two?

It was the closest and highest mountain in the state. It has the most glaciers in the lower forty-eight states. It's a natural. You can't help but see it from Seattle. We got an offer to guide on Rainier in 1948. Bill Dunaway was guiding in the summer and he needed help taking clients up to the summit. So we formed a guide service and got the concession from the Park Service. We did a year

with Bill and then my brother and I did it while in college.

It paid well. We'd also take people to the ice caves, so it paid several thousand dollars during the summer which was pretty lucrative. But we hadn't thought that we could make a life out of it.

When did you start working at REI?

In 1955. When I went to REI and started to work there, I was the only employee. It was a small room, only about ten by twenty feet. People wondered what I did for a living. They couldn't imagine I was paid enough to make a living. It was a co-op. I was the only employee in the place for quite a while. I had to lock the door to go down the hall to pee. In 1955 I think we broke $85,000 in sales. At that time it was still almost all climbing. We did get a line of ski gear, but not much. I think the budget was $5,000 for skis. Lloyd Anderson was still working for the city as a transit engineer.

At that time I guess it would have been hard to imagine what REI would become.

I would agree although I knew it had great potential; just the stuff that we sold and the fact that it offered a dividend. I had also worked part-time during the winter at Osborne and Ulland, a sporting goods store, so I knew the ski business and the sporting goods business pretty well.

Did you envision yourself growing with REI?

No, I didn't think I'd stay there twenty-five years. I knew it was a good deal, and then as it continued to grow I had a percentage of the profit so it was very worthwhile.

How did you begin to expand REI?

Well, we had a good product and actually we were the only ones that had climbing equipment at that time, anywhere in the United States. People didn't have any source for that sort of equipment except in Europe. We had a lot of Army surplus. We sold army climbing ropes, clothing, even army crampons stamped out of aluminum which wasn't very good. We had army ice axes, army carabiners, but we were also bringing in equipment from France, Switzerland and Austria. We put out a little mailer, and people began to order from various places. We'd have twenty-eight to thirty-five percent growth each year. We'd knock walls out and it just kept going. But at that time there were more professionals than students and youth, people who had the time and money.

It was after 1960 that you moved to the present location.

We had a flood down at our warehouse. Seven feet of water everywhere. God, it was terrible—mud in the sleeping bags. We had a big sale, moved up to Capitol Hill and had a little more room. At that time we didn't think we'd need all that room and tried to rent it out to people. Then I climbed Everest and we really began to grow.

It was also during that time that you and REI took an active role in the environmental movement.

We didn't have that ethic to begin with. We used to climb and drop tin cans and juice cans down the wall to hear it tinkle. Then we began to bury the tin cans and orange peels under the summit rocks. You'd pick up the rocks, there'd be stuff under them, and you began thinking, "Geez we'd better carry some of this out." That's how it started, and it didn't really start until the late 1960s.

I recall that you led a number of cleanup climbs around the Snoqualmie Pass area.

We did that, got the governor to go in, and got a lot of exposure. We cleaned up some lakes, planted trees around REI, chopped the concrete up on the sidewalk. We took some Central Area kids up into the mountains and did a lot of things in the city. We got some Central Area kids up skiing.

It was also during your tenure that REI began to do much more in the way of quality testing.

We were being attacked unfairly by Larry Penberthy. He wanted to start a business of his own and he put some pitons in acid to weaken them and ended up directing quite a bit of publicity towards us. We knew we had good stuff and had to prove it, show it to people. We set up test controls in our warehouse and tested all biners, ropes, and stuff like that.

Having been with REI in its infancy, what do think of what it's become?

Well, it's a two-hundred million dollar-a-year business. There are twenty outlets. When I left there was seven. I opened the first one in Berkeley. I saw other stores spring up around the country, and I thought we could best serve our customers that way and it's worked okay so far. There are some things I see that I don't like, but all in all it's serving a lot of people. What we tried to do was get people out and give them a good product for a good price. That ties into my philosophy. You can educate people about how to take care of the out-of-doors, but you've got to get them out. It's like a church. If you get them out, they're going to know it and like it.

How did you get chosen for the Everest expedition?

My brother and I had been climbing a lot, and when we were guiding we went up and down Rainier quite a lot. Then we did McKinley, and I just got a phone call from Norman Dyhrenfurth asking if I'd like to go. I thought it would be nice to go to the highest mountain in the world and said yes. That was in 1961, a couple of years before we left. I became equipment coordinator for the climb.

Did you have any doubts about making it to the top?

No, I didn't. In fact I was the one guy who said he could do it. We were tested by the Office of Naval Research and I made the statement that I could do it. I was pretty confident. When Jake Breitenbach was killed the second day we were up there, it caused some real soul-searching to see if I could justify going back up. I had a couple of kids, but I had always been lucky climbing. I just thought that the route wouldn't fall on me for some reason, and it didn't. I didn't know I would be the first picked to climb it. I just thought, "I'll do everything I can to get somebody on the summit," so I did every dirty job I could think of. That's probably why Norman picked me.

Did you anticipate the impact the climb would have on your life?

No, not at all. It opened a lot of doors I would not have imagined would open. I think that after reaching the highest point on earth, I was a little less concerned about reaching summits. I think I could stand back a little and be more objective and not quite as feverish about getting to the top of various mountains. Up to that point I was more or less a peak bagger. I would do anything I could to get to the top of any mountain.

On your next two big expeditions, the K-2 expeditions, you were the leader, assuming the Dyhrenfurth role.

That's the best way to make a successful climb. Well, Dyhrenfurth tried to make it to the summit on the first assault on Everest, which I didn't do on K-2. He tried to go on the first assault but couldn't do it. That didn't hurt the expedition, although I think there were questions in some people's minds about why he should do it when he wasn't that strong.

On K-2 I didn't think that I needed to be in that position. We had failed on it before, so when we went back in '78 I really wanted to get the mountain. I was blamed by the American Alpine Club and some different people for not making the summit the first time. There were some questions about my leadership, and not from people you could respect, but some rabblerousers, and some people who were jealous who said I didn't treat the porters right, which was a bunch of crap; people who weren't over there and didn't have any idea what was going on. And so in order to make it go, I felt it was best to put aside my personal desire for the summit.

Was it frustrating going into it knowing that most likely you weren't going to make the summit?

No, because I didn't care. I'd been higher than that (laughs) on a higher mountain. I'd broken the altitude records, gone to the top, higher than any American. I didn't feel, as I said before, the hunger for reaching the summit. I felt the hunger for having a successful American expedition.

In both those expeditions you had collected a group of people who were strong climbers, and independent personalities. How as a leader, do you keep the group together?

Egotistic and independent, most climbers are that way. The first time I went with people who weren't used to the Himalayas, some local people who were afraid of the mountain; it just boggled their minds. And they weren't prepared, like they said, to die. It's one thing to talk in the States about how good you're going to be over there in a strange country. And almost everybody loses their will to go to the summit. Eventually they'll say, "Let's go home" and some say it very quickly.

But ultimately, even on the successful expedition, it was still a matter of keeping a lot of egos in check.

That's true. They're all egocentric. This Peace Climb with Soviets, Chinese and Americans that I just got off, you've got the Soviet egos which are huge, the Tibetans have egos and, of course, the Americans have egos. You still have to look for people who are team players. There are some who have such high egos that they can't work as a team and so I just don't take them. There are some people I may have made a mistake on initially, but I would never climb with them again.

When you found out that the climbers had made the summit on the second K-2 expedition, was the satisfaction similar to that which you had experienced when you stood on top of Everest?

Actually I didn't have much satisfaction on the summit of Everest. The temperature was thirty-five below zero and winds up to fifty miles per hour, and we were out of bottled oxygen. I say this in my talks, but they asked Gombu in New Delhi what was the first thing he thought of after having reached the highest point on the earth, and he answered for me when he said, "How to get down." That's all we were thinking, so we didn't really have any excitment until we reached base camp. The thing is that you really are worried about getting down. You think that the mountain might come after you after you've been on top of it.

Well, you may have that ultimate confidence needed to get to the top of the world, but those are still imposing peaks.

You bet they are. They all are. But you have to respect them all, even Mount Kennedy which I did in 1966 with Bobby Kennedy. You can get in trouble on those things. You've got to be constantly thinking about the slope you're on . . .

What was it like taking essentially a beginner up a mountain like Kennedy?

Well, I've done that quite a bit. I took the governor up Rainier. I'm used to looking out for other people, that comes from my guiding. The first thing we learn as guides is that the client will probably try and kill himself. The second thing is that he'll probably try and kill you because you're roped to him. You really learn how to watch what's going on.

The Peace Expedition on Everest was probably your most complex organizational effort. How were those climbers chosen?

The Soviets ran marathon climbs and picked

the five best they could out of the country. The Chinese picked some of their Chinese and some Tibetans and we ended up using the Tibetans; they were the strongest. And I looked around the country, put a couple of ads in climbing magazines, asked for applications and then went through applications.

Were you able to climb with the full team before embarking on the expedition?

We had a shakedown on Rainier and on Mount Elbrus in the Soviet Union. We had two weeks in each place, getting acquainted and giving the Chinese a little bit of technique, and just working things out climbing roped together.

Was there a member of the Soviet or Chinese team who spoke English?

No, we used interpreters. So we worked with radios. A couple of the climbers had some English, but very little. It created problems. We had hand radios and we could talk with an interpreter below who could translate what a climber was saying up above. When you're climbing, you don't need to talk a lot. Sign language is fine. It doesn't take a lot of conversation.

Did you find that as the climb progressed the various teams began to meld, and was that a difficult process?

No, it wasn't. We had said that we wouldn't go to the summit unless we had a Soviet and Chinese climber with us. That was a condition of the climb. I said to our team, "When we do that, you can get the mountain for yourself." We had enough oxygen. So everybody knew that they had to get those first three in order for them to do it, but then that they would have a chance. We had enough supplies for it, stocked our camps heavily, and set up our logistics so that we could operate a real assault if we had good weather. And then our team was so strong that instead of sending one rope of three on the first assault, we sent two ropes, a total of six.

The weather was calm and clear. It was incredible weather and we had it for four days so we put more people on the summit than any previous Everest expedition. Twenty on the summit. The first Soviet woman on top, the second Chinese woman on top. Five did it without bottled oxygen. We didn't lose a finger or a toe. It was a great success. We also took two tons of garbage off the mountain. I spoke to President Bush from base camp.

Any possibilities for further expeditions?

I'm taking a lot of people up mountains who haven't climbed before. They're older, they're rich. They're seeing that their lives are going to end without any adventure. A lot of people want to experience the mountains. And I feel that the mountains, the outdoors, are the best place for people to be. They haven't been programmed for centuries to sit in the ess position for eight hours a day or travel in Nepal on big, asphalt trails. They need to get out, and their heads are better if they do get out. I'll get up Rainier a few times this year, and then I'm taking some people up Kilimanjaro, just a walk, but it's a nice part of the country. We'll go to the Serengeti and see some animals. We'll do that in October. Jesse Jackson told me to get together with some of the people, blacks on Kilimanjaro, so maybe we'll follow up on that.

Do you still get the same satisfaction that you did when you were younger?

Yeah, I still like the Cascades and Olympics. I look at the Olympics and Cascades from my home. I now have two little boys, and they're about due to start going out in them. I still have fond memories of walking up some of those trails, and so when I hike those trails I like to do them alone. I go up some of the mountains like the Tooth, and it's really nice. The trails are really crowded, you're not quite as alone as you were, but you can still find places. I can hike from Paradise and in ten minutes not see a soul. That can be on a busy weekend.

So you encourage your children to climb?

Yes. My six-year-old and eight-year-old have both roped up and climbed. It's dangerous, but what I've gotten out of it, they can find enjoyment in, too. I've got five boys. The oldest two have done Rainier and climb and ski. I encourage it. I still think that Nature is a wonderful teacher. It's fair. There's gravity, cold, avalanches, but it's fair.

It's been almost thirty years since you climbed Everest. What changes have you noticed in climbing?

Well, I'm hoping climbers are more environmentally conscious. Some countries aren't yet. You go in some of the camps where some of the expeditions from other countries have gone and it's a mess. But I think it'll come around that they'll clean up after themselves. Some of the most fun is doing it as small as you can. I couldn't have done that with the Peace Climb, but small expeditions are good. More people can afford them. I think that if you can travel light, you can do less damage.

I never had the ethic that I conquered the mountain. That's asinine. You climb it and enjoy it. It's your friend, not your enemy. I've always felt that, and I think that ethic is more important. It's a challenge of course, but the challenge is your own physical weaknesses. So it's arrogant as hell to think you've conquered a mountain. You're lucky as hell to get up and back down again alive. The mountain is a friend. It's just like the animals. It's God's creation, not man-made. I find in Tibet and some of the mountain, Sherpa people, there's a real communion with nature. I see that as important, something we've lost.

CHAPTER
21
TOM HORNBEIN

*A*s a teenager living in St. Louis, Tom Hornbein gazed at a grainy black-and-white photo of Mount Everest and imagined how it would be to plant the first flag on its summit. His was a not an uncommon dream, but 20 years later Hornbein stepped across the threshhold separating daydream from reality when he and Willi Unsoeld became the first men to traverse Everest: up the unclimbed west ridge to the summit and down the South Col route; a remarkable mountaineering feat at the time; one still regarded as a classic, difficult route.

Everest, the West Ridge, Hornbein's account of the '63 expedition, featured a stunning cover photograph of the West Ridge. The ridge is sharply delineated by clouds butting up against snow-plastered rock; the summit lies who-knows-how-far beyond the horizon. It is a color photo but there is only rock, snow, clouds and a dark sky. In the foreground two climbers follow the snow-scalloped crest that leads to a soaring rock buttress, their choices limited to advance or retreat. Unlike a younger Hornbein who looked at Everest and thought, "Yes," I looked at the picture of the west ridge and blinked, my aspirations shifting abruptly from mountaineering to the wild world of professional golf. Himalayan climbing looked too damn cold, steep, and scary. Hornbein and Unsoeld spent the night just below the summit of Everest. That night out would cost Unsoeld many of his toes, but he would return to the Himalayas. Hornbein would not.

Tom Hornbein exchanged one passion for another: climbing for medicine. Chairman of the anesthesiology department at the University of Washington Medical School, he has done pioneering research into the effects of altitude on humans. Hornbein still climbs, but characterizes it as, "binge climbing."

"I'll get out once or twice a year into the Cascades," he says.

When I was a kid Mallory was one of my heroes, and it's odd to think that you're a hero to someone else. I'm just a little guy. I had an opportunity to do something. I was there and I was lucky.
— Tom Hornbein

107

"I can still climb as good on rock as I used to because of these new "glue" shoes. I'm quite timorous about leading, but I was when I was in my twenties."

There is nothing in Tom Hornbein's outward appearance that screams, "Everest Mountaineer." Great alpinists, unlike many great athletes, often shrink to anonymity in civilian clothes. Hornbein is maybe 5-7 and slightly built. He is fit as he enters his sixties. It is Hornbein's eyes that reveal the incendiary intensity necessary for greatness. They are luminous blue and seem capable of enticing answers from the unanswerable questions.

The interview takes place at an upscale restaurant on Seattle's Capitol Hill during the busy lunch hour.

▲

When did you move out to the West Coast?

I came out to Seattle in 1957 to intern after medical school. I thought it was kind of a nice place and decided if there was anything that met my professional interest that I could see coming back.

What were your first trips into the North Cascades?

It's kind of hard to resurrect that year. I recall an internist who wanted to climb Mount Rainier. We went up via the Ingraham route. I remember getting incredibly sunburned for not being smart enough to wear long pants on the way down from Camp Muir.

The people I climbed the most with were John Rupley, Don Claunch, Herb Staley and Fred Beckey. There were a couple of climbs I did with Fred. Up from Castle Rock there's a cliff way up on the hill that we named Midnight Rock after Fred and I spent the night sitting out on a little ledge there, having tried to climb up something. I think it was the first time anyone had ever gone up there. It was a mess getting down. There were times you never touched the ground for vast distances; I don't mean on the rock but the jungle below.

I guess the only other thing we did during that time was climb the Mowich Face on Rainier— Fred, Rupley, Staley and I. That was an interesting event. Fred wasn't feeling very good, and we bivouacked on this moraine that dropped down into the Mowich basin. We only had these see-through army sleeping bags, so it was a cool night. Fred allowed that he really didn't want to climb the next morning. That morning the rest of us took off, but after awhile here comes Beckey, seeing the prospect of a first ascent disappearing from under him, catching up with us before we had gotten very far.

Now, Fred is a good guy, different but exceedingly competent and conservative. He's a fine mountaineer. I was with Fred on Huntington, and even on Midnight Rock, the measure of his caution was very apparent. He's capable of knowing fear and knowing how to respond to it. We're very different in terms of personality, but, I wouldn't have any hesitancy about climbing with him.

When did you decide to try an expedition?

I'm not sure it's a decision; maybe it is nowadays. In a sense it was a thing that happened. There was the trip to Huntington in 1957, and a couple of years later Nick Clinch, whom I had known at camp in Colorado, invited me on a trip he was putting together on Masherbrum in 1960. At that time there weren't many climbers who were physicians, so that was my function.

There are lots of physicians who climb today. Part of that is due to the general popularity of climbing, but it may be that the subset has increased disproportionately. I think that some people go into medicine, in a sense, with the perspective of a mountaineer. I know I did. Everything I have done has been colored by the mountains, not the other way around. My research has been, as a physiologist, concerned with how people respond to high altitude. When I started, my choice of specialty was a bit of pot-luck; certainly at the time it was a rather primitive type of specialty compared to today. But the fit has been a perfect one. Everything starts with the mountains.

In what ways did Everest change your life?

I think in very major ways that I would have never anticipated. If I had I probably would have thought twice. I had misgivings about going in the first place. When I came back I wanted to put the climb aside and prove myself in my professional career which I was just beginning. But there was the notoriety which, in a way, felt like a handicap. I surely enjoyed what Everest took me into, some of the kinds of people I met. Unquestionably it opened doors, made contacts and created visibility. So, for even someone who didn't want to be a hero, it was pleasurable.

There were other impacts, that after twenty-five years you begin to reflect on a bit. I can now, for instance, describe how everything was integrated to my mountaineering. It all is. I use and abuse Everest mercilessly as a metaphor. The last week of the audio-respiratory course for our second-year medical students I give a two-hour lecture: the first hour having to do with the definition of altitude and limits; the second of which is very philosophical and has to do with commitment, risk acceptance and things of that sort. It's a bit like being in church on Sunday, I suppose. But these poor students find it inspiring after these weeks of being hounded by volumes of knowledge that they're supposed to soak up. I'll see some of these students fifteen years later and they won't remember my acid base lecture, but they'll never forget that talk.

The book, *Everest, The West Ridge*, is the catalyst to a lot of this. I didn't appreciate it at the time—and I don't climb with the sense that I am climbing for other people—but when I was a kid Mallory was one of my heroes, and it's odd to think that you're a hero to someone else. There was a lot of troubled denial of that fact for years, because I'm not a hero. I'm just a little guy. Nothing about me that is fundamentally different from any other guy, at least those who are stubborn. But I guess I am different in a certain sense. I had an opportunity to do something. I was there and I was lucky. As a Nepalese dignitary said, "Luck is what you make it." I didn't say, "I'm going to Everest so I should help young people, to inspire their own ethics." I went for purely selfish reasons.

In the book, you listed a raft of questions that you were posing to yourself.

You can see at the end of the book where my head was at that time, real doubt. I really felt that way. Part of it was the thing ending, Willi being gone, and having to go back and confront real life again.

Something else that comes across strongly in the

book was the bond formed between you and Willi Unsoeld, and that sense of loss when he was airlifted out ahead of you. Have you ever again had that experience with a climbing partner?

You know, in some ways—and I've never thought about it this way—our relationship on Everest was almost like having an affair, because we were so close together, living with each other in ways that just don't happen except with your wife. That was kind of unique and very special and has undoubtedly colored the nature of relationships from then on. We saw each other—Willi, Dick Emerson and myself—not frequently, but it never felt like it mattered. You always felt like you were close. Both Willi and Dick Emerson are dead, and it sounds crazy, but even now there are times when one would just love to hear them or see them. But at the same time, it's almost as if you can. You never forget those characters.

I think your book gets as close as the subjective mind will allow to being objective. It must be difficult to portray yourself that honestly.

When I returned from Everest I knew I wanted to write a book and I knew why, and I don't think it was predominantly for notoriety. I knew that James Ramsay Ullman's book was going to be a very hero-worshippy kind of book. I think he looked on mountaineers, even though he climbed some, as sort of unreal. Certainly that is the way he portrays them in much of what he writes. What I had found about this experience that was so incredible—I mean the climb itself was incredible—was more the politics of the climb, the interpersonal relationships and the logistical complexity. It was a very intellectual kind of thing.

The expedition worked out well, because I think it was a pretty good party, even though we were competing on different routes. I thought, "That's what ought to get into the book, not all this devil-make-do and greatness stuff." There was an attempt to be caring and respectful of people which is one of the gripes I have about some of the modern mountaineering literature. But at the same time I wanted to tell it like it was, because that's part of the beauty of such an undertaking; the fact that you do disagree with each other, but that you have ways of dealing with that and working it out.

Have you considered writing again?

I think about it some, but I wrote that book for a purpose. The time may come when I will write for the fun of writing. I like writing and I write fairly well, but there just aren't enough hours in the day to indulge myself in that and do all the other things I want to. That includes my work which is part of my passion. It's my climb right now, with just as much uncertainty and challenge.

I was invited to give the major talk at our annual national anesthesia meeting before seven or eight thousand people; the topic was using mountaineering as a metaphor for risk taking. I believe the ability to accept risk is a critical element in being a good anesthesiologist. Much of the time it's like piloting the airplane. All you've got to do is stay awake. That's important, but sometimes all hell is flying around you and you've got to be cool and thinking, capable of responding to high stress in a very deliberate mode.

With your other interests, passions, have you allowed yourself the time to climb?

I've continued to climb, but the character of my climbing has changed. I'll get out once or twice a year into the Cascades, usually a backpack with my wife, daughter and older kids if they're interested. We have this old man's group. They are all in their early to mid-forties, and they treat me with appropriate gentleness. We go out and get in one decent climb a year. Our last climb was on Argonaut Peak, a fairly strenuous rock climb. The capacity to move up and down some of that stuff is still reasonably good.

So your family climbs?

My son is a fairly serious climber. I never climbed in my heyday at his standard. Those standards didn't exist then. He's not a hotshot rock climber; he can climb 5.10-11. He's just a real fine mountaineer, with a lot of savvy and wisdom. He works for the Denali Guide Service.

One of the things that you mentioned often in your book was the separation from your wife.

That was in some ways harder because the relationship was tenuous anyway. It finally came apart about five years later. I think that the expedition was the straw, though it wasn't the cause.

In the book—and I don't know how serious the other members of the expedition were—you were perceived as a bit of a fanatic, the driven one. Was that a part of your personality?

Oh, I think that *is* a part of my personality,

not was. It's much better packaged than it probably was. My faculty perceives me as very intense and stubborn, and I do too, in my mind. Those attributes aren't different than they were then. I'm more socially able to intersect them with people in a constructive way perhaps. But part of that is role play, then and even now. Willi and I had really defined a certain kind of relationship with the South Col group, where I would be the extremist and he would be the peacemaker. So, to a certain extent it was conceived, but it was easy to play the role, no question about it.

Do you enjoy competitive sports?

When I say that I'm not competitive, friends who know me sneer in disbelief. I guess it depends on how you define the term. I don't see myself explicitly competing with other people. Most of my competition is internal. You don't like to lose, but to compete in a win/lose type of situation just isn't where my pleasure in physical activity or most other things comes about.

Kathy (his wife) has gotten into triathalons, not as an athlete. She likes the T-shirts. I've sort of been her coach. I run and bike with her. About a year ago I learned how to swim and actually entered a triathalon myself; came in last. I had a flat tire, although I was second-to-last coming out of the water. The point was not to record any great times but just to keep Kathy company. I felt nothing but intimidation about swimming before the summer of 1988. Pete Schoening has a cross-lake (Washington) swim every August with a huge breakfast at the end of it. It's a great social event. It's been satisfying to know that you can still learn to do something reasonably well.

A couple of generations of climbers have emerged since you climbed Everest, since you were at your physical peak. Is it hard to identify with or comprehend what's being done today?

The evolution is not hard to comprehend. It's what older climbers were seeing when they saw Fred Beckey. That's inevitable; what Dick Emerson defined as the need for uncertainty as to outcome. As certain standards are set, there is a need to define new unknowns, set new standards.

I would have never imagined the caliber of rock climbing today. These people are really human spiders. It's incredible, and yet I see it so I believe it. I can understand it, but I can't identify with it personally. Could I have done it if that had been the standard then? I suppose if I had prepared to commit as much to it as is necessary.

My guess is that you would find very few Renaissance men among today's rock climbers. You really have to commit to it as if you were preparing to be a champion.

You really have to. If you are going to climb at the competitive cutting edge, that's a full-time job just as in any other competitive sport. You can argue whether mountaineering is a sport, but rock climbing on artificial walls is.

All that is very comprehensible. The thing I have difficulty with—and I can't decide whether it's age—is what's happening in the Himalayas in terms of risk taking. It almost seems to have transcended something that relates to accepting reasonable risk for reasonable gain, replaced by a fanaticism that lays life flat on the line in a way that has not been characteristic of mountaineering up 'til now; holocaustal, as on K-2 and Everest a few years later.

I look at free soloing and I can appreciate the level that these climbers have reached and the confidence in their abilities, and yet I look at the objective dangers that seem to give one no chance.

I guess I understand that better if I make an assumption because I did a little soloing in my younger days. Climbing has its hazards anyway, even if you're climbing roped. The kind of soloing I did on the east face of Long's Peak was well within the limits of my technical ability. And if I make the assumption that these guys who are climbing 5.11-12s unroped, where any little thing would be the end of them, are climbing as much within themselves as I was—which is an awesome thing to believe—then I have to accept that what they are doing is reasonable. If

those climbers are climbing right at the edge of their limit, with little margin, then that's Russian Roulette.

Some people would believe that, for you, standing on top of Everest was the high point of your life. For some climbers, one summit must be replaced by another.

I suppose we need to get our challenges somewhere, and some people continue to confine their challenges to that arena. I found mine elsewhere. I have other interests.

At a talk I recently gave, a woman came up to me and said, "Well, that must have been the pinnacle of your life. Nothing can compare with Everest." When you get down to the fundamentals of that trip, it was a juicy climb, but in different ways, there have been experiences that have been every bit its equal.

A few years ago I went on a climb to China, and although we didn't succeed in climbing the mountain—we got dumped on by a lot of rain—it was the nicest trip I've ever been on. There were just five people, including my son. It was the loveliest experience. We didn't have a leader. We just sat there Quaker style and sometimes laboriously worked out where we were at; coming from slightly different perspectives, but with basically the same approach to risk taking. The risks I took on Everest are just not a part of my life anymore, at least in climbing. I have too many other things going on.

How does it feel to have a couloir on Mount Everest named after you?

Well, the Hornbein Couloir is much more auspicious sounding than Hornbein Avalanche Track. It is strange to have a piece of real estate on Everest named after you. But nice.

CHAPTER
22
JOE AND CARLA FIREY

« I've climbed Rainier only once, and that was years ago. You want to be on peaks that are in amongst the rest. You get on top of a volcano, like Baker and look over

at Shuksan, which is only 1,500 feet lower, and it looks like a piddling little bump, not scenic at all. »

— *Joe Firey*

The Firey name probably appears in more North Cascade summit registers than any other save Fred Beckey's. Beginning in the mid-1950s, Joe Firey, his late wife, Joan, and their daughter, Carla, traversed seemingly every acre of the Cascades from the Canadian border—and often north of it—to Glacier Peak. Along the way they made countless first ascents. Looking through the guide books it appears that the Fireys and the many friends who accompanied them were seeking the last adventures in the Cascades, not the hardest climbs. A typical Firey trip might include some steep snow, some mid-5th class climbing and interesting, often esoteric, approaches. The Fireys seemed to like a good bushwhack, although Joe says, "I won't say I enjoyed them. You just can't avoid them in the Cascades."

Joan died of cancer about ten years ago, and Carla, because of her art studies and shaky knees, has focused most of her attention on rock climbing rather than long trips. Joe, now in his early 70s, is retired from the University of Washington where he taught mechanical engineering. He still gets out regularly on extended climbing and skiing trips with the same friends he has been climbing with for a few decades. He has focused on the Coast Range in British Columbia lately. "In the Cascades you have to hike all the way in", Joe says. "In the Coast Range we can use a chopper to get in and save ourselves four to six days hiking."

We meet at Joe's home in the University District. Leaning back in a squeaky chair, Joe talks easily about his mountaineering experiences but doesn't volunteer a great deal of detail. He talks about his trips as great fun or adventures. Often he directs questions at Cliff or myself, especially about areas he has yet to explore.

Carla arrives from the dentist about an hour later. As her father is stocky, Carla seems physically delicate, but almost two

112

decades earlier I watched from a comfortable heather bench as she tried to overcome the crux of a climb on Midnight Rock, the Easter Overhang. She would jam with her right foot and hand while scrabbling across the face with her left. Two feet, five feet, almost ten and then she would fall, and try again. When I left, she still trying.

She remembers the climb and says, "I used to be much more competitive, although there was always someone better, even among my group and it really motivated me to try and be the best, or among the best."

▲

Is there an area in the Cascades you haven't explored?

Joe Firey: I haven't been between Snoqualmie and Chinook passes. That's not much of a mountaineering area. One of the big advantages of getting here in the '50s was that very few people were climbing then. I think the big change occurred when Whittaker, Unsoeld and Hornbein, and that bunch first bagged Everest. After that people started noticing mountaineering as a sport, although it's still a sport that's not too popular.

When I read about your climbs I get the feeling the Fireys didn't mind a good bushwhack.

Joe: We didn't used to. I try to avoid them now. I don't mind some of it as long as there isn't too much devil's club.

I mentioned that because I remember reading a description of your traverse from the Colonial-Snowfield area to El Dorado. On that trip you chose to descend from Snowfield and ascend the McAllister Glacier near its icefall. It seemed like such an unlikely route choice.

Joe: That was not the way to go. When we got ready to leave Colonial to go over to El Dorado, the weather got really poor. We stopped on a swampy bench above the McAllister and hoped the bad weather would improve. It quit raining, but the clouds still hung real low. We could see the McAllister Glacier and figured there must be a way up out of there. There was but it wasn't a very good way. I wouldn't do it again, but at the time we couldn't see the other way. That is a real choice area though.

Have you done much climbing on Rainier?

Joe: No, I've climbed Rainier only once, and that was years ago. One thing I noticed when I did climb Rainier—and the same is true of Baker or Adams—is that when you get on top it really isn't that scenic. You're above everything. I really like the scenery which is a big attraction. You want

to be on peaks that are in amongst the rest. You get on top of these big volcanos, and you're above everything. Gosh, you get up on Baker and look over at Shuksan, which is only 1,500 feet lower, and it looks like a piddling little bump. Besides the rock on Rainier is pretty crumbly.

(At this point Carla Firey joins us.)

What do you do to stay in shape?

Joe: Well, I go ski touring in the winter almost every weekend. Your options are kind of limited in the Cascades. There are some good trips around Crystal, and if the weather is halfway decent there are some good tours from Paradise. This past spring we skied up the back side of St. Helens. Very nice skiing. We also got a chance to look down into that horrendous hole.

So it's just a matter of getting out. You don't do any other kind of exercise?

Joe: I suppose I should. I know a lot of people who run into problems with knees and ankles, but from running, not hiking. I think it's all that hammering. I'm really too lazy to take up that kind of thing, just running along. I probably get out every other weekend, but over the years I've gotten slower. Not that I was ever fast, but I could move along reasonably well then.

Do you guys jog? Well, don't run downhill. You'll pound your knees to pieces. Talk to Lloyd Anderson. That's what stopped him from climbing. He was real strong. Finally, those funny cushions in the joints of his knees got mangled completely.

Carla Firey: Joan had knee operations, Irene Muehlmans too. I wear knee braces and use a cross between a walking stick and ski pole. Joe's never had any knee trouble, but he's never run. I think I inherited Joan's knees.

Did hiking and climbing seem like a natural thing to do for you when you were younger?

Carla: I just assumed it was what you did.

Joe and Joan would show slides of their trips when we were quite young, even before we went out much. Also being that I was the first child, I assumed that even more than my siblings—they are still interested in the out of doors, but not like me.

When did you get interested in rock climbing?

Carla: The first couple of times I went out with Joe or Joan, they would take me on third-class-type climbs where there wasn't a lot of snow, something in the Tatoosh Range. They didn't take me on too many trips before they and I decided I should take the Mountaineers' basic climbing course and learn the basics of safety and so forth on my own. I always preferred the peaks where we'd do some rock scrambling, third, fourth or fifth class. That traverse of the McAllister Glacier was really the first year that I did more. I hadn't graduated from high school. That summer I did the traverse and right after took a rock climbing course and gained a great deal of confidence. The next year I did more alpine climbing in the Cascades.

Did you have a lot of trust in your parents?

Carla: That was certainly an interesting issue. I certainly had complete trust in them. Between those two summers there was a change from complete trust in your parents to realizing that you really had to make your own decisions, take responsibility for yourself, and no, they were not infallible.

Were there many kids your age climbing?

Carla: A few. The University of Washington had courses at that time. Bill Sumner and others were teaching, and I decided to take their rock climbing course. Before that I only knew a couple of people my age: Bruce Albert and Steve Ansell. The instructors were quite capable.

Carla, the last time I saw you—must have been seventeen years ago—was at Midnight Rock. I remember watching you attack one of the routes, moving up ten feet, then falling, struggling up and down. You must have been on that pitch for over an hour. When we left you were still at it and I was struck by your tenacity.

Carla: I remember that. It was a disastrous day. Al Givler was apparently amused that I kept trying. Sometimes I think, "Well, I don't have that kind of determination now." At that time I could do 5.9 and the Easter Overhang was 5.10a, about one step higher than what I could do.

In the early '70s there weren't many women climbing at your level.

Carla: No, not really. There was Julie Bruegger, of course, and Catherine Freer.

At that time you did a flurry of first ascents in the North Cascades. Did you venture outside the country on expeditions?

Carla: No, not exactly. I was never really interested in that sort of thing. I think Joan's involvement in the Annapurna expedition kind of solidified my feelings about that kind of activity. Joe was always kind of negative towards it. It just doesn't seem like fun. I have been to Peru and the Soviet Union. Other than that, the more ambitious trips were those Joe organized in the Coast Range.

Joe: Those aren't real expeditions; two- or three-week trips.

Carla: Those were just like bigger trips. I do not like snow and ice climbing. I like rock climbing. I like traveling in the mountains but am not comfortable on ice. It's just one of those things, and I think it happens to plenty of women at this age, that you recognize that some risks just aren't acceptable.

I'm not one of those frenetic types who can put a lot of energy into many different things. If I put a lot of energy into rock climbing, it really takes away from the time I spend in the studio. I keep asking myself over and over again, "What's important?" and the answer's always the same. As a result I don't give as much time to rock climbing. Jim (her husband, Jim McCarthy) and I belong to the Vertical Club and that kind of workout, just doing it for the sake of working out, has made it real easy to maintain a certain level of climbing fitness where I can go out and climb 5.10 and it's not too much of a problem.

Do the subjects of your paintings revolve around the mountains?

Carla: They're not specific landscapes. I really approach them from a formal standpoint. The composition of the values, colors, forms, is how I work on it when I'm actually working on the painting. There was a piece I did last May that was an interior. There was included in the interior an area that could be read as a landscape although it wasn't terribly specific. I have been thinking recently of specifically starting with the idea of including a mountain landscape.

I was just wondering if your experience in the

mountains and where you live are in any way an inspiration for the work you do?

Carla: Alpine landscape certainly does intrigue me as a motif. But not a painting of Mount Rainier, which is more illustrative. There are issues having to do with what Joan's body of work represents to me versus my own; Her work was more literal, illustrating a particular place. I started out deliberately thinking that I was not going to do that. I did do a portrait of the Southern Pickets, and it did turn out nicely. I used photographs for reference and used watercolors and then sold it for a moderate amount of money, considering I was just a beginning painter. I did it, because it was something Joan was thinking about doing and hadn't gotten around to doing. It was kind of unfinished business, but I knew afterwards I was never going to do that again.

Did you ever do much technical winter mountaineering?

Carla: For several years, while in my early twenties, I assumed that at some point I will learn how to ice climb, but I really don't feel like doing it now. Well, I never really got around to feeling like doing it, and I cannot properly ice climb. I simply do not know how to use the tools. The stuff is sharp and heavy. I think it's ridiculous.

So that sort of limited what you could do in the Cascades or forced you to do things you didn't want to do.

Carla: You mean carrying packs. I have never heard of anybody who really enjoyed carrying a heavy load.

Joe: I haven't either.

Does your husband prefer rock climbing?

Carla: He likes it, but sometimes I think left to his own devices he might prefer to do more alpine climbing, although he's never voiced any frustration.

Do you two make a good rope team?

Carla: Well sometimes. We used to do quite well when we were doing some more ambitious climbs. Actually the last year we haven't climbed together. It's often better to climb with your friends than with your spouse. We went climbing in Chamonix this winter and did rather well. I think he's more conservative than me despite the fact that, this year particularly, I was in the worst shape I have been in for a really long time. It used to take two to four weeks. Now it takes the whole season. I hope that next season I'll get into the

mountains more, work out a little more. I just can't let it slide. I just can't get away with it. Of course we'll get lots of sympathy from Joe.

Joe: You won't get any tears from me.

It must be frustrating to watch the standards for "State of the Art" rise always out of your reach.

Carla: I have never felt, even if other people might have thought otherwise, that what I was doing was state of the art. When you feel that way, and somebody gets really good really fast, it doesn't really affect you as much as if you were one of the top climbers.

I have always been acquainted with people who were close to the top, so it wasn't alien. The scene has changed tremendously, but I haven't had that sensation of being left behind. When I was in my late twenties I did climb quite a bit in Yosemite, and again, there were women doing harder things than I could do. I was close, but not that close.

When you look at the scene, younger climbers, do you find yourself making judgements in the same way that another generation of climbers must have made judgements about you?

Carla: When you're in your twenties you're a lot more aggressive socially, but I think I was more focused on trying to do this hard climb rather than climbing better than so-and-so. When I started to look at people—and this was starting to be true even around 1980—seeing women who were becoming quite good, it was obvious that they were built differently, ate differently. They ate a low-fat diet to keep their weight down to keep themselves as light as possible.

You look at these sport climbers, and some people have accused certain climbers of being anorexic. I don't think you could perform at that level with that sort of problem. Although somebody told me that a well-known Yosemite climber is anorexic. I've heard that in ballet there are anorexics. It could definitely fit.

Obsession is certainly no stranger to climbing, but that sort of obsession is one you would not associate with the sport.

Carla: But you can't be sure. Some of those people are so thin.

Joe, what did you think of the new generation of climbers that emerged in the late sixties and included Carla?

Joe: Oh, that's kind of hard to say, because I didn't really climb in my early twenties. Those were the war years, so no one was climbing much. I guess the only thing I noticed there was that a lot more people were climbing in the mountains.

Carla: I kind of remember that you and Joan were somewhat critical of technical rock climbing. This is my opinion and you may disagree, but I think that Joe and Joan thought that rock climbing was a lot more artificial than going out and experiencing the wilderness which was fun. Joe has always had a recreational orientation towards climbing, which I have now adopted. He believed that you go climbing to have fun, not as something you specifically trained for.

Joe: The people who get into rock climbing—that's a different sport than mountain climbing—their interests are different. But I don't think I was critical.

I guess I am amazed at the standard of climbing today.

Joe: Nobody now says that this or that route is impossible. That was once said. If you went back into the 'Thirties people would say, "Well, you can't climb this route." Nobody says that anymore, because routes are being knocked over, extremely difficult routes.

I think of the change that occurred at the Town Wall. All those routes used to be aid routes. Now most of them go free. And they still look the same to me, damn steep.

Joe: They do some amazing things nowadays.

Carla: I think that if you do a variety of climbs in the easy 5.11 range, you have a sense of what is involved. Or if you do boulder moves on artificial walls, you have a better sense of what they're actually doing, even though I don't know what 5.13 is like at all. I can remember thinking, "If I can just do 5.9."

I do think it is different if you're a woman, because the standards are different for women. There is a double standard. It's not the usual kind of double-standard you experience in society. The double standard is there partly out of the interest of fairness, and partly out of, who knows? I mean, Lynn Hill thinks women should be competing at the same level as men. Well, you wouldn't have any women making the finals. If you're going to attract women to the sport, you're going to have to have that double standard.

Climbing 5.11 is fun for me, and I would love to stay in shape to do that sort of climb more than I can. The thing about a 5.11 being much different than a 5.10, it is, a different kind of excitement. There is so much difficulty all wrapped together. When I say 5.11, I must say that I am way back in the 5.11 crack climbing phase which is eight to ten years old; thin cracks. So I guess I am dated.

Joe: Unfortunately I'm really dated.

CHAPTER
23
ALEX BERTULIS

The 1975 Mountaineers annual included an article on a complete traverse of the Pickets done in 1963. It sounded like a great trip until the author, Alex Bertulis, began recalling the series of Dulfersitz rappels down the vertical 2,000-foot north face of Mount Terror. After almost a day of rappelling with no sense of how many more rappels they faced, Bertulis and his partner ran low on anchors and started cutting off pieces of the climbing rope.

The Alex Bertulis I meet bears little resemblance to the wild man I pictured while reading that article. The 51-year-old architect, conservatively yet casually dressed, is relaxed, smiling easily in his Seattle office.

« Architecture always had the priority, although I must admit that sometimes my architecture

suffered because I went on a climbing expedition and then got fired. »

— Alex Bertulis

Recently returned from a wind-surfing expedition to Patagonia, he lifts his pants leg to show ugly gashes from a collision with a coral reef. Maybe there's a bit of that wild man in him yet.

Bertulis retains a slight Eastern European accent, even though he left Lithuania as a small child after World War II.

Bertulis has first ascents in the Cascades, Rockies, Alaska, Africa, Europe and the Himalayas, and was instrumental in arranging the first Soviet-American climbing exchanges early in 1970. He is equally proud of his firsts in architecture, which include many buildings incorporating energy conservation features.

At the time of our conversation, Bertulis is coordinating a Lithuanian-American expedition to Mount Everest for 1992. When Bertulis talks about the disintegration of the Soviet Union, and the Lithuanian independence movement, it is clear that he still retains a strong tie with the country of his birth. When referring to Lithuania, he says "we."

Do you remember your first real hard ascent?

I would say that the climb that got the local, leading climbers attention, namely Fred Beckey and Eric Bjornstad, maybe Steve Marts, was a traverse of the Picket Range, a ten-day traverse, which entailed the third ascent of Mount Terror, the descent of the north face which took a day and a half of rappelling.

I remember reading your account of that trip and being amazed by this marathon descent. Weren't you slowly running out of . . .

Yes, rope, or rope anchors and so we were cutting up pieces of our climbing rope. We made the eighth ascent of Mount Fury, and the twelfth ascent of Mount Challenger. It was quite an adventure. We went very light, without stoves, moving all the time. We ate dried food, or if we went down lower, we built a fire because we did have a little pot. But quite often we stayed above any fire zone. It was, I think, the first north-south traverse. I made the trip with Half Santoff, who was oblivious of any concern, because he thought I had been there the year before in the Northern Pickets and that was good enough. So he was always relaxed, and I was always thinking, are we going to make it?

I really had never met anyone who had been there. The guide book was very rough. We had no tent, but I had a super light two-pound sleeping bag. We had two Army ponchos, because they're compatible. You can make a shelter out of the poncho, or use it as a ground cloth, or even as a poncho. That's the way we traveled with very light packs so we could climb with them. Therefore, we moved fast. It was one of my most memorable trips.

I think Eric Bjornstad had at that time the Coffeehouse Eigerwand. That was the hangout for climbers. I think he was impressed when he heard we made this traverse. He introduced us to Fred Beckey, and we came to their next slide show.

Who did you climb with to gain your skills? Who were your climbing role models?

The people I climbed with from then on were primarily Fred Beckey, Eric Bjornstad, and Steve Marts. Of the three I would say the climber who set the highest standard was Steve Marts, even though he was a lot less experienced than Fred Beckey. And his role model was Royal Robbins. I guess he had just done a summer in Yosemite and came back starry-eyed. So there was this school of Fred Beckey and Ed Cooper who were siege climbing, and there was the Yosemite School. I drifted quickly to the Yosemite School rather than staying in the Fred Beckey School. Fred Beckey had bad habits which took a long time to break. So we made fun of him a little bit during that time. But I did climb with him, enjoyed climbing with him. I did one siege climb with him, a route on the Squamish Chief, and that was my first and last siege climb.

How would you characterize a siege climb?

Well, you fix ropes, and then you come down during the night, come back a week later, whatever, and continue climbing; prusiking up what you did before and continue that way. A two-day climb could take a month, or whatever. That was a tactic we were ready to abandon. It took Fred longer. But the reason was not so much that he couldn't do it in one push, but—and this is my personal opinion—it gave him the opportunity to climb more peaks and more new routes at the same time.

The unwritten etiquette at that time was, if you put a rope up on the route, the route was yours until you finished it. This rule didn't last very long, but at that time it worked. So Fred went around starting all these routes. He was afraid somebody else would get to them before he did. It stopped when people finally would bypass his rope and put the route in anyway and leave a little thank-you note.

You were involved in the early climbs on Liberty Bell, and in fact had done a lot of the hard work on Liberty Crack. Why were you unable to complete the climb?

I think I went to Africa, and so I couldn't complete it for that reason, but Steve Marts and I reconnoitered the east face. The first time we hiked in there, the shortest access was from Twisp over Copper Pass and down the eastern slope. One time when we did that we found another climber up there on the regular route fooling around. His name was Frank Tarver, and we asked him how he got there. We hadn't seen him or his tracks. He said, "Oh well, my car is down there." We didn't know that the North Cascades Road was already pushed in. So we not only had to suffer that, but also hike back out the way we came in which was a full day hike.

But you did come back and do the Independence route.

I think that was the following year when I came back from Africa. We came back in 1967, I guess it was. Don MacPherson and I ended up doing the route. In fact I think Steve Marts and Frank Tarver—I'm not positive it was them—but all four of us were going to do the climb. We were ready to do it early, like in May sometime. But there was a big storm over the Cascades. We could see the dark, raining clouds, so we waited near Mazama where the clouds couldn't reach us, and we waited several days. I think Tarver and Marts ran out of time, just waiting. Don and I were unemployed at the time, so we just sat there until it looked like reasonably good weather and jumped at the first sign of blue sky. I remember when we got there, that all the overhangs the first day had icicles hanging from them.

How did you scout out the route? Was it a pretty obvious line that you could see?

I didn't do the scouting because there were two other guys who made the first attempt, and they deserve credit for pioneering the lower third. That was Hans Baer and Tom Quinn, I think. They got up to a ceiling the year before and said they left a water bottle up there. That little ceiling afterward was named the Baer ceiling. They weren't able to come with us, and also we weren't trying to steal anyone's climb. Everyone knew and we asked, "Who wants to go?" We were all friends, so just by process of elimination and default Don and I ended up the two survivors to make that climb.

We spent over three days on the route. We never fixed ropes. We went right from the start.

What's it like spending that much time on a huge face?

The weather was really good. I liked it, and I was psyched. So I was super confident and I remember Don was finally getting psyched out. He had problems, mentally. In the end we were both jubilant when we reached the top. In fact the lower half was so difficult, in terms of minimal nailing, you know like A4 and hard 5.9. In those days 5.9 in alpine boots was pretty hard climbing. We were just stressed out. As it turned out we persevered and that last day we did, actually, half the climb.

When did you begin to look to climbs outside the Cascades?

I always looked outside the Cascades. I think most climbers do look outside their home range.

In those days the Himalayas were closed. So there were the Alps. I had already climbed, or made an attempt on a peak in Alaska in 1964 with Fred Beckey and made a first ascent with him, in the Wind River Range, Spider Peak. That was fun.

But then Leif Patterson, being Norwegian, told me about this Trollryggen, a big face, about 5-6,000 foot face on one of the fjords. He wanted me to go there with him, and I committed myself to go with him in the summer of 1965. I was saving money up for that trip, and my girl friend, who had used my car while I was climbing the Squamish Chief got into an accident in Vancouver. And we found out neither one of our insurances covered the accident, so I had to pay damages on two cars. That knocked out my trip to Trollryggen which Leif then did, an awesome ascent.

I postponed my overseas ambitions by one year, worked hard and went to Africa to climb in the summer of 1966 and then during the winter I climbed in the Alps. Suddenly my overseas horizons were broadening very fast.

Were you postponing your career at that point to do those climbs?

No, I had already finished school and was working in architectural offices as a draftsman and designer. I was pretty good at it so I could work hard and fast at it, put in extra hours if I wanted to. I lived very frugally in those days, as all climbers do during that period. So I saved lots of money.

Did you take a leave of absence?

No, I just quit. You just quit and off you go. If I had more demand for my architecture, I think I would have ended up climbing a lot less and would have been better for it. Architecture always had the priority, although I must admit that sometimes my architecture suffered because I went on a climbing expedition and then got fired. Or I wasn't around when a client came knocking on my door with a job. But as a rule I have always put my architecture career before my climbing career.

When you came back to the Northwest did you become interested in doing winter ascents in the Cascades?

Yeah, I was always interested in winter ascents. Even while I was living in California, I did Grigornio in the winter just because it's fun to do things in the winter. And of course Fred Beckey was getting into winter climbing real hot and heavy during this period, so we were keeping in touch regarding our winter agendas. I made an attempt on Mount Robson one year with a fellow named Dick Springate, and it was unsuccessful because we hit a big storm on New Year's Eve. But I met Leif Patterson on that trip. and we agreed to make our next attempt together. That was in March of '65. I told Fred Beckey he was welcome to join us.

I remember we kept in telephone touch with the people at Robson Ranch. In those days we didn't have satellite photos. So when they said, "Yeah, the weather is good," Leif and I just jumped on the train from Vancouver to take off for Robson. Fred was someplace in Colorado, and he left phone numbers around where he could be reached. I left a message and said, "Leif and I have left for Robson." It was an epic chase for Fred.

When he found out we were after Robson and the weather was good, he said he dropped everything and just hightailed it from Colorado to Seattle, called everyone under the sun who could join him. He finally found Tom Stewart, who was working for Boeing and then drove like a bat out of Hell down the Alcan Highway.

As we were poised just below the summit, Leif and I, we saw three people wandering up the Robson Glacier. And it was Fred, Tom Stewart, and Eric Bjornstad. We didn't know for sure who the three were, but we figured one of the three had to be Fred. So we reached the summit almost at the same time and then took what was a nice reunion at high camp. We considered it a team climb. I didn't mind them being part of our team, because we weren't competing. Boy, Fred just broke all records on that one.

Was there generally this sense of camaraderie among the climbing community in the Northwest, and did that change as more climbers came onto the scene?

I think there was a sense of camaraderie among certain players and not among others, notably Ed Cooper and Fred Beckey who were very competitive in that sense.

With one another?

Especially with one another, but I think also with anybody at large. They were very possessive of their climbs. And I never completely understood it or participated in that. There was that competitive backbiting that existed, but it ema-

nated from the two and there was a little fallout around them. But among the rest of us there was a camaraderie and respect.

I remember the climb you did on Bonanza with the Soviets? Had there been other climbing exchanges?

No, that was the first time that Soviet climbers were here, the very first time. I had my eyes for many, many years, like everyone else, on the Himalayas, but I also had my eyes on the mountains of the Soviet Union which very few people were even aware existed. Having come from that part of the world, I knew they existed. I was trying to figure out how in the heck we could establish contact during this very Cold-War period with the Soviets. We were able to make contact through visiting Soviet scientists, some of whom happened to be climbers.

The first trip started in 1974 and we went over there. Everybody was elated. It was a big breakthrough. At that time, I guess I could have led the expedition if I'd wanted to, because I was the guy most involved with making it happen. I was a great admirer of Pete Schoening and knew that he had made an attempt to climb there like fifteen years earlier and was turned down. So I asked Pete if he wanted to be the leader and he said he'd be delighted. It was a relatively successful expedition with a lot of diversified climbers, from moderately experienced to very experienced.

The following year, six Soviet climbers visited all the major climbing centers of the United States, starting in the Shawangunks and going over to the Tetons, Yosemite and the North Cascades. In the North Cascades I was assigned to host them. They said they would love to do a first ascent. I said that was a big ticket to ask. We'd all like to do first ascents. But I had this hidden route, which I had made at least one attempt on, on Bonanza. So I said, "Okay, we'll go in and do that route." It turned out to be just what we wanted. They really liked it.

The following year six of us went over. We had a very good team that year. We did a lot of great climbs, many new routes. When I went back in 1989, I went back into some of the same areas to visit, and local climbers told me, "Here's the Lowe Route, here's the Barber Route." They named these routes after us, because it made such an impact, and they're so proud of those routes.

We broke ground for them.

Do you feel different as a climber than you did twenty-five years ago when you were putting up new routes in the North Cascades? Have your skills eroded much at all?

Well, I think that, no, only my physical ability has declined like in all sports. I'm not half the soccer player I used to be but I still play soccer.

Twenty-five years ago I would stick my neck out a lot farther and get a thrill out of doing something extreme. I have become a gentleman climber. Even though I get stuck into some harder situations inadvertently, I'm not out chasing hard climbs. I do love the mountains, and I do a lot of climbing now with my children or people of the younger generation, and sometimes I get involved with guys who do harder climbs and they simply invite me along. I'm very happy doing the classic climbs I like doing a lot; Liberty Ridge on Rainier, the north face of Shuksan, a few other climbs like that.

God, I went to Joshua Tree last November, and I couldn't believe how hard the climbing was. I enjoyed it. It was exhilarating, although I've never been a boulderer-type rock climber of the Joshua Tree mold. My love has always been climbing in the high peaks in alpine style. And if there is some hard climbing that has to be done along the way, great.

Are your children becoming interested in climbing?

I had one daughter who was very interested in climbing until she grew up. We did many climbs together. Now I have two sons, and the younger of the two is very interested in climbing. And it's a nice circle to come back and do the same climbs you did twenty-five years ago with the next generation. There's something very worldly about that, you know.

*F*red Stanley's first rock climb was on Jello Tower at Castle Rock, an introductory climb for many aspiring climbers. He says of that climb, "On the rappel the rope got stuck and I climbed back up, unsnagged it and climbed down without any problem. I don't know whether I was roped up or not, but it didn't bother me to go back up without a belay on. It took me a while to get smart so I was scared."

As was the case with many of the best climbers living on the east slopes of the Cascades, Stanley found his way into the Sherpa Climbing Club. He recalls bugging the Praters or Dave Mahre about once a week and asking, "If you're going on anything can I tag along?"

« We had a tent that we set up at Washington Pass that summer. We just left the tent there with sleeping bags and climbing gear and everything, and nobody ever touched anything. Those days are long gone. »

— Fred Stanley

In the fall of 1963 he accompanied Jim Wickwire and Dave Mahre on a climb of the northeast face of Stuart. "That was a real eye-opener as far as getting out on bigger rock climbs. There were places where I really wondered, 'What am I doing here?' The first pitch the second morning, I wasn't physically warmed up for it. Dave climbed up it and didn't have any problems. I went up there and was so wiped by the time I got to the big belay ledge, that I almost felt like I was going to puke. But I recovered from that and the rest of the day was just great. It was intimidating to look up the north face of Stuart and think, 'How many Castle Rocks is that stacked one on top of the other?'"

In the next couple of years, Stanley established his rock climbing credentials with new routes on Dragontail, Stuart, Prusik and Liberty Bell, the now classic Liberty Crack. In his chapter on Northwest climbers, in *Climbing In North America*, Chris Jones called Stanley "Perhaps the strongest free climber of the period" (mid-1960s). Stanley also took part in expeditions to the Pamirs in 1974 and K-2 in 1975. The tensions on the K-2 expedition were exposed to the world in Galen Rowell's book, *In the Throne Room of the Mountain Gods*. It read like "All My

Mountaineers," the melodrama played out at 20,000 feet rather than in some klieg light-lit studio. At the time I remember rooting for Stanley and another Ellensburg Sherpa, Fred Dunham.

For the last decade Stanley, who works at Central Washington University in the computer science department, has confined his climbing to occasional weekends. "Physically, I'm a wreck. But I see no reason that, given the opportunity, I couldn't climb at the same standard I was in the 'Sixties, or even better."

Stanley and his family live in a big Victorian home, a quick drive from Monashtash Ridge, a long, open ridge that is a conditioning hike or run for all the Sherpas in Ellensburg. We do the interview at his kitchen table, a comfortable place conducive to long conversations.

▲

What was the Washington Pass area like when you first climbed Liberty Bell?

In that summer of 1965 they had bulldozed a road pretty close to Washington Pass. We couldn't drive it all the way at that time. Steve Marts had a little Renault. With three people in it, you had to stack the gear on the roof. One of the times he hit a rock with his gas tank, punctured a hole in it. We thought we better get out and look at it right away. Sure enough gas was dribbling out of his gas tank and here we were miles from any town, with no way to repair it. We tried to figure what we could put in it to plug it. We ended up carving a plug out of a bar of soap that he had in his glove box. Damned if that didn't fit just perfectly, and he drove around Seattle for a few days after that until he got it fixed.

We had a tent that we set up at Washington Pass that summer. We just left the tent there with sleeping bags and climbing gear and everything, and nobody ever touched anything. Those days are long gone. We just left the stuff up there and came out with our packs. Next time we brought in the food we needed. Like having your own little base camp.

Did you do that climb in one big push?

Steve had been there before and had started the climb. He and Alex Bertulis had gotten just above the first big roof. That part of the climb to just above the roof was fixed when Don McPherson and I went back. At that point we just prusiked up and continued on. If it had been me, I would have never done it. I had never done anything like that before. But Steve said, "Sure you guys can do it. Let's go." So away we went.

For that climb I got some ripstop nylon and old army tubular webbing off a parachute, and sewed up a hammock to sleep on. We prusiked up

above the Lithuanian Lip that day. Steve led what is now a hard free pitch. Then Don led another long pitch and quite some time before dark we found what looked like a good spot for putting in anchors—two or three pitons and bolts—and spent the night there. That was a new experience. It was a beautiful night, with the moon sweeping across the face. The only problem was mosquitoes that seemed to be following us up to the top.

What was the response to your new route on Liberty Bell?

I don't think there was that much of a response. Afterwards I became aware that other people were interested in the climb. I heard a story that at one time Fred Beckey had tried Liberty Crack, and somebody had gone up and thrown his ropes off or had used them. Our climb was the start of a lot of activity up there. Although a lot of people were interested, I'm not sure it was considered a classic at that time.

I didn't really seriously think about climbing other places until I went to the Pamirs in 1974. We were just a group out of a very large number of people invited to what they called the International Climbing Camp that summer. There were probably two- to three-hundred people, not all climbers; quite a few nationalities: Austrians, Germans, French, Scots, British, Dutch, Japanese.

You got caught in an avalanche that summer.

Just prior to that, a bad spell of weather had set in, creating a big avalanche hazard on what they called the Krylenko Face. It's a big wide-open face, not a front-pointing slope, but steep. We were headed down off the mountain at the time the avalanche hit. When we had come down from that pass the afternoon before, there had been a real metamorphosis in the snow from the morning. It had set up into a real thick, wet slab on top of some corn snow beneath. Peter Lev was in our group and he is an avalanche expert. We dug down in there, took a look at it, and he said, "I don't think we have to worry much about this." But Bruce Carson and I had a bad feeling. I remember that night in the tent waking up off and on thinking about that slope up above.

The next morning, it turned out to be pretty nice, but one of our stoves wouldn't work, and we futzed around with it trying to get it to go. We decided that here we are six guys with one stove, and we better not try and go on without a stove. So Al Steck, who wasn't feeling too good, decided to come down with John, Bruce and me. I felt we should get off the slope and let it stabilize a little bit and come back.

My recollection of the afternoon was that a big storm was coming in. The sun was beating in pretty hard, a little bit of snow starting to filter down. Just then we heard this big boom behind us. Apparently, an earthquake must have set the avalanche off. Standing there on the mountain, I felt no earthquake at all. I looked around, and all I can remember is seeing snow coming down from everywhere. It looked like a mile and a half. In the whole basin, snow was coming down everywhere. I thought, well I'll try and ride it out. When it got close I just lay down and was just gently lifted up. I can remember a couple of times ending up on the surface and seeing the avalanche alongside me which was moving a lot faster. I ended up being pretty much on the top of things, a leg kind of stuck beneath me. I really don't know how far I was carried, but I suppose it was a hundred yards. Bruce, John and I pretty much came out on top of it. Steck was nowhere to be seen.

We hollered and hollered. Al had been off on my right when this thing started and when I was on top of that snow I could see that everything on my right was moving faster, so I figured he must be down lower. I headed down and finally got a weak reply to my yelling. Here he was with one hand and his head stuck out of the snow. I got over and cleared a little snow from his face and made sure he was alive. I told him I'd get help right away. John and Bruce came running down. John Evans was a real good friend of Steck's and is real husky. I was trying to help a little bit, but he just shoved me to the side and finally got Al dug

out. Al was all contorted, with his legs bent up behind him and sideways. His chest felt real bruised. He was able to walk pretty much under his own power.

We wondered what had happened up above with the people left up there. There was another one of our parties that had just gotten up to our camp before we had headed down, plus a British party—Doug Scott was with them—but we couldn't get an answer out of anybody up there. We hollered and hollered and figured they were goners, because we thought for sure they would be able to hear us. Our main concern was trying to get Al off there, so we headed down with him. We ran into some Japanese climbers who had been outside their tents when the avalanche struck, and they had lost some of their equipment but were pretty much out of the way. They helped us a bit, and we got Al down to the next camp below, and he was feeling a little better.

Bruce and I headed down to base camp that evening to give everybody the bad news. I think within one hour after we had gotten there, we finally had some radio contact with Evans and the other people, and lo and behold, everybody who had been at the camp had been able to make their way back down safely. It was a big avalanche and for nobody to have gotten killed in that was a miracle. It looked like the whole amphitheater was sliding.

Your next expedition, to K-2, was with a large group as well.

The group itself was not extremely large. We had eight climbers, and experience shows that a lot of people end up getting sick, or for one reason or other, don't feel really fit to climb. I think that by the time you got the opportunity to reach the summit, if you had two people feeling good out of eight, that's doing pretty good.

There must be a point, on a mountain like K-2, when being out there that long begins to work on you in negative ways.

I don't know that the time works on you negatively. I think it's more the events that occur that work on you. If you're out there and things are going good, you can spend a lot of time out there. We had lots of difficulties with relationships between climbers, even before in the states, so it really had nothing to do with being out there that long, but those kinds of things carried over into the expedition. The chemistry didn't work out.

Often if there were problems between two people, it wasn't necessarily mutual. It was one person and not the other. It bothered me and it must have bothered other people in the group to see those sorts of things happen. It was not a pleasant experience to go out and be with a group of guys where there was that kind of bickering going on.

Do you think that is a matter of luck in the choosing of expedition members?

Looking back, I don't know. At the time I felt that Schoening and Bob Craig had done an extremely good job choosing members for the trip to the Pamirs. They had really made a major effort to find people they thought would work together. The element of luck is still there, of course. When you think of nineteen people, there has to be some. The trip I went on the next year to K-2, I thought I was going into that climb with my eyes wide open as to the possibilities. I saw right away when we got together on Rainier the winter before that there were some things going on that I didn't like. I anticipated problems, but I didn't think it would get as bad as it did.

I kind of came into the K-2 climb late. What I'm trying to say is that there were people on that climb who were very focused on the climb itself, and I think in my case, although I very much wanted to climb the mountain, it wasn't something that had been driving me for the past five or ten years. I think I wanted as much as anyone else to get to the summit of the mountain, but there was more to the trip for me than that. One of the things I had always hoped for, after two or three years of climbing, was that

this group of guys I had been climbing with around Ellensburg—Wickwire, Dunham—I always hoped we'd be able to get together our own expedition and go to the Himalayas sometime and everybody just have a great time together. The way it turned out was as close to a thing like that happening for me as anything ever would. So I was really interested in that aspect.

I don't think it should be said that my primary objective on the expedition was to not get over there and climb K-2, but it wasn't something that was burning inside me for years. I think that the fact that I was getting over there and climbing with some of my friends was important.

After that did you feel soured on expeditions, or did you still want to try again with friends?

I didn't feel soured on expeditions. When they went back in '78, I really felt, gee, I should be there with those guys. I'd really like to go back there again. Under the circumstances, with what had happened in '75, I was sure I wasn't going to be asked to go, and in the second place, it wouldn't have been much different.

Do you get out climbing much with the old Sherpas?

The old Sherpas? I am an old Sherpa. Physically I've gone downhill. But I see no reason that, given the opportunity, I couldn't climb at the same standard I was then or better. It's not so much being out of shape, but tendonitis here, a bad back there—not climbing related but general wear and tear over the years. I think climbing has done more for me physically than anything else.

CHAPTER
25
FRED DUNHAM

*F*red Dunham and Jim Wickwire grew up in Ephrata; Dunham remembers their first climbing experience, a scramble in nearby basalt coulees. "We went out and had a pretty good party, as young men do, and the next morning we went for a hike. We were all pretty well hung over. Jim and I climbed quite a bit farther than the rest of the group. We got to talking about climbing then, and from that we tried to do some climbing on our own."

He and Wickwire climbed Mount Cashmere, but the descent of their first mountain almost proved to be Dunham's

« I've tried never to go out and say I have to do this. I go out and I want to do it. I think there is a difference in philosophy that you have to do it. You're going to be more prone, I think, to make mistakes in judgement. »
— *Fred Dunham*

last. "We climbed it with no real problem," he says, "although we had virtually zero experience. We stepped into the head of the gully to start down. The snow was soft enough that we stopped to take our crampons off. I sat down on a rock that was covered with verglass and it slid off immediately and I fell the entire length of the gully, about oh, nine-hundred or a thousand feet. I did a lot of flipping and rolling and I went down inside a real deep runnel, about two or three feet and when I got to the bottom of it, I kinda of tobogganed around a berm built up on the rock buttress to the side of the gully. Had I gone out over it, I would have gone out into the rock and ruined the day." The last line is delivered deadpan, betrayed by the merest hint of a smile.

Dunham and Wickwire tagged along with the Praters and Dave Mahre, and within a year he and Wickwire had not only learned a bit about climbing but made a number of first ascents as well. "I think it's that way with a lot of people who are serious about climbing," he says. "The first time you do it, you realize the benefits and just the fun of being out in the mountains. I think, being from a really small town and having spent a lot of time out, that we probably knew things that, maybe, some kids growing up in a city environment now don't learn."

Dunham quickly established his climbing credentials with

ambitious climbs on Mount Rainier, including the east rib of the Willis Wall. It was on those sorts of climbs that Dunham learned the value of moving quickly. He emphasized that fact several times during our conversation in an Ellensburg restaurant. "If you're fit, you're going to be able to move faster through danger areas and will be less likely to be caught in bad weather."

Like the other Sherpas I interviewed, Dunham exudes a quiet confidence, and he tends to describe tense moments in the mountains as exciting rather than scary. In fact he never remembers being really scared.

▲

It wasn't long after you started climbing that you began looking at the north side of Mount Rainier.

Jim and I started climbing every weekend, every time we could. Jim was going to school then, so I did more than he did, at that period of time. The first time I went into the north side to try the Willis Wall was 1961. So a year after I started climbing I tried it. Luckily the weather turned bad. There were a bunch of us: Gene Prater, Barry Prather, Dave Mahre, Jim Wickwire. That would have been a large bunch on the wall. At that time all the climbing on the mountain was still done with support parties and all that kind of stuff.

One of the interesting things on that trip was that when we went up there we built pretty extensive little rock shelters up on the edge of the Carbon Glacier where it extends from Curtis Ridge. Several years after that we had a slide show with a naturalist who said he had found these amazing stone shelters up on the north side of Rainier. He was trying to attribute them to people who were a lot older than we were.

So what was your first difficult ascent on Rainier?

I guess the first one was the Willis Wall. I did other routes, several of the standard routes, before then. We did the Mowich Face the week before we did the Willis Wall in '63. It was a conditioner and just a matter of trying to get in as much climbing as we could.

So what was the Willis Wall like?

It was a fun climb. Did you talk to Jim about it? It's always interesting to see if memories are the same. He documents quite a bit, so his document might be different than my memory. Jim, Dave Mahre and I were really fit. The fourth member of the party, Don Anderson, wasn't as fit as we were and it was hard for him. We had worked really hard at the Wall, through 1961-62, had been over there quite a number of times but had never had a decent shot at it.

The morning we left, the weather wasn't any good either. In retrospect, it might have been better to wait, but we left camp, which is at about 8,300 feet, around 10 o'clock on a Thursday night. We had a long slog to get up to the base of it. One of the crevasse crossings was really wide and thin, and we belayed across it. We climbed through the dark, had a little bit of rockfall once we crossed the schrund, not bad. We diagonalled over to get on what they call the eastern rib and got up on top of that. That was really spectacular because the sun was up. From there it was a traverse across to the exit crack area. When you do that you're right in under the shadow of the ice cliffs above you.

That must be a bit intimidating.

It's really exciting, if you've ever been up there when ice has been coming off. We've watched pieces break off the entire cliff and sweep the face. There might have been a few spots where you would have been protected, but essentially once you get above that rib, you wouldn't be. One of the things I can remember really well is a place where we crossed some really hard polished water ice. I remember stopping there and looking up. At that point you're committed to it and all you can do is move as quickly as you can.

We worked our way to the space between the two ice cliffs, and there's a moderate rock pitch. They call it the Traverse of the Angels. I think we went on hands and knees across there and that puts you on the ramp up between the two cliffs. By that time we were in snow and sleet. We finished the climb in that kind of weather. We got to the summit of Liberty Cap and Anderson was coming down with pulmonary edema. The three of us were really fit and were planning on bivouacking there, but when Don came up, we recognized the symptoms.

I had been involved when Tom Horn crashed his plane on Rainier in '59. I knew that the other guy had died of pulmonary edema. I realized we had to get down now. From the top of Liberty Cap we had Jim head on down. He was just fired up to keep on going, and he had to do a little transition in his head to decide we weren't going on to the summit. He turned down and Dave and I got on either side of Don. From Liberty Cap you can drop down quickly, a thousand feet. Well, once we'd dropped that 1,000 feet, he'd recovered a lot. It's just really remarkable, what the elevation can do.

We got down and didn't have any idea where we were. We didn't recognize portions of the Mowich Face that we'd climbed through before. We were still in the storm, and it was the kind of storm that if you sat real still the ice would build up on you. It was kind of neat. Our ice axes had a coating of rime ice about an inch long. We just kept going down, picked a route and ended up on the south Mowich. We got down off the glacier to the creek sometime Sunday, I believe. We were fairly stretched out. We stopped and said, "We're not going to get anywhere tonight. Let's find a spot." Somebody said, "Well, this looks like a good spot." Someone else said, "Let's go on. We'll find someplace better." So we went about fifty feet, stopped again and lay down right where we were.

We had two sleeping bags with us. We got a fire going. Dave was partially snowblind at that time. He had taken off his goggles to see where he was going and his eyes were smarting pretty good. We went out the next morning to the west side road. We got up on the road, a little better than a day overdue, so we flagged down the first car that came by, and told them they needed to take us to the nearest phone. We threw our gear in the car before they could argue. They were interesting folks from Enumclaw, and they'd never been up to the mountain. The first time they get there, these guys jump in their car. I still enjoy that kind of climbing.

I enjoy the mountains for the mountains themselves and the people who are there. I don't need an excuse, I don't need to go to the mountains to satisfy anything except just going to the mountains.

All the Sherpas have been involved in mountain rescue. One rescue that Fred Stanley told me to ask you about was the Mark Weigelt accident on Stuart's Ice Cliff Glacier.

Mark and Earl Hamilton were climbing together. There were two guys ahead of them. Bill Sumner and Clark Gearhart were below them. Each of these parties were independent of one another. The first two had just gotten off the top of the gully, and Earl and Mark were climbing right up the middle of it. Mark was a really strong guy, real bold.

Personally, if I had been climbing that day, I would have been off to the edge of the gully, which would have made a difference. If you looked at it you could see where rockfall funneled right down the middle. They got hit. Mark was killed outright, and was left hanging on an ice screw five- to six-hundred feet above the schrund at the bottom of the gully. One of the guys on top had climbed back down the gully while Clark and Bill climbed up. They had been able to lower Earl down to a bench, off to the side, a pretty good spot. He had a depressed skull fracture as it turned out.

We flew in, and the next morning, I got in a M.A.S.T. chopper and they flew me in around the mountain. I could see what the situation was, and the pilot flew in tight. He was a Vietnam-era pilot. He got in close enough to scare me and him to death. But he flew us right into the base of the climb. As soon as he got close enough to the schrund where Bill, Clark and Earl were, I bailed out. I wasn't very comfortable getting out of the chopper. He didn't have more than a foot of blade clearance on the rock. He was real tight. We got Earl, slid him in and got him out of there. We looked at the situation and decided there wasn't a whole lot we could do from that position, so we down-climbed the glacier. We were down-climbing the glacier when the Forest Service flew an Allouette helicopter and gave us a ride out to the end of the road on the Icicle Creek side. I told them that the last communication I had with the other chopper was that I needed help and they would be coming in for me. I had to get back to the other side of the mountain, so they flew me back over.

Now all this was happening in Chelan County, and the sheriff's deputy felt like his toes were being stepped on. In one of my better moves I told him that he should go with us. The deputy, the pilot and I flew in. We headed for the west ridge of Stuart and swung in close around the north ridge and then popped in to the Ice Cliff. It's pretty spectacular when you do it that way. I told the deputy, "There's the guy we have to bring out. Now, we can turn it over to you guys, and we'll go home, but I've got to get off on the other side of the mountain." The sheriff's deputy didn't say a word, so they let me out on the south side and I met the other part way up the couloir. We went out that night and tried to figure out a plan of attack. By that time we were in no hurry.

We got ahold of Tacoma Mountain Rescue, and they had a hydraulic winch system made out of a chain saw motor. We got four or five of them to come over and an Allouette ferried us in to the south side of the mountain to within a hundred feet of the top of the Ice Cliff. We rigged ropes and anchors and Fred Stanley and I went down on lines; I think we had six-hundred feet of line. We had a cadaver sack with us and our motorcycle helmets for better protection. We got one blast of rockfall when we got down to him. The only reason we didn't get hit was that we were able to run back and forth at the bottom of that anchored 600 feet of rope. We weren't really able to get him in the cadaver sack, so we looped the cable around his feet and the winch pulled him up feet first. The hardest part was getting out of the chopper the first time. In retrospect I wouldn't do that again. I think that rescue on Stuart was the most complex one I've ever been on.

CHAPTER
26
RON MILLER

Ron Miller has been a climbing companion for almost twenty years. I've accompanied him on several rock-climbing trips, and he has quietly endured my sometimes left-field approach to climbing. He once watched me zig-zag desperately up the Canary route on Castle Rock placing protection at every turn. By the time I pulled myself onto Sabre Ledge, I had created so much rope drag that I could pull neither rope nor Ron up. I had discovered Static Climbing, but Ron was not impressed as he had to run down to the car, grab our extra rope and give it to climbers who were heading up a nearby route.

Ron is not a balletic climber; he climbs with a precision and attention to detail that eliminates the possibility of error. He anticipates without losing track of moves immediately before him. He does not hurry, and hence he rarely falls, although he did break his ankle once stepping off a curb in downtown Everett.

Miller made several first ascents in the North Central Cascades during the late 1960s and early 1970s. After that he seemed to give up on hard climbing until after he had reached 40. He turned almost exclusively to rock climbing and in the last five years has climbed better than ever. On almost any weekend you can expect to find him at any one of the many rock climbing areas in the Northwest.

So many of us were in it, because we knew that someday it might be Mountain Rescue coming for us. So it was the least we could do. This is our payback.

— *Ron Miller*

In a crowd of strangers Ron will usually drift into the background, although he is a great storyteller. For many years Miller has been associated with Everett Mountain Rescue. Although less active in recent years, Ron is still looked to for his leadership on any rescue he takes part in.

The interview took place in Miller's house in Snohomish, between games of pool.

Mountain Rescue is a pretty thankless job, if you're not in it for the publicity, even if you are for that matter. What were your reasons for joining?

So many of us were in it, because we knew that someday it might be Mountain Rescue coming for us. So it was the least we could do. This is our payback. There were some who thought they might make a name for themselves. Those were the ones who caused the conflicts. Because of a conflict with the sheriff's department, for a while, Everett Mountain Rescue wasn't getting called. When some of the rescues became quite technical, I think some of the other search and rescue units were pushed to the edge of their limits which was rather dangerous. Nowadays there are a lot of qualified people in those other units, search and rescue, not mountain rescue. They didn't really have the training in the mountains.

I do remember a number of times, going on a rescue and it would start to get a little bit technical. If we were all involved, the other units were glad to just step back and let people take over who knew what they were doing.

Politics was a real problem with Everett Mountain Rescue and the sheriff's department.

We had quite a problem. There were a couple of people in our unit who really loved to see their names and pictures in the paper. They were always the ones who leaked the story. We'd be told "Nobody from our unit says anything. You don't give your name. You don't tell anything. We'll have a special spokesman." And they didn't care. They'd still do it. "So and So says . . ." And that's what you'd read in the paper.

We had to take a woman off of Mount Pilchuck in the winter. She had fallen and stuck her ice axe through her neck and killed herself instantly. Her name was Flora Green. We struggled for several hours packing her out.

A bunch of us put in a lot of effort just bringing her down. We'd almost reached the parking lot and Jim Leo from the Everett Herald was there waiting to get a picture. There was a certain member in one of the rescue groups, an aspiring politician, who had been waiting for some time to get her out. As soon as we got in sight and Jim Leo began to get his cameras out, this particular person runs up to the litter, grabs one of the people by the collar and jerks him down and throws him out of the way. He grabbed ahold of the litter, turns toward the camera, Jim Leo takes the picture. As soon as the pictures are taken, this particular person says, "Okay, you can get back on the litter", and walks back to his car. I used to have the picture. There he is looking like Mr. Macho Man. There were several of us on the litter who were just pissed.

You would get calls at all hours in the morning.

After 11 p.m. when the phone rang, I knew what it was, Mountain Rescue. I'd hope that it was a wrong number.

Have you been in situations where somebody was still alive, just on the edge, and you brought them out?

Most of the rescues I've been on, the victims weren't on the edge. They were either bodies or "let's get them out. You're going to be fine, pal."

How do you deal with bodies?

I've never gotten used to it. You just accept it, but it does kind of wreck your day. You're glad it wasn't you.

You have to think about it in terms of yourself, to a certain degree, "It could have been me."

Oh yeah. I remember a few incidents, people doing the same things you do, going across the same type of terrain that you'd go across, say, unroped. One little slip and 1,500 feet, gone.

I was involved in a rescue at Lake Serene one winter. There was a father and his three sons who were traversing around the lake. They went eighty percent around the lake and found out that it was barred by cliffs. They were wading waist deep in snow at that time and were becoming exhausted. So the eldest son hiked out for help. I remember hiking in and rappelling down the cliffs, Bob Marcy and I. We were trudging through waist-deep snow and finally located the father and one son just sitting on the snowslope. We were just elated.

They were just sitting there staring off ahead. I remember Bob Marcy racing ahead a few feet of me and reaching over and grabbing the guy and saying, "Hey, pal you're going to be okay," and realizing that this guy was stiff as a board. But they looked completely normal, both of them. They died of exposure. When they had stopped, they were near exhaustion. The one son still had something left so he went for help.

Were you guys ever in a situation where you felt pushed to the edge of your limits during a rescue?

1

(1) Mount Rainier's impressive north side: Liberty Ridge in the center, Willis Wall on the left. Rainier's last great problem, the "Wall" was finally climbed in the early 1960's.

(2) Sherpa Nawang Gombu and Jim Whittaker, first American to climb Mount Everest.
(3) Backbone Ridge above the MacAllister Glacier. The ridge remained unvisited until the late 1960s. (4) Willi Unsoeld.

2

3

4

1

(1) Alex Bertulis leading on second day of first ascent of the Independence route on Liberty Bell, May 1966. (2) Joe Firey (left) and Glen Denny on Dusseldorfer Spitz in the southern Pickets. (3) Jim Wickwire leading in Stuart Glacier Couloir on Mount Stuart, June 1966.

2

— Gene Prater Photo

1

2

(3) Ed Boulton in bivouac at 12,700 feet on Willis Wall. (4) Alex Bertulis at 11,000 feet on west rib of Willis Wall, February 1970

(1) Dave Mahre belaying Jim Wickwire on Mount Rainier's Puyallup Glacier, July 1965. (2) Jim Wickwire on central rib of Mount Rainier's Willis Wall, May 1971.

3

4

Probably not. There were some where you definitely felt a little bit nervous. But I've always had the ability to think things out ahead of time.

Did you find yourself in a leadership role most of the time?

Most of the time I found myself in that position. I was very seldom an operations leader, I didn't go to enough meetings, but yet when I'd go out on a rescue, they'd usually say, "Ron, you're in charge."

Did Mountain Rescue have a number of practice sessions?

That's what they tell me. (He smiles)

Did you ever have to rescue someone you knew?

No. Most of the people I knew who got hurt were all dead. I don't like the idea of bringing out my friends when they're dead. There were plenty of times when I was going out that I thought it was going to be someone I knew, because they were supposed to have been up in the area we were heading to.

Have you ever been on a rescue when people were fine, but had just been stupid?

Up on Twin Peaks in Snohomish County, a woman was with a Mountaineers group and they had hiked up between the two summits. The leader had decided to turn back. The woman decided she wanted to go for the summit, so she took this sixteen-year-old kid and went for the summit. After a while she decided it was too dangerous and they shouldn't be doing that. She decided that rather than taking any chances they'd just stay where they were and Mountain Rescue would come up and get them. She told the kid that.

Mountain rescue was called out and we started hiking up. As we climbed the slope she was too scared to go down, we had our ice axes strapped to our packs. We were just kicking steps up the snow—we didn't need our axes. This is the slope she wouldn't come down. The rest of her group had waited all night and finally gone out for help, which is what she figured would happen.

I was fuming that she wouldn't even try. She didn't want the responsibility of a sixteen-year-old kid. But the terrain was easy, and they had ice axes and a rope. We tied them in and brought them down. When we got them down, the sheriff wanted to know what it had been like up on the mountain. Did this woman have any business being up there?

It was a consensus among us that she didn't belong in the mountains. This was the third time in a month that she had to be rescued. What really got me going was here she had been rescued and we had worked our ass off up there. And I'm walking past her by her car. She pulls out this great big rack of hardware and she's telling this other guy, "Let's climb Vesper tomorrow." Now Vesper is a Class 1 route and she pulled out a rack and was sorting it out for the climb. Within days the sheriff got a court order preventing her from going into the mountains in Snohomish County. This must have been ten or fifteen years ago.

What was the most technical rescue you've ever been on?

The one I had to sit and watch from the car, because I was sick, had the flu. That was the one where somebody had fallen on the Town Wall, at Index. Kenn Carpenter was basically in charge and he did a heck of a job up on top setting up the different friction belays. I would have been the one going over the edge if I hadn't been sick.

Another time there was a girl who fell at Sunset falls. She came ashore on the other side and tried climbing up the cliffs on the other side and fell. She broke a leg or something. When I got up there, the Alderwood group was over on the other side with her. What we decided to do rather than lift her up the cliffs, was to set up a Tyrolean and go across the river. This was around midnight.

The sheriff took a gun and shot a line over to the other side and then we started stringing lines. The Alderwood team had gone around the backside and rappelled down to her. The rescue was right there by the fish ladder and we were able to drive a truck right up to the fish ladder. We let out a whole bunch of cable and attached it to the Tyrolean. We stretched out the lines, a couple of them, taut and put a litter on it and we had the guys on the other side pull the litter across as we lowered it down by slacking off the line.

They put the girl in it. I had them set up a belay on the litter, so as we started setting tight on the line with the winch, the Tyrolean would get taut, with a belay on she doesn't go sliding out in the middle. We communicated with the guys across the river by radio and when she got across she was about ten to fifteen feet in the air and we told the guy on the winch to lower her down an inch at a time and we lowered her right down into our hands. It was just so slick.

How would you compare Everett Mountain Rescue with other rescue units?

I wouldn't compare us to Boulder, Colorado or even Seattle. They just had too many people, but we were good. There wasn't anything that came up that we couldn't handle and that's what mattered.

▲

CHAPTER

27

JIM WICKWIRE

The sun has not yet come up when we meet Jim Wickwire in downtown Seattle. Grabbing muffins and coffee, we walk briskly up to his law office. Wickwire is planning a trip to Menlungtse, an unclimbed Tibetan mountain; shortly after we sit down in his office, he lays out aerial photos of the peak and traces the route for us. It is a steep face and long ridge, about 5,500 feet of sustained 50-degree ice and snow, a daunting route on a massive mountain. "It's a great peak," he says. "Climbers I know think it is one of the best objectives left in the Himalayas."

« I don't think climbing should be glorified. It's what some people do to satisfy themselves. I suppose it's the risk that makes it interesting. Some people will wax eloquent about the beauties and joys of the

mountains—and I do—but to the extent that some people talk or don't talk about their religious experiences, I'm the kind of guy who tends to keep that to himself. »
— Jim Wickwire

Wickwire points out the west summit which was climbed by Chris Bonington. It is 600 feet below and about a mile away from the true summit. "I talked to Chris about it, and he was really pissed that they didn't get to the summit. He said, 'Well, you should just repeat our route.' I said no, because that would be an anticlimax to just go up his route and walk over to the main summit, so we're going to try this route right to the main peak."

There burns within Wickwire the young man's passion to climb to the edge and peer over into the void, even as he nears 50. In 1978 he realized a long-held dream when he climbed K-2, and he paid a price. Benighted just below the summit, he huddled in a bivy sack in sub-zero temperatures at 27,800 feet, fearing he would be swept off the mountain or simply die of exposure. At first light he talked himself down to the last camp. Wickwire returned to the states weakened by pneumonia, pleurisy and frostbite. He would also undergo lung surgery. Flying home to Seattle, Wickwire had written in his diary the words of Maurice Herzog, "There are other Annapurnas in the lives of men." Wickwire then wrote, "Ahead lies the task of identifying and surmounting these other Annapurnas."

Although he was most likely thinking metaphorically, several real mountains lay ahead, including two attempts on Everest.

Like most great climbers, Wickwire has succumbed to the ineluctable siren song of the Himalayas. Many friends have died—he has watched four friends fall to their deaths—but Wickwire says, "Mountaineering is such an important facet of who I am. I don't think climbing is anything particularly special, but I think that people do lots of different things in life and what they do is part of who they are."

When asked what he gets out of mountaineering, he says, "There is something about doing something that is challenging, where you are kind of overcoming certain fears. I think too there's probably a little of the thrill junkie aspect to it in the sense that when you're out at risk, there's some psychological benefit. I suppose it creates a sense, in terms of mortality, that you are pushing at it a little bit, defying it. And you get a sense that life's a little bit more satisfying."

▲

Did you have any accidents or near-misses in the Cascades?

I remember one trip. Dunham and I had gone up to retrieve some gear we had left at the base of the Willis Wall. We were going up the Carbon Glacier, and it was real icy and the crevasses were obviously out and you could see them. I had the only rope and Dunham was up ahead of me, almost out of sight, as we climbed through these seracs. I was following his tracks and came to this bridge between two crevasses, and I slipped. I headed down into this crevasse which was about forty feet deep and had a pool of icy water at the bottom.

I ended up on the edge holding on by my hands. As I came back out I thought, "Holy shit, I could have gone in there and he'd never have known where I was." I didn't know how deep the water was and I had the only rope. It was just sheer stupidity. Those kinds of accidents are what get you ultimately. When you're on a hard climb, you're so concentrated that you're not going to get into an accident. It's when you let up, take it easy . . .

I was with Ed Bolton on the Willis Wall in 1971, May, when we got caught out in a storm for two nights. We had no real gear with us—a bivy sack but no sleeping bags. The second night we got into a snow cave just under Liberty Cap close to 14,000 feet. That night they were recording winds close to sixty-five miles per hour. It was horrendous.

Any second thoughts at that time about being a climber?

No, no. You don't have those reflections. You're there to get through that situation and survive. And we had the snow cave. Bolton was obsessed with the notion that we were going to get packed in and suffocate, which apparently has happened, so he broke out of the snow cave, and we ended up in the entrance in the bivy sack. The snow was just blowing by, almost a ground blizzard. You could see the stars above at times, but we were getting packed in by the snow, and then the bivy sack broke apart. We ended up pulling it over us for the rest of the night.

By the morning I was worse off than he was. I was hypothermic to a degree and had a real problem getting down. But you have to. Either that or you die. You know the consequences of not trying to continue to get out. So we managed to get down to Schurman Hut and broke into the hut just as the storm broke for another four days. We were on the mountain for eight days, and people were beginning to give up on us because there had been no word.

Cascade climbing diminished for me in the late '70s and I began to concentrate more on Alaska and the Himalaya. From a rock climbing standpoint, I was never really right up at the top, so I never went down to Yosemite. I knew at some point I was not going to be the world's best rock climber. I had always been real strong on snow and ice and had always had this desire to go to the real big mountains. It stemmed partly from my high school reading and partly from the natural progression from climbing in the basalt coulees of eastern Washington, to getting into the Cascades and then thinking about McKinley and other Alaskan ranges. It was pretty easy to think about the Himalaya after all that.

I began to think about getting over there in the late '60s, but I was just out of law school, married and had five kids.It wasn't until I was thirty-two in 1972 that I went to McKinley on an expedition. Once I got off on that first one in '72, it somehow broke the ice, and I was able to virtually go on an expedition every year, and sometimes two, for the next several years.

Was it a difficult transition to make from Cascade climbing to the Himalayan peaks?

The altitude was more of problem than technical difficulty, and I always seem to do real well at altitude. I'm lucky I guess. I've never had a headache. A lot of expedition climbing is mental. I would find on expeditions that you would have to have a lot of patience. You had to have a certain mindset. If you were going to have a good experience that was one thing, but if you were going to climb the mountain that was another. You'd find that some of your companions with whom you'd done Cascade climbs, when you got off on an Alaskan or Himalayan expedition, for some reason—their wife, girlfriend or whatever—would lead to the kind of thinking, "I wish I wasn't here. Why did I come on this climb? Why am I away from home?" So you'd tend to see people's motivation change during the course of an expedition.

For me it's really been a search to find the ideal companion for expeditions. You know how they're going to function on an expedition. John Roskelley has turned out to be probably the best for me, because for some reason, we really get along. Despite the fact that I'm nine years older, he seems to want to climb with me. There's never been a cross word between us, which is pretty unusual, and that's what you're looking for. Roskelley is incredibly careful, and so you know that the risk of something happening is substantially reduced.

How has climbing affected your family life?

I was lucky, in a sense, in that my wife has been very understanding over the years, knowing the risks involved. In the years when the kids were younger, it was much harder to leave, but they are all grown now.

Did your children develop any interest in mountaineering?

Zero. I've got one daughter who's a little bit interested, but I wouldn't say it's serious. And it's not something you encourage. I don't know whether I'd want one of my kids to climb, as much as I know about climbing. In my whole life of doing it, I'd worry about my kids.

Your parents weren't interested in mountaineering. Did they worry about you? Did they under-stand what it was you were doing?

I'm sure they worried, and I think they understood. I've had no one, friends, relatives or wife, ever try to talk me out of climbing.

How have you balanced your professional life with your passion for climbing?

It's been very difficult. It's been fairly easy to do the Cascade climbs, get away for weekends. But the expeditions have been harder. I've gone on about fifteen expeditions, Alaskan and Himalayan, and have been lucky in that I've had one particular client. I've been doing work for one of these Alaska native corporations, formed under the Sullivan Act of 1971. As a lawyer, when you have a multitude of clients that have all these different problems that need to be addressed, it would be very difficult to leave for a long period of time. It has been easier to leave that one client who is also aware of what I do although not particularly happy about it. From time to time I have gotten a little heat from them about my climbing.

I tend to use my sabbatical and vacation time to go on climbs. In 1984 I went to Everest the last time and was gone for three months. I didn't take another vacation for about two and a half years. I tend to work very hard when I'm not on these trips, and if you were to add up the hours I've billed over a five-year period, it would stack up with the other guys in the office.

Have you found that being a lawyer and being an expedition climber you've had to say, "Maybe I'm not going to be the best lawyer?"

Oh yeah. If you're trying to do those two things and excel in them, each is so demanding, that you're probably going to sacrifice the excellence in one or another. It would be nice to have had the opportunity to do what Messner has done. He's not any physical marvel. He's just a guy who had a goal, and he's so able to translate his goal into reality that he's been able to drag his body along.

Climbing really is all mind, well, to a large degree. It's not as if you're playing for the Seattle Seahawks and if you're not right there at the top physically, you're out, you're gone. You can still do Everest. You just do it slower. Climbing, at least in the big mountains, is something you can do into your forties and fifties.

Athletes and coaches are always talking about the qualities they take from sport to their daily lives. Do you find those qualities in climbing?

Sure. If you've been in a particular mountain situation, particularly some of the tragedies I've been associated with, or a storm situation, any time you're really stretched, getting through those situations intact, I think, paves the way for dealing with just about anything that your normal life throws at you. If I know some situation is coming that is likely to be difficult, professionally as a lawyer, I think, "Well, it can't be anything like what I experienced in the mountains, and therefore I can handle this."

I don't want to make too much of it, because I think climbing tends to get glamorized to a certain extent. The fact that you are here is a little bit of that. I don't think climbing should be glorified. It's what some people do to satisfy themselves. I suppose it's the risk that makes it interesting. Some people will wax eloquent about the beauties and joys of the mountains, and I do, but to the extent that some people talk or don't talk about their religious experiences, I'm the kind of guy who tends to keep that to himself.

If you had grown up on the west side of the Cascades do you think you would have joined the Mountaineers? Would that have been good for you?

I don't think I would have joined the Mountaineers. I am essentially not a joiner of large organizations. My history with law firms is that after working for the third largest firm in Seattle, I left in 1975 to start my own firm with three other guys. We built that up into the '80s, but after the death of Chuck Goldmark, one of the partners, and the climate of law firm mergers in Seattle, we ended up doing this merger with a large San Francisco firm. Although I didn't leave that firm because I was unhappy, the notion of being back in a smaller setting appealed to me. I like small firms. I like small expeditions.

I don't think I ever want to go on another large expedition. The last one with Lou Whittaker on Kangchenjunga was too large. I was headed off to Menlungtse with Roskelley, Steve Swenson and Alex Lowe, just the four of us, and it had a great self-contained feel to it. But at the last minute we changed plans and went to Kangchenjunga. We switched to an expedition that had ten American climbers. In addition, Skip Yowe of JanSport had four Indonesian climbers who were there to provide some financial support. They were interested in a Himalayan expedition and gathering information, and they paid for that privilege. There was also a large cadre of Sherpas, and at any one time we had twenty-five people at base camp.

There is a trend away from large expeditions, but you still see the larger ones. Mostly what you see are the commercial guided trips. People who want to climb McKinley, Aconcagua or Mount Vinson, or even Everest, who have the money but don't have the organizational capabilities will find a Phil Erschler to guide them. And they pay him a lot of money. It seems almost a throwback to what went on in the Alps in the 1800s when the British would hire Swiss guides to take them up the alpine peaks.

Going into K-2 now, going up the Baltoro glacier, you're right in the middle of a war between Pakistan and India. There are military camps, helicopters all over the place and even occasionally howitzers flying over you. Then you have the garbage factor. You go into K-2 and the campsites along the way have been there for eleven years. Even in 1978 it wasn't good. The shitfields and turds you found at Paiyu were just unbelievable. It's pretty hard to diminish that impact if you're going up the same valley that everyone else is going up. So you're constantly looking for a place where there isn't a lot of human intrusion.

I guess I like smaller expeditions because there really isn't any need for a leader because you are all equals, and if you have two, four or six people you make decisions without anyone having to take charge. On climbs in the Cascades we never had a leader; it just wasn't something you thought about. At different times somebody would rise to the fore to lead a difficult pitch. There's a kind of ebb and flow.

After the number of times you've been to the Himalayas, can you get the same kind of satisfaction from the Cascades?

Sure, after K-2 in '78 I had lung surgery, and it wasn't until the next August in 1979 that I went up with three people to climb Mount Baker. I had never climbed Baker before, and it was amazing coming up the normal approach to Baker and getting on that first snowfield. It was as if I had just stepped from the glaciers on K-2 to the glacier on Baker. I remember being struck by the similarities of the mountain environment: rock, ice, snow, glacier. It's the same if you're in the middle of the Karakoram or the North Cascades. And it was a very satisfying feeling being back on a glacier, walking up a glacier but half a world away from the last glacier I'd been on.

1976 **1992**

What would Edmund Meany think of sport climbing, free soloing, plastic boots, Friends, and movable ceramic handholds? Would that dignified gentleman be tempted to climb routes dubbed Non-stop Erotic Cabaret, Eraserhead, or Freeze-Dried Lizard Antlers? Meany wrote in 1910 in *The Mountaineer,* "We wish to save old names and to bestow new ones of an appropriate kind where no names are known." Three Prune Camp was probably the most outlandish name ever dreamed up by Meany and his fellow Mountaineers. This was a man who wore a tie and jacket climbing, wrote poetry on the trail and conducted Sunday worship services on summer outings. Meany and the modern climber would most likely find some common ground, but then again, sorting through the rack of technological and philosophical differences to find shared values might prove insurmountable.

Many older climbers can't comprehend what has occurred in mountaineering in the last 15-20 years. No longer are there a few bold climbers setting the standards. There are hundreds of climbers on the cutting edge, which often seems, to those left behind, razor thin.

In 1985 a British Columbia climber, Peter Croft, alone and unroped, climbed every peak from the north ridge of Stuart to Prusik Peak's west ridge in one day. Twenty years ago each of those climbs was at least a full-day's undertaking. Sixty years ago they were thought impossible and weren't even seriously considered at the turn of the century. In the last decade there has been a ski descent of Liberty Ridge on Mount Rainier, winter ascents of the steepest North Cascade walls, the Ptarmigan Traverse skied in a day and parapents taking climbers from the tops of wilderness peaks to parking lot in mere minutes.

Modern mountaineers certainly have advantages not available to previous generations.

1976 1992

Dirt logging roads and paved highways have unlocked the Cascades. Liberty Bell is a half-hour from the car, Sloan Peak a half-day and helicopters will take climbers virtually to the base of Mount Slesse's northeast buttress. Climbers are no longer crushed by the weight of pitons carried in wood-framed Trapper-Nelson packs. Carabiners the size of the human ear hold the weight of falling climbers, the falls checked by small metal belay plates, which along with the belayer are anchored to the rock by devices that look like miniature cogs in an engine, effortlessly slotted into cracks and just as easily removed. The climbers are dressed in feather-light, skin-tight waterproof (almost) outfits made of the latest synthetic super fiber. Today's climber seems stronger, faster, brasher, more irreverent, less interested in ties to his or her mountaineering past. Good lord! What have they done to our sport?

Generational amnesia is a common affliction. "Those damn kids . . ." falls easily from the lips of older climbers who at one time chafed under the judgemental glare of climbing elders. Twenty years ago, climbers who smeared their hands with chalk were considered sacrilegious, while forty years ago, climbers were assailed for their crazy piton-pounded routes. Sixty years ago a generation bemoaned the fate of climbing if pitons were used at all, and the original Mountaineers looked askance at those daring climbers who went out and climbed almost by themselves in groups of two and three. I found myself choking on "those damn kids" as I lost my tenuous finger-lock on state-of-the-art climbing and increasingly viewed the changes through binoculars—the dreaded armchair mountaineer.

By my comfortable chair I had copies of *Outside, Climbing, Backpacker, Off Belay,* (the new) *Summit,* (the late, lamented) *Mountain Gazette, Rock and Ice.* A nearby pile of books, many of them published by the Mountaineers press, took me to the tops of every 8,000-meter peak and into the privacy of the tents of the expedition members as they bitched about everyone else on the team. With my remote control I could tune in Wide World of Sports, the Discovery Channel or A&E and watch free solo climbs of big walls and sport climbing up the side of the hotel at the Snowbird, Utah, ski resort, without working up much of a sweat.

Often the people I read about and watched on T.V. were Washington mountaineers. Almost every American expedition to the Himalayas or Karakorams in the 1980s included a Washington climber. John Roskelley seemed to be on every expedition during that period, pushing the limits of what was possible above 25,000 feet, and without oxygen. Jim Wickwire spent an unplanned night just below the summit of K-2 and lived. More than ten Washington climbers stood on top of Everest, including Phil Erschler, who did it twice. In 1990 Jim Whittaker led a Chinese-Soviet-American Expedition that put an astounding 20 team members on the summit of Everest. Mountaineers were getting to the tops of the big peaks, via the hardest routes, many without small cities of support, without oxygen, in record time.

Closer to home, rock climbers were making a mockery of the icon of my climbing youth, 5.10. In 1970 it was the highest rating. Anything after that was the nebulous Class 6, aid. By the late 1980s, the best rock climbers were aspiring to something called 5.14, which was abcd, abcd, abcd, abcd past anything I had ever dreamed of climbing. Once a climber had mastered a 5.10a climb, there was 5.10b, and so on. And The Jackson Five be damned, climbing abc was not as simple as 123. Microscopic smears on smooth, vertical rock became acceptable footholds, and fingernail-sized ripples of granite the equivalent of a bucket handhold.

On any week day you could find some rockmeister at Index Town Wall free climbing a route that had been an aid ladder to previous hotshots. Rock climbing seemed to cleave from

mountaineering like some scary Arctic iceberg, laying waste to tradition, stirring up ethical controversies in its wake. The new generation of rock climbers wanted rock and they wanted it now, no approaches, no nasty weather. When the weather was bad in Index or Leavenworth, they could be found at Smith Rocks, Yosemite, Joshua Tree, Red Rocks or any other of the new rock climbing areas springing up all over the country.

Rock climbing became a sport almost unto itself, with its own particular language. Traditionalists would deny that the new generation of rock climbers could in any way be a part of the mountaineering community. By the late 1980s, Seattle had the first indoor rock climbing gym in the United States, the Vertical Club, and for many members the club was as close as they would get to real mountains. But at the Vertical Club you might find Fred Beckey bouldering next to the latest techno-wizard, and an executive, too, who found the artificial walls more exhilarating than aerobics.

In 1980, REI welcomed its one millionth member and doubled that number by the end of the decade. REI outlets can now be found all over the country, in cities as diverse as Anchorage, Boston, Atlanta, and Austin, exporting a bit of the Northwest to the rest of the country. But the belief that REI was somehow our store, a mountaineer's store, has long since passed—the same way the Cascades have ceased to be the province of a small group of climbers.

REI could be almost any chain store in any mall in America. It has grown like the climbing community, like the Pacific Northwest. The store no longer serves the homogeneous community it once did. It couldn't and survive, let alone thrive. As a result there is unending space for clothing and a cubby hole for climbing equipment. Any of the smaller outdoor stores still open for business in Seattle have to cater to a broader clientele in order to serve the mountaineering community. REI still offers the yearly dividend to its members, donates a portion of its profits to various environmental causes, supports expeditions, and offers reasonably priced clothing and equipment. It may be harder to detect, but REI still has a bit of Lloyd Anderson in it.

Strip away the gaudy fashion, the jargon, the technique and flashy equipment, and the Cascade climber of the 1990s probably shares more with Edmund Meany or Cora Eaton Smith than he or she might at first realize. The joy that one experiences on top of Mount Shuksan, Adams or Si is no different today than it was in 1907, no matter what the route. It is elemental emotion, whether expressed through poetry or boom box rock-n-roll. The spiritual rewards derived from walking through a Douglas fir forest or lupine meadow are the same, no matter the religous prism they are filtered through.

In the end it is the mountains that tie us to past generations of climbers whether we feel the gentle tug of the past or not. Once we step onto a Cascade glacier, trudge up a switchbacked trail, or rope up at the base of a granite cliff, there is a place for us at the campfire, next to Edmund Meany, Art Winder, Fred Beckey, or Ome Daiber.

CHAPTER
28
PIRO KRAMAR

*P*iro Kramar is gardening when I arrive at her home, which is hidden away in the woods at the end of a winding gravel road on the west side of Vashon Island. After our conversation she takes me on a tour of the grounds. Many arduous hours have gone into the landscaping, although great pains have been taken to retain a natural look. There are cats and dogs aplenty.

It is evident that, even in her mid-50s, Piro Kramar is still climbing-fit. She works at it. As we tour the yard, she shows me the chimney. The Swiss stone mason who built her chimney created it so that it would serve as a climbing wall. He even embedded a piton in it.

Kramar also runs, and she carries heavy packs up Tiger Mountain and Mount Si. She says, "I used to do curls, especially stuff for the lower and upper arms, but in the spring when we do a lot of gardening, I don't think I need to do an awful lot that way. The worst thing that you can't train for other than climbing is fingers. You remember the first time out at Peshastin in the spring? It doesn't take more than a day, but I get psyched out the first day. Then the next day, it's so nice when things flow right back."

For the conversation we sit in her living room which has a wonderful view of the Sound and the Olympic Mountains, when skies are clear. Mountainscapes by her dear friend, Joan Firey and Joan's daughter, Carla, hang on the walls. An exercise bicycle sits next to the large picture window.

« I did McKinley in '77, and when I came home, Joan said that she had talked to Arlene Blum, and how would I like to go on Annapurna. I said sure, why not? When you're invincible, you know, that sounds pretty good. »
— *Piro Kramar*

Kramar is engaging; candid, thoughtful and very funny. There are hints of her Hungarian past in her voice. She moved to the United States as a young girl but didn't start climbing until she was an adult. When Kramar moved to Seattle she became acquainted with the Fireys, who introduced her to their special exploratory climbing style. She and Joan became close friends and climbing partners. They shared some first ascents and a few misadventures. They were both members of the 1978 expedition to Annapurna.

A Seattle eye surgeon, Kramar has always tried to balance

141

her climbing with her profession. She says, "I would think that climbing and opthalmology are my two big loves, but I would not want to have one and exclude the other."

▲

Tell me about Joan Firey.

Joan was a relatively complex person. You almost got the impression that she was pulled in several different directions: having fulfilled the motherhood, wife-type role, she really felt very unfulfilled at the age of fifty-some years. You almost got the impression that she thought time was running out, and, by George, she better do this and that. She didn't have the same chance as a youngster starting out. That was true with her climbing. I'm sure you heard or read that she was very vocal about the fact that although she had done all this climbing, it was always with the guys and always with Joe, and he always led. And although she could do every bit as good as they, she never knew whether she would be able to lead.

That sort of translated into her art. She didn't really know whether she would be able to be anything more than a copycat. One of her uncles was a rather well-known painter in San Francisco. So that sort of runs in the family. Towards the end, she was trying, other than representative paintings which was marvelous, but she somehow belittled that, because it wasn't "original." So she did go into different abstract modes of painting.

(Piro points to a painting that Joan did that is hanging in her living room.) That's one of the best climbs she and I ever did, Asperity, in the B.C. Coast Range. We did the second ascent by a new route. We got up on top and there was this little sardine can, and we opened it and it was Beckey and two other guys who had come up from the other side.

On Asperity this was probably the first time she had decided that we could really do this climb. We were on the Pilot Glacier, there must have been about a dozen of us. This was the year Nixon got impeached, 1974. It was the usual Firey crew: Dave Knudson, a whole bunch of other people. And we did one of the Serras one day. I hadn't realized that Joan had her eye on Asperity all this time. She and I went off just scouting around, and we were able to see the whole Radiant Glacier. We sat there tracing out the route up Asperity; how we would be able to

make it up the glacier. So we went back to camp and decided to do it, the two of us.

We stayed overnight at the foot of the glacier and discovered that we had forgotten our cooking pot. We had one of these little Svea stoves that you had to fiddle with. If you were a pipe smoker you liked that kind of activity, you know. And all we had was the metal container for the gas, so we decided to put all the gas we could in the little Svea and try to go with that and clean out this pot. That gas container became our cooking pot. I belched gas for about three days. It was just horrible.

The next day we made it up to the top of the Radiant and camped there and got some snow. The following day the folks on the Telet could come out to a little notch and see down onto us. The third day we went up and climbed Asperity. It was the first time I had ever climbed a new route. I decided that this was the ultimate in climbing. You don't know if it is going to go or not, but we made it up to the top. I would say we were probably not speedsters. We came down, spent the night at the glacier, the fourth day we came down. The little bridges we had crossed were gone. There was always that feeling like, "Oh, how are we going to get out of here?"

Joan was just in seventh heaven. She could do it and show the guys. There was a lot of that in her, trying to prove herself.

We did a climb in the Southern Pickets, what was the name? It had one of those fearsome names, like Forbidden, Torment.

Terror?

There you go. We climbed Terror. It was six weeks after Joan's knee surgery, and we left our tent near McMillan Spires and decided to bivy. We thought we'd spend one night out on the ridge, but to come back to the tent there was this razor ridge where we actually had to a cheval, straddle this razor edge ridge. We made it up just below the summit of Terror, got snowed in and didn't make it up to the summit. We ran out of food, had wet clothes, went down the other side and promptly got lost. We just got fogged in and so spent another night out.

It was just the two of us, an absolute nightmare. I think I had one sausage left and some nuts. Joan was a big smoker and actually I smoked in those days too, unbeknownst to my parents. Here we were trying to light this wet pack of matches. We were so stupid that we didn't even have a waterproof container for matches, so we couldn't start a fire. We were under this rock underhang and sort of a semi-cave. We could not start a fire and Joan had a headlamp, so she rigged up her headlamp and put her matches inside so that she could dry them. And she was finally able to dry them so that we could both have a smoke (much laughter).

I still thought we were lost, but I didn't say anything. Unbeknownst to me, Joan, during the night, worked out where we were. There was some kind of nubbin that she suddenly saw when the fog had lifted. But she didn't tell me, so all night I was anticipating bumbling around the next day. It was the first time I had an experience that I subsequently found out is a fairly well-known defense mechanism. When you're miserable you actually split yourself off and there's another person there. There were three of us in that little overhang, absolutely three of us. Joan and I were over there miserable and I was fine. Apparently it is a fairly well-known reaction. At the time I was wondering what the hell was going on. I knew there were only two of us, but I could see that other person.

The next day she said, "Well, we'll just have to go down." We could not, by the way, go back to our tent. We had to abandon the tent, because we were just below the snow level. We were totally wet and there was fresh snow just about a few yards above us. We would have had to go across this razor edge rocky ridge which was about a half-mile long and it was still snowing. We had to stay alive. By that time it became clear that this was survival. Joan wanted to go back up and I said, "Joan, you can't keep up with me. Look at it. It's icy, snowy up there. I'm not sure we'll make it up there. We cannot spend another night out higher up. There's no way." She finally realized that it was true. Later she told me I had been right.

Joan was really slowing down because of her knee. So we just abandoned the tent and came out. I remember I was just amazed at that woman, limping along. She and Dave Knudson went back two weeks later and hauled our stuff out. Dave still remembers the smell when he opened that tent. He thought he was going to pass out.

When I talked to the women who climbed in the Thirties, and all of them were associated with the Mountaineers, I got the feeling that some of them were very good, but none of them ever led. None of them, at least to me, ever admitted that was something they ever wanted to do. When you started climbing, had things become more democratic?

Oh yeah, if you wanted to. Certainly if you were shy or insecure, the guys never had trouble taking over, but there was never anything like, "No way, you're not going to lead this. You're just a weak woman." I never felt that, and certainly with rock climbing, we were always leap-frogging. That was no problem. I think Joan didn't mean necessarily this kind of leading, where you lead pitches, but actually leading a climb, organizing it. That was very important to her.

Did you do any climbs outside the Northwest before going on the Annapurna expedition?

I did McKinley in '77, and when I came home, Joan said that she had talked to Arlene Blum, and how would I like to go on Annapurna. I said sure, why not? When you're invincible, you know, that sounds pretty good.

It was a full year of hectic preparations. All my free time in fact, I got almost no climbing done that year—was spent gathering the medications, writing to pharmaceutical companies, getting samples. When you get donations from pharmaceutical companies, you don't get a bottle of penicillin, you get these little paper/plastic containers with two capsules, so you have a mountain of this stuff which you have to sort through. That was a tremendous amount of work for everyone. We were sort of isolated up here, because most of the party was in California. I took a leave of absence and everyone was really supportive. I think people here are used to people taking off on climbs.

Did you find that expedition to be—enjoyable is probably the wrong word to use.

Yes, it is the wrong word. Looking back I think there was so much work, and I don't mind work, but after all climbing is what we're there for, and when I think back, I think I had three days of superb climbing. That's it. The rest was grunt work, and scared work. It took so long to get to the point—and this is the problem with this kind of pyramid type of expedition versus the alpine style— so long to get it built up, that I think I was burned out, and I just wanted to get away. And Joan kept saying—by this time I realized I was picked for the first summit team —"I don't understand it", and I said, "I just want to go home." But she said, "Now just think, it's eight hours, eight hours, no more." Well it was more than eight hours, but I was surprised that here it was, the moment we had been working for, and I didn't want it.

It seems to me that climbing in the Cascades is almost always done with friends, people you've formed long-time associations with and it's comfortable. An expedition throws you into an unnatural community.

I don't think that's such a problem, because you know, unconsciously, that your survival depends on each other, so that even though someone might drive you nuts for some reason, you find another reason to like them. I certainly did not dislike anyone. In fact I liked them, at that time. But since the expedition, and I don't know if I'm the only one, but I've had practically no contact with them. Part of that is probably the different generations. I was older than most of the others.

But those three or four months are still intact, still sort of special. But it was certainly interesting that at the time, on one of my lazy days at 18,000 feet—I carried two days and rested one—I got a *Newsweek*, several weeks old, and we heard the pope had died. There was all this hubbub about who the next pope would be— would there be black or white smoke coming up? Who cares! Nothing had any relevance outside that little conclave. I was really embarrassed, myself, that I didn't seem to care. We were so focused in on the climb, that it was almost frightening. I think that was the reason, that when we came back—it was my first expedition—I was totally unprepared for, I guess the best word is dislocation. You just feel that you don't belong.

Had you allowed yourself much time after the return before you went back to work?

No, I came right back. Actually it was good. It took literally months to get back into the swing of things.

In reading the book I got the impression that the moment you discovered your finger was frozen that the decision not to go for the summit was not hard to make.

It was a gut reaction. It was no thinking, nothing about, "My God, I'm a delicate eye surgeon" sort of business at all. I was simply scared. And I had never experienced it before. I had never seen it in anyone. I suspect that if I had been with some climbers who think nothing of having a black finger or toe—there are many of them, and they go back—they could have reassured me. But I saw this white thing and then the stories start to spin in your head, especially on Annapurna. I had no idea how severe it was, whether I would lose it, get it infected, get it amputated. I just didn't know.

I did know enough, and this was later as I was laying in the tent, and I swabbed it with antibiotic ointment and bound it up. As I was lying there, the worst thing that could happen was that I would thaw it out and it would freeze again. Because we actually used that in therapy. It's the double freeze/thaw technique. And I thought, geez, that's the last thing I need now, is to freeze it again. And I think that was a big factor in me turning back. And I think that's something I will always be a little ashamed of, that I backed off the second time. Not the summit climb, that doesn't bother me. It's when I didn't go back up to find the two gals. Vera would have gone on. But I said, "This finger is getting cold. It's just aching. And I know they're dead. There's just no way they could be alive." And very definitely I was thinking about myself, there's no doubt about it.

Do you think your decision would have changed at all had you really been still focused on the summit.

Yes. You know nobody has ever asked me what would have happened if both the other gals for some reason or other could not have gone on. Nobody's asked me that. I'm sure I would have at least tried it. No, once we were past what I had climbed before so many times, it was very different. It was tiring, sure, but all in all, we were pretty gung ho. I think I would have tried then, and I suspect I would have lost part of the finger. Then obviously, you don't think, "I've got to go," it's the fact that everyone else is sort of depending on you, and that's where the communal guilt gets on your shoulders and you think that you at least have to try. But I didn't have that pressure because these two gals were in pretty good shape.

Were you at a point where somebody could have soloed to the top?

I don't think so. Maybe Allison (Chadwick-Onyszkiewicz) could have. None of us had really this kind of experience before. In fact I think it would have been stupid, because Vera

(Komarkova) told me that she's never going to climb with oxygen again. In fact she hasn't. She climbed another one or two 8,000-meter peaks subsequently.

They went up fine, and then they came down. They still had oxygen, and she said suddenly the oxygen gave out and she fell, absolutely fell in her tracks. Fortunately it was a slope and deep snow and she just sat down. But she said, "If this had happened on a technical descent, no way." It was just such a sharp deprivation that it really scared her and she said, "Never again." I think she did climb Ochoyo without oxygen. Now there's a remarkable gal.

The second expedition to India a few years after that was a little bit in between the pyramid and alpine style, and that was more enjoyable. There were just a few of us. We had no Sherpas.

When you returned from Annapurna you still wanted to go back?

Oh, Vera and I were planning Dhaulagiri for two years later in 1980, and we were making the plans to climb the Pear route. And I had real doubts about, well quite frankly, putting my folks through that again. Dhaulagiri had that same reputation for being a very dangerous mountain. When the India thing came up, Arlene assured me that it was a much safer mountain, and I thought, well, maybe I can do that. Interestingly enough after we climbed Bhrigupanth, which was a first ascent, the two camps I think that we were on people got killed on later, by avalanches. We felt so safe there. It was just like on the ridge on Annapurna, the Dutch Rib. Four guys got swept off at the end of the Dutch Rib where we had had Camp Three. We had felt so safe but the wind got them, swept them off the following year.

In the Cascades there's a certain predictability, but in the Karakoram or Himalayas one's ability to predict conditions is severely limited.

The old saw about getting back to camp by noon and you'll be okay is false. Any time can be bad.

After that climb on Bhrigupanth, did you undertake any adventurous trips?

I haven't gone outside the country, no.

Was that a conscious decision to scale back your climbing?

I decided I would not go on another expedition. It's just not my style at all. As I said my ideal is the alpine type of climbing, but at this point I'm not really sure I'm strong enough for that; technical climbing with a big load. I'm pretty sure I'm not up to it.

Could you see yourself living outside the Northwest?

That's an easy one. No.

How much a role do the mountains play in that decision?

Oh everything. I like the mountains of Washington. And I like the idea of living on the edge of the states versus somewhere in the middle. I hardly ever go to the ocean, but I just like that idea of being outside.

CHAPTER
29
CHRIS KOPCZYNSKI

*C*hris Kopczynski remembers meeting John Roskelley at his first climbing class. Kopczynski, 16, was a couple of years older than Roskelley and wasn't impressed. "I didn't think much of him. I didn't think John would ever be a mountaineer," he laughs.

Later, looking for someone to climb Chimney Rock, in Idaho, Kopczynski talked Roskelley into going with him. "I made the first lead up the peak," he recalls. "Then John said, 'Hey, let me lead.' He had on jeans, kind of hunting boots, and a jean jacket. I didn't think he was that strong or capable, but I gave him the hardware and that son-of-gun, he's got the most beautiful natural ability. His judgement was real good. He went up, bypassed the hard parts and went on harder parts. He hit in about two pins, and I asked him, 'What did you do in the chimney?' and he didn't even know he went through a chimney. I thought, 'God this guy is good.' And I thought, 'Stick with this guy and I'll get up the big peaks.'

"We climbed 150 mountains together. We had some great climbs: the north face of the Eiger, Makalu, and 50 peaks in the North Cascades, all throughout the Canadian Rockies, first ascents some of them, a lot of white knucklers."

((We got up there (the summit of Everest) early, a clear day. I just sat there memorizing the scene. I felt so good. Then I thought about getting down, but, god, when we

were going down, it was like in the Canadian Rockies. We sat there and relaxed. It was like we were on the side of Mount Spokane.))
— Chris Kopczynski

Almost from the beginning, Kopczynski was drawn to Everest, convinced that someday he would climb it. The dream became less fantasy as he and Roskelley improved their skills. He made it in 1981, and a few years later he came close to becoming the first man to climb it twice.

Since summiting on Everest, Kopczynski, a building contractor in Spokane, has sought to climb the highest peaks on all seven continents. In 1991 he climbed Mount Vinson in Antarctica and accomplished his goal.

My conversation with Chris Kopczynski was done over the phone. There is something in Kopczynski's folksy and friendly voice, as with Roskelley, that implies confidence, not the rash bravado of young climbers on the make. It's a quiet assurance that comes with years of experience, from watching close friends die in the mountains, from knowing one's limits. Kopczynski seems to know when to quit: he has turned back a number of times when things didn't feel right.

When I mention that John Roskelley has taken perhaps a permanent hiatus from serious climbing, Kopczynski says, "He's done so damn much. It's got to end someday. I kind of feel the same way."

▲

Do you remember when Whittaker climbed Everest? Did that have an impact on you?

We followed that real closely. We went to his lecture when he came to Spokane. I told my dad I wanted to climb Everest. He thought I was nuts, but I just kept dreaming about it. I knew I could do it. It took a long time, fifteen years.

Did you and Roskelley discuss your climbing aspirations?

Oh yeah. John always wanted to do the Eiger, which we ended up doing, and I always wanted to do Everest. I kept trying to talk him into doing Everest without oxygen because I thought we were both capable of doing that. It turned out we almost did it that way on separate expeditions. I knew that was coming, because I could feel it when I was climbing on Mount Rainier and I knew it was possible to do Everest without oxygen.

When I talked with John, he really seemed to have a preference for the Canadian Rockies over the Cascades.

I really do. The Cascades are beautiful, but I like the Canadian Rockies a little better because they have more ice climbing. I like the mixed climbing, kind of like Mount Robson where you can climb on rock for a long time and you can climb on ice, pretty good ice.

What sort of driving were you guys looking at when you climbed in the Canadian Rockies?

Well, believe it or not, we climbed Mount Robson in a three-day weekend. We started at six o'clock at night after dinner, then we drove all night—about thirteen hours—got out of the car, climbed the mountain in about two days and then got home Monday night about six. That was a long ways. I'd never want to do it again. You have to get it perfect. It was very common in the Sixties and the Seventies that we'd take off at dinner and be back early Monday morning. You did an awful lot of climbing. You needed two or three guys.

The 1974 expedition to the Pamirs has always

stuck with me as a result of reading Bob Craig's book which I always considered one of the most moving accounts of an expedition.

That was a pretty good book. That was the way he presented it. But it was a tragedy! You can't describe that, although he did a pretty good job. I can't describe what a feeling everyone had for those Soviet women. I was on the radio at base camp, listening to these gals coming over the radio, pushing a button with their frozen arms. It was just a hopeless situation.

That sense of helplessness was really apparent in the account.

Steck and Chris Wren were sitting in their tent a thousand feet away and didn't even know what was going on, but they couldn't have got to them at all.

Had you had those brushes with tragedy before in the mountains?

No, not death, no. That was the first time I was close to that, Gary, and the Soviet women. Gary Ullin was a great guy. I got to know him pretty good. He was a talented guy.

That first encounter with death in the mountains is bound to make you take a hard look at your climbing.

The amount of experience I had before that, ten years of real intense climbing, kind of hardened me. Roskelley, sort of the same way. We could look at all those things—except for Gary Ullin, which was a total accident—that were brought on by emotional decisions, poor judgement. You could see it. What really affected me was after the Pamirs, there must have been six people who were on that trip that died later in separate accidents. Bruce Carson was first, Marty Hoey, the two Brits, Boardman and Tasker. Oh my God, there were three or four more guys that over the next fifteen years died, and that affected me more than anything. I lost two more just last week, Dan Reid and his wife, Barbara, died on

Mount Kenya. I had been on Everest with him the second time. Sundari, the guy I climbed Everest with, he committed suicide.

I guess when you climb at that level you understand those risks, you have to.

The thing is if you keep pressing it and keep pressing, the odds are going to catch up with you. There are only so many times a person can go through the Khumbu Icefall or go to the extremes that you have to with 8,000-meter peaks. And unless you're Messner and totally driven and have the natural ability and the judgement with it, it catches up with a hell of a lot of people.

I wanted to ask you about the movie made of the Pamir expedition, Storm and Sorrow. What did you think of it?

It wasn't too bad, actually. They portrayed Roskelley real accurate. I'm the guy who fell, and Molly Higgins saved me. That was in the script. It didn't really happen (laughs). We were climbing to the top of Peak Lenin. The stuff that is shown in that movie didn't happen that way. They sent out letters, and little contracts, said they were going to use some of the people's names. Other people's names they weren't going to use.

After the trip to the Pamirs, you and John climbed the Eigerwand. What was that climb like?

I thought it was one of the neatest experiences I've ever had. We had only six days left on our excursion, so we were going to do it. We came back from the Pamirs and we just went up and did it. Two-and-a-half days up and a half-day down. We took the classic route up. I didn't realize that we were the first American team to do it.

The Eigerwand is one of those climbs where you have a real clear image of the route before you even start because so much has been written about it.

Oh yeah. That was the neat part. All the the history: Sedlmayer, the death bivouac, Toni Kurz, the Hinterstoisser. You'd find these pitons and you'd know that Sedlmayer, who led the first climb, pounded them in. We'd chat about that awhile.

Did you find that it was less difficult than you had expected?

We were pretty pumped up, but I found it every bit as challenging as anything I had read about it. I didn't find it less difficult at all.

So after that you did Makalu.

Makalu wasn't until 1980. After the Pamirs

I trekked into Dhaulagiri, Annapurna, the Lopsang Valley, scouting out routes. I did a lot of climbing in the Canadian Rockies up until Makalu.

You must have begun to really believe that if the right opportunity came along that Everest would really happen.

I kept trying to get on the list for any Everest climb. I tried in 1976. I thought, "Hell, there's no way I'm going to get to Everest," because I didn't know the politics involved. And it was booked up for so many years. Right after Makalu. We were actually climbing on Makalu and we got a letter from Jim Morrissey that said they were going to the east face of Everest. I did know Morrissey, and Roskelley said he'd help me get on the expedition. At the same time, when I got back, I found out that John Evans was the climbing leader for the medical expedition to Everest. So I immediately called him and I was the last one chosen. They waited until three weeks before they left, and told me I was going to go.

During the course of the expedition, did it become apparent that you were going to get a first crack at the mountain?

It's just like war. Your teammates are all trying to get a crack at it at the same time. It kind of becomes a survival of the fittest really. Who can hang out the longest up there, because there's no question about it. It's a tough son-of-a-bitch.

Having talked to several Everest summiteers, I find myself asking, "How did it feel standing on top?" For those of us who have never been there, we feel there must be this sense of elation, but the response from almost all those men was, "We just wanted to get down." Now, with you, after having pointed to the summit of Everest since you began to climb, was your response the same when you finally made it?

Let me tell you, I really enjoyed every minute of it. I was on top only about twenty to twenty-five minutes, but I had an absolutely crystal clear day and I was feeling really good. I couldn't have felt better. My mental capacity was there. We were up there at eleven in the morning and we had perfect conditions to get up there. We got up from the col in four hours and twenty minutes. So it was far faster than I imagined I could.

I had taken all these records of all these guys who had done 250-300 feet an hour, and I figured I could do no better than that, but, god, we had perfect conditions. We got up there early, a clear day. I just sat there memorizing the scene. Then I thought about getting down, but, god, when we were going down, it was like in the Canadian Rockies. We sat there and relaxed. It was like we were on the side of Mount Spokane.

It's rare that a peak of that magnitude allows you that luxury.

Yeah, well, it was still like a fifty-mile-per-hour wind on the final summit ridge. But you got out of that wind, then it was nice. It was still so clear. You could pick out the little villages. Sundari could see his little house in Tibet. There wasn't a speck of dust. You could see the Rongbuck Monastery.

Why did you go back?

You mean the east face? Well, I looked down it, on the way down, and I thought, "Shit, that's a piece of cake." I figured I was thirty-three at the time and had one more shot at a serious climb, and I thought, "I'd like to be involved on the Chinese face of that." It turned out to be a successful expedition.

It seemed like a much stronger team.

Oh, it was a fantastically strong team. I have mixed emotions about it, even now, going back that soon. I had a chance to go to the summit again and I got freaked out when a couple of guys died right ahead of me. I decided not to go because of that. It was two Japanese and one Sherpa. Lou Reichart was all in tears. I wanted to be the first American to climb it twice, and I was all set to go. Maybe that's why I'm still alive, because I decided not to. But it was a good trip anyway. We proved that we could climb that thing on that side.

Did you have any more expeditions after that?

Since '83 I climbed the highest peak on each continent. I figured that was a realistic goal for me. I couldn't compete with Messner. Only Messner can compete with Messner, doing all these 8,000-meter peaks. But with the seven summits, I always wanted to travel to those places. I completed that, and that's it. They were hard enough.

Was it a conscious decision on your part to back off, relatively speaking, after Everest?

I'd had enough of my friends die, but that wasn't it as much as a person's got to know that you have to back off it sometime. There was a point in my life, from twenty-nine to thirty-three, where I was really strong. Then I could feel it ebb, from thirty-five on up. I was losing a little bit of my physical strength.

And all this time you were balancing job and family. How do you do that?

Well, a wife who worked really hard, supported me in my endeavors. She's not a a climber, but she would keep really busy while I was gone. We're both in the same family business. She'd run the shop and keep things going while I was gone. A really good trouper about it.

Has she ever had a desire to trek in with you?

Oh yeah, we've climbed several peaks together. My son is really interested in climbing, but I don't encourage it too much. It was great for me, but I'd rather have them play tennis. It has been a great thing for me, but let's face it, it's dangerous. It wasn't for me, still isn't, and I don't think it was for Roskelley. But I'm fortunate to hook up with a guy who felt the same as I did, about safety and had a real strong sense of good judgement and didn't make emotional decisions. We just clicked.

I am late for my interview with John Roskelley, I have just locked the keys in my car which is parked at the gas pump of a busy Mini Mart on the outskirts of Spokane, and the car lights are on. The last thing I want to do

《 *I found that basically when I was in the heat of battle, I got really cool and calm and really enjoyed it. I didn't enjoy it when I came to the point where I was going to be killed. It's always going to the base of the wall, standing there, but the*

is irritate John Roskelley because, well, he has this reputation. I have read Ridgeway's K-2 book and Roskelley's account of the Nanda Devi climb. John Roskelley, one of the premier Himalaya climbers of the past two decades, has been portrayed as blunt, pugnacious, and driven, among other things, and having little patience for what he perceives to be incompetence. Nervous, smelly sweat dampens my shirt as I fiddle with a trembling coat hanger, which amazingly catches the lock, flips it up and lets me back into my car.

Pulling into their driveway, I am met by the Roskelley family. John is holding their nine-month-old daughter, Jordan, and beside them are his wife, Joyce, and son, Jesse. A gracious, friendly, All-American family. John and Joyce do seem a bit harried, and I find out shortly that Joyce is scheduled for back surgery the next day. She is getting ready for a doctor's appointment but still finds time to brew a pot of coffee (extra strong) before leaving.

moment I get started and get my hands on the rock and go for it, the butterflies essentially leave until I stop for a belay and I look above me and I have to wait there. If I could just keep going, I would never have a problem. **》**
— *John Roskelley*

John is house-husbanding, tending their farm, and trying to finish two books. Expeditions have been put on hold indefinitely. About his last trip, to Menlungtse in the spring, Roskelley says matter-of-factly, "Menlungtse didn't make it. The southeast ridge proved to be just what Bonington predicted it would be, very hung over, corniced. We got to 21,000 feet, essentially the easy section, and then it turned horizontal on us. I didn't have the nuts to cross this one cornice, and neither did Child. He didn't even look at it hardly. I just decided it wasn't worth it. There were only two of us left. Wickwire and Duenwald dropped out."

When asked if he has any expeditions in the works, Roskelley answers quickly, "Not a thing. I can't think of one peak at this particular point that I want to get, that I would spend all that time, all that money and all that effort to go after. Not a one."

Not a surprising response from a climber who, in the last 18 years, has averaged almost one major expedition per year: trips to Everest, K-2, Kangchenjunga, Nanda Devi, Dhaulagiri, Makalu, Trango Towers, Jannu, Tawoche, Gauri Sankar, Cholatse. Many of the climbs have been on demanding, dangerous routes, and there have been brushes with death.

At the same time Roskelley obviously chafes at the constraints of domestic life, and perhaps the act of writing, which, he says, in many ways is as mentally challenging as the actual expeditions—far duller though. He appears to be in excellent physical shape, ready for a trip should the right climb and partner materialize. In the epilogue to his new book, *The Last Days*, Roskelley admits that he doesn't want Menlungtse to be the coda to an otherwise distinguished Himalayan climbing career.

During the conversation many of Roskelley's more notorious traits are revealed: feistiness, candor (some might say tactlessness), and brutal honesty (some might say intolerance). It could be the kitchen setting, the wiggling baby girl he holds in his lap, or the self-deprecating humor, but those qualities which have earned him staunch allies and enemies in almost equal number, seem softened—perhaps better packaged—at the kitchen table. A thoroughly pleasant conversation. I stopped sweating hours ago.

▲

Did you compete in team sports in high school?

I was a good athlete but not real acceptable to some coaching techniques. I didn't mind hitting someone in football, and I didn't mind wrestling, but I think each individual takes a certain type of teaching. I take a very soft hand. I rebel at strict coaching, the "you do this or else," type. That's not the kind of person I am. So team sports did not turn me on, but climbing, downhill skiing, hunting appealed to me because of the individual aspect.

Were the climbing course instructors for the Spokane Mountaineers more soft-spoken?

Oh yeah. I still remember those guys. They always treated you like an adult, where a coach always treated you like a kid. If you were on a rope, they treated you like you were going to learn something. They never got heavy-handed. You were an equal. I'm convinced that had I been given more individual teaching, that I would have turned out to be a superb team-sport athlete.

But then you might not have found mountaineering.

True, but the people who got me started were these instructors and they were older, fifty-five and older, some of them. But they had gone through the whole game, and they knew how to present the subject and treat you as an individual. They figured if you were there, you were there on your own ability and desire.

Growing up on the west side of the Cascades, I tended to think of climbers in Spokane as being deprived.

No, I felt like you guys were deprived. Consider that the Spokane area only has a population of around 300,000, but we've produced some of the best mountaineers around the states. I'm including myself, but there's Kopczynski, Kim Momb, Jim States. We've got three Everest summiteers, and guys who have done a lot more than most. We've also had some really excellent rock climbers come out of here. But basically we have the training for mountaineering here. Any rock climbing we did was for mountaineering. We didn't rock climb for the sake of rock climbing.

Chris and I started at the same time, but we didn't get to know each other until the first major climb we had in the Mountaineers, which was Mount Shuksan. Chris was an athlete and I was just kind of your generalized, individual punk. I was more into running around and having a good time with my friends and not concentrating. He was a wrestler, baseball player, so for him to mess around with me was not good. His parents didn't like it at all.

Initially, climbing for me was getting away from home for a weekend, going out and having a good time with the guys. God, I got tied in with a group when I was about seventeen years old. They'd buy me a few beers. I'd have a great time.

I was with guys ten to twenty years older and they'd treat me like an adult. My dad would never give me a beer. I had a great time, listening to their bawdy jokes. We'd get to climb and a lot of times they'd crap out because they'd be so drunk, but I still had a great time. I think that was the bottom line. I didn't get into the climbing thinking it was a serious deal until about two years later, until I was eighteen. There was no particular climb or moment, I just started going more and more. Then I cut out the goofing off.

Did you start looking for climbs that hadn't been done?

Chris and I began to look for more difficult routes, but our techniques were so backward. The Spokane Mountaineers was not really a forward-looking group. I'm sure the Mountaineers in Seattle had belay techniques with Sticht belay plates long before Spokane Mountaineers did. They didn't become institutionalized until I got back from Yosemite. The advances in Yosemite were so far above what we were learning. We were absolutely dangerous. Chris and I were trying these routes that demanded a lot more technique than we had.

Did you have a sense that your technique was dubious?

I didn't realize how backward we were until I started going to Yosemite Valley. I went to Yosemite in 1967-68 and there was a hard-core group of guys down there. I didn't think there was anything down there I would have a real hard time doing. I was a good nailer, but I didn't know anything about runners or harnesses. I didn't even have a harness. So it took me a short time to pick all this up.

I wasn't particularly intimidated by the climbers down there, because in learning mountaineering in Spokane you became very fast at what you did. That didn't mean you picked up techniques faster. It meant that every time you stepped out of a car you were moving through brush, over rock, over terrain that rock climbers just balk at. They go back to the car.

I didn't know a thing. I still don't. I don't care what's out there. I hardly knew what a Friend was. I somehow kind of rely on this attitude of "I'm gonna do it no matter what, whether I've got to use my own technique." Sometimes I just refuse to move forward, mostly out of expense. I will not buy some of that stuff that is so expensive. I've got every piece of mountaineering gear imaginable through my expeditions, but when it comes to strict rock climbing, I won't go buy a new pair of rock shoes.

I'm not a real graceful rock climber, although I guess I compare myself to the guys like Kauk. Boy, those guys are absolute wizards, so smooth, so flexible. But that's their life, and I don't have any problem staying with them or running them into the ground when it comes to mountaineering.

You did some climbs in the Washington Pass area?

I worked in Twisp for two summers building Sun Mountain Lodge, the two years after I got out of high school. The only thing I can think of that I did first up there was going up that gully up to Liberty Col. I don't even know whether they consider that a first ascent or what. You know I haven't even looked at the guide book. Fred Beckey called me up and he said something about doing something on the South Early Winters, and I told him, "Yeah, I went in there and I did a route with Bob Christianson and never saw a sign of anyone going up there, and I went direct up the center," and he said, "Well, that was a first ascent."

I'm not concerned about where I'm headed as long as I get there. I've always had a real aversion to guidebooks, basically because I think the author instills his fear in you, and I don't care to be scared before I leave the car. I'd rather get scared when I'm up there. Beckey's guidebooks are infamous for what he sticks in there. He sticks a lot of, "You go towards the horrendous crack on the left side to the right of the open book . . . " Beckey is a detail person but, god, there's fifty open books up there.

Were you nervous in tight climbing situations?

No, I found that basically when I was in the heat of battle, I got cool and calm and really enjoyed it. The moment I get started and get my hands on the rock and go for it, the butterflies leave—until I stop for a belay and look above me. If I could just keep going, I would never have a problem. I never had to watch other people lead anything. I lead everything. Chris and I had an understanding that I would lead and he would follow, unless it was mountaineering. He would occasionally lead an ice pitch.

Did you have much interaction with climbers on the west side of the Cascades?

I never even thought about those guys over on the west side. I met Del Young. He was climbing with Catherine Freer, and they were both about eighteen or nineteen. Chris and I were about to start up Angel Crack, at Castle Rock, and Del walks up with this gal and she leads it. My eyes got about big as saucers. Heck, I was embarrassed to lead the thing until they left. I didn't know whether I could lead it. It was the first time I had been on rated climbs. I was really hesitant to stick my neck out in case someone saw me. But I never thought of competition with the climbers on the west side. God, if they even thought about us, that was a credit to us. But we never thought about them.

We were into our own thing over here; going up to Canada. I was a lot more competitive with the Canadians. I've never been competitive with the western Washington climbers. I didn't really think the Cascades were that big a deal. They seemed so small, such short climbs. Where I was going up to Canada and doing four-thousand-foot faces, over here, the only thing that's four-thousand feet is the Wickersham Wall—no, what is that thing on Rainier that Wickwire keeps going up? Willis Wall! And it's as rotten as hell, and I just didn't like that at all.

Did any of your early trips end in disaster?

Most fiascos involved whether to leave the house or not. If it was raining in Spokane, we'd figure, "It can't be raining up north." And usually it was worse, a downpour.

One time we drove a 1947 International truck, put Chris's motorcycle on it and drove to Lake Chelan from Twisp. We left the truck, put the motorcycle on Lady of the Lake and went up to Stehekin, where we took the motorcycle as far as you could get, left it and went up and climbed Sahale, Boston and Forbidden. When we came on back down a porcupine had eaten the seat off the motorcycle. That was a rough ride down.

I got beat up by a grouse on that trip. I was so beat from climbing all those peaks. We had eaten all our food the first day. That was the biggest problem Chris and I had was that we'd eat everything the first day. We came down the trail and a mother grouse jumped up in my face—must of had chicks around—and she fluttered around my face. I was so exhausted I couldn't raise my ice axe to beat her off. So she just literally beat me with her wings. And then we get down to the motor-

cycle and it's eaten alive. What a trip!

When did you begin thinking about expanding your climbing horizons?

I didn't really think about it. I graduated from WSU in 1971. I got a bunch of different jobs that winter and in 1972 I worked for the Bureau of Mines and didn't climb at all. I happened to be out bouldering sometime in January. Del Young, who was on the Dhaulagiri expedition, was out bouldering. He was living over here and going to school and told me about the expedition and that there might be a couple of spots on it. So I applied and got chosen a month before the expedition left, which was kind of hectic. But I managed to get the money with a bank loan.

So it wasn't anything you really planned for. It was an opportunity that came along.

No, I wanted to go do the Eiger and some of the big peaks in the Alps. I figured I'd like to go to the Himalayas only because I had read *Annapurna*. But consciously I didn't think I'd be doing it. I summited on that Dhaulagiri trip. Even though I'd frostbitten my feet and lost parts of the toes, and spent a long time convalescing, I thought, "Well, I really enjoyed that." And I wanted to go back. I knew I was competitive. I was climbing with fifteen other guys who were supposed to be some of the top mountaineers in the country, and I just perceived that the competition wasn't great out there (he laughs).

I was really competitive, and I was extremely strong and dedicated, if I wanted to be. I hadn't been in 1972 because I had just gotten married. It just occurred to me that there was a lot out there and the Europeans were knocking them off. The Japanese were knocking them off and there were no Americans. I'd just been on one—we'd just climbed Dhaulagiri—but really the big stuff was being done by other countries.

I was impressed with what Unsoeld and Hornbein had done. Let's face it, that's probably the greatest climb Americans have ever pulled off. They were some tough climbers there. I think had I been with a team like that in '63, my attitude might have changed. They were tough. Unsoeld was tough in 1976 when he was fifty years old. He'd have made it to the top of Nanda Devi if his daughter hadn't been killed. Schoening was tough as hell. Schoening and Unsoeld were mountaineers. They weren't rock climbers. They were mountaineers.

Now, you've got the bug, but how are you going to make a go of it?

I had set up a climbing shop of my own before I left for Dhaulagiri, and then I went back with everything purchased and ready to go. I worked at the store for almost a year and decided that was not what I wanted to do. During that period I knew that Pete Schoening was going to Russia, so I called him on a weekly basis. He finally invited me and I went to Russia in 1974. By that time I was just working as a laborer on a construction job. And that's what I wanted to do so I could keep on climbing.

In 1975 I went to South America, organized my own little three-man trip to climb there. Lou Reichart got me on the 1976 Nanda Devi expedition. I just kept hunting around and seeing if climbers were going, and then in 1977 I went to the Trango Towers, but I had already organized a trip to go with Chris Stanberger, who died that year, to go to Makalu. I took his permit, and went over there with one other guy, passed kidney stones on the way in, and almost died. I didn't even get to the peak.

I came back from the '77 Makalu trip and got an invitation from Galen Rowell to go to Trango, so I went over there and we did the first ascent alpine style. And that's kind of the way things were headed. I can't claim any responsibility whatsoever. Messner got that going, and some of the other climbers. I knew I didn't want to do Dhaulagiri-type expeditions with Sherpas. I was getting an aversion to using anybody beyond just American climbers. I felt, "Why are we using Sherpas when we're supposed to be over there challenging these peaks by ourselves? How can you call it an American expedition when you've got Sherpas carrying you to the summit?"

In 1978 I went on a K-2 expedition and went to Jannu, the north face, with one other guy. I go with Kim Schmitz to Jannu, and just two of us go halfway up the face of Jannu. I go back with ten or eleven climbers to K-2; god, and problem after problem on K-2. It lasted for three and a half months. The weather was terrible, the route was dangerous, and there were personality conflicts. That one went all over the place.

1979 was my absolute best year. I summited on Gauri Sankar first, went to Uli Biaho and summited on that. Both were really fine expeditions. In 1980 I went back to Makalu and with four guys from Spokane—no sherpas, no oxygen—knocked it off. Then in 1981 I went to McKinley with one guy and ran three-quarters of the way up the Cassin Ridge and got cerebral edema, went blind. We rapped the entire route while I was going blind. As a matter of fact I set the rappels up because my partner didn't feel comfortable with it. As I got my eyesight back, every minute or so, I'd quickly pound in a piton and try setting up the route. Then my eyesight would go, and I would be completely blind. After I got about three-thousand feet down it got so I wasn't blind. Let me tell you, even though I was going blind, and setting up the rappels, I had a knife hooked to my neck and I was cutting all the fixed lines all the way down. I detested the fixed lines.

You must have wondered if you were going to get out of that one.

I did because when I first got it, we were stuck in a storm for two or three more days and ran out of food. It was looking grim.

So here you were going blind, suffering from cerebral edema, but still making a political statement.

Not a political statement. I never make political statements. It was more ethical. There were five or six fixed lines hanging off every area, and it just irritated me that I couldn't go up a route and not see it cleaned. It was terrible so I cut them all.

Then I went to Everest that fall in 1981. It was the east face, and I ended up bagging out of that one because I felt the weather was too bad, the team was not up to the route; they were dangerous. Some of them were good climbers, but they were absolutely off their rockers. I thought the season itself was terrible. Some seasons are just not good in the Himalaya. So I bagged out, and I caught a lot of heat. I had a sense that I was going to be put in a position of heading up to the camps up high, and the avalanche danger was absolutely terrible.

The weather was continually coming in and dumping on the east side. I just had a bad, sick feeling about what these people were doing. They accused me of stealing equipment, a lot of horrible things afterwards. I guess I talked Kim Momb into leaving with me. I was afraid they were going to kill him, too, because of the things they were pulling. They were disorganized. The leadership was down the tubes, and everything added together there were going to be some real major problems.

Were you still in the position of having to go where the opportunities were, or could you pick and choose?

Basically that has been the biggest problem with most Himalayan climbs. You have to go with whoever has the permit. On Nanda Devi, I would have loved to do that with a team that was qualified, but there wasn't one. Luckily I was able to ask States to go, and that was a boon for me. Uli Biaho was my own, Makalu was my own, Gauri Sankar was a good team—it was great team actually—but the Sherpas were not qualified to be on there. The Sherpas were our teammates, we had no choice. The Nepalese said, "You have to take the Sherpa-American group." Protemba chose the team. They were all a bunch of young tigers, and I would imagine some of them were qualified, but it was dangerous because they had never been on fixed lines and jumars. It was a real experience.

In 1982 I went back with Galen Rowell and a couple of guides and did the first ascent of Cholatse. In 1983 I went back to Everest and tried the west ridge. I got pulmonary edema at 26,000 feet. I barely managed to get down off that ridge alive. So I turned around in 1984 and got to 28,000 feet without oxygen on the north side of Everest. I knew exactly why I got pulmonary edema on the west ridge. I'd had a fever, chills at 24,000 feet, didn't go down and take care of it properly, just kept going up, and I should have gone down. I went back in '84 and had no problem. It was just too damn cold. I'd have froze my feet and hands.

In 1985 I went to Kangchenjunga. Kim Momb and I should have summited but didn't. We just lost it at the top, and I think the problem was carbon monoxide poisoning. We were always sick, all of us, kind of nauseous with vomiting. It affected our ability to drive forward. We could have gone to the summit the next day and we just didn't do it. It was just stupid. I can't believe we didn't do it. In 1986 I went to Bhutan. I didn't get anywhere. I had one of the greatest teams: Chouinard, Ridgeway, Roach, and they were all chiefs. There were no Indians. It was just really a funny team.

In both 1987 and '88 I had major back problems and couldn't do a thing. In 1989 I went to Towoche with Jeff Lowe and knocked that one off. This year I went to Melungtse and fouled up.

I don't see anything down the line. I could go. I could not. It all depends. If Jeff Lowe was to call me and say he wants to do some peak in the Himalayas this coming winter, I'd jump at it. Anybody in the United States call me except Jeff Lowe, why I'd say no. Actually, number one, you've got to have the team. You've got to have the people you're confident in, that have the same ability you do, the same drive, and want it as bad.

I've only found it in two or three climbers in the whole United States. One of them is Jeff Lowe and the other one's dead, Kim Momb. I've known throughout the years that this was the case but just never paid any attention to it I guess. After climbing with Jeff on Towoche I realized right there that you have to have the right people. On Menlungtse we did not have the right people. We would have probably summited with the right people. It's the team that really makes the difference. We could have knocked it off with two guys if the right two guys had been there. Perhaps two of those guys could have knocked it off without me being there. It's the chemistry of the team. That's what makes the climb.

What's it like standing on one of those summits?

It's different every time. The main thing is that your thoughts are more on getting your tail off. I'm not one to sit around and think about it. I'm not mystical. I'm not religious. I don't give a rip. The route is more important to me than any summit. So I basically get there. I enjoy it. But my main thought is, "Okay, how do I get down?"

How do you deal with the tragedies that occur?

Well, I really haven't had many. I've had Ullin. I didn't really know Gary that well. That was a mistake on all our parts. With Nanda Devi Unsoeld, I wasn't there at the time she died, and I had built myself up for knowing that something was going to happen. I was waiting at base camp for these people for ten days and knew that something had gone wrong. But I figured it was the Indians who had problems. I don't have a problem with that kind of thing. It would be different if my son or father got killed. I'd feel a hell of a lot worse.

I didn't get to know Ullin. It's not that I'm callous. But I haven't developed a real rapport or friendship with a lot of those people. I feel bad about those deaths, but I don't see it as being a devastating thing for me. We all accept the risk when we go over there. I don't think a lot of these climbers think much about it.

Have you always wanted to write?

No, I didn't think I'd ever write another book after *Nanda Devi*. My dad talked me into it, basically. He said there was money in writing books. Now I know he lied to me (he laughs).

With the Nanda Devi book I tried to nail myself as hard as my partners. I wasn't trying to be all right all the time. You know I had to be honest. I was looking at these people and they were pulling bonehead moves. I could see where States was coming from sending Marty out. Right or wrong that was my opinion. And I'm writing the book, and there's nothing I can do about it.

Peter Lev got down my throat about the book. He saw it in a different light. I said, "Well, write a book about it. I put as many opinions in as I could, including yours. I asked you questions and you wrote me a letter back." And I sent it to him. I tried to get everyone's opinion, but it's tough. Everybody's seeing through two different eyes.

Do you have any goals left as a climber?

I don't believe I have any specific mountain goals. I haven't got any set. I think I'm waiting more for a good partner. I haven't had a good partner in years. I've felt that loss. There's no camaraderie. I'm listening to myself a lot.

What do you look for in a good partner?

It's difficult to say. Kim Momb was a good partner for me. He was young, enthusiastic. A person who could bend with the wind, essentially. He just didn't come at you and say this is the way it's going to be. We negotiated everything. He was really fun to be with, more of a playmate than anything else.

Jeff Lowe is a totally different kind of climber but had the same characteristics as Kim as far as being able to read what was going to happen next. Kim was a trainee of mine, a protege. So everything he did, I knew what he was going to do next. Jeff Lowe and I came out of the same background, mountaineering, the same generation, the same desires, so he and I could read each other the same.

How about Jim Wickwire?

Jim and I get along real well. That's one of the nice things. But he's in a different generation. He's reached that point where he doesn't want to do it anymore. He's decided his work is more important. He's gone out on the last couple of climbs hoping he was physically able. Mentally he was, physically he just wasn't able to stay there. And it's hurt him, but it's awakened him. So we're not able to, we won't go on any more climbs together, except for maybe around here. If I go to the Himalayas I've got to have someone my age or younger, preferably younger.

31

JIM NELSON

*J*im Nelson flops down onto one of those sofas which threaten to pull the sitter into the land of lost coins and pencils. He is wearing jeans and a white T-shirt that is a little too short. Although the sofa is comfortable, the conversation, at least initially, is not. Jim Nelson does not like to talk about himself or his climbs, at least for public consumption.

Despite having chosen to make climbing his profession, Nelson keeps a low profile even though his climbs include impressive ascents in the North Cascades, Alaska, Canada and the Himalayas; many of them done in winter. Nelson works as a guide for Alpine Ascents, leads climbing programs for REI and is also employed by Marmot Mountain Works in Bellevue.

His long-time friend and climbing companion, Dan Cauthorn says, "Jim is too low-key for his own good. His dedication to mountaineering and some of the things he's done, he won't tell anyone about it. Then he gets all bent out of shape when other people get all the attention and whatever comes with publicity. When you line up everything that's happened to him, to the hard climbs he's done, to the close calls with death, and the relationships he's had, it's pretty amazing, but he's stoic."

((When I was going to college, I realized I was a climber and foresaw that I was going to be climbing for a while. And, later, if

I wanted to go back and do something else I would. So I dropped out of school.))

— Jim Nelson

Nelson becomes truly animated when the talk turns from him to the issue of climbing ethics. He is neither purist nor pragmatist. His is a laissez-faire approach to climbing, but he emphasizes, "It's important that, as a climber, you're honest. There are climbers who call free what I would call aid climbing. I don't have any problem with how anybody approaches free climbing, hanging on the rope, etc. But to call it free climbing!"

His irritation extends to manufacturers who make product claims they can't back up. Of Gore-Tex he says, "It's good stuff. I have no problem with the product at all. The fact is, it's not waterproof."

For the most part, Nelson seems intent on avoiding those

fractious debates. That he takes pride in his climbs is obvious; but equally apparent is the fact that he doesn't place too much importance on what he does. "With a little natural talent for rock climbing, you can be well below average and still do any of the climbs that I've done. They're not that hard. I mean, we don't hesitate to use aid, whatever's the safest. We're out there to do big climbs, to push ourselves, but also have some fun, too."

▲

From the beginning did you see yourself as a rock climber, alpine climber?

Cauthorn and I were mountain climbers, all the way. Rock climbing was the jazziest part of mountain climbing but . . .

It wasn't an end in itself?

It sure wasn't . . . The hairy thing was the heights on rock or whatever.

Did you have any climbing accidents early on?

Cauthorn and I were up on Slesse in 1978, just getting off the glacier onto the rock, climbing up a ramp. We were going from no exposure to fifty feet of exposure in just a couple of steps, as we traversed across this ledge. And there was this snow patch on the ledge. Going across the snow patch, I slipped off and dropped fifty feet over a rock cliff and down onto this glacier. I ruptured my spleen. I remember landing standing up, then collapsing to break my fall as much as I could. I was airlifted out by helicopter. At the time we couldn't really diagnose that I had a ruptured spleen, but I knew I was hurt.

What was your response to this accident. How did it affect your climbing?

It made a big impact on me, for sure. It definitely changed the way I thought about climbing, as far as safety, but I was back into it right away. I didn't have any problem mentally.

When did you decide that climbing was going to be a career for you, with guiding and such?

I don't know. When I was going to college, I realized I was a climber and foresaw that I was going to be climbing for a while. And, later, if I wanted to go back and do something else I would. So I dropped out of school.

Do you suggest the climbs to clients?

Usually, if I'm dealing with people I've guided before, I. suggest the climb. I work for Alpine Ascents, and I do programs for REI. A lot of the clients we have through the REI program are usually the less experienced climbers. Usually it's their introduction to climbing.

Have you had clients freak out on you?

I don't guide climbs if I haven't ever climbed with the people before, unless it's something like Baker. For those we have two guides, as much as possible, and we gear the climb to the slowest climber. But if I'm going out with somebody, say to climb Forbidden Peak, it will be one-on-one, so it's no big deal. We take them, they pay us, and if he gets freaked out by exposure, well, you just try to keep him within his abilities.

You've done some pretty impressive winter ascents.

I started going out in the winter right from the beginning, climbing up around Snoqualmie Pass with Cauthorn (Guye Peak, Chair) on a regular basis. Then we'd go up and try to do Stuart.

It seems in the winter, especially in the Northwest, you really have to be ready to go when the conditions are right.

Or you just get lucky. In the Stuart Range we had a lot of good luck with the weather. And I have the flexibility with my job at Marmot Mountain Works, at least after Christmas. The owner, who's been there about eight years, knows that if there is a spell of good weather, he kind of turns away when I take off.

What are the best winter climbs you've made in terms of difficulty and adventure?

I guess the Northeast face of Stuart, Early Winter Spires, Slesse, Nooksack Tower. They were fun climbs.

What were the descents like?

We came down the Ice Cliff Glacier on skis. In the fall it's one of the most extreme ice climbs around, but in the winter you can just ski it. When we did Stuart, we skied out in horrible snow conditions with big packs on. At one point, we got to the bottom of the first hill, took a rest and were thinking how are we going to get out of here. The snow was just terrible. All of a sudden I said, "Let's leave our packs here, ski out and come back when the road melts out." So we cached all our weight, just skied out with light packs and came back in a couple of months. I didn't particularly need the gear for awhile. I've got gear cached up in the North Cascades.

Have you ever been caught in an avalanche?

I got caught in an avalanche going for Mount Sir Donald. Traversing across and up to the col, at the base of the northwest ridge, a slab broke off above us, carried us away. I took my pack off and went swimming. I was with Jim Martin on that one. He was trying to get me to go up to the Rockies, around Banff. He thought they were great. I don't like the rock and, plus, I know it's a different kind of snow/avalanche condition from the Cascades, and I'm just not comfortable with it.

You get used to a certain area. I mean, I go out every weekend in the winter. Me and Cauthorn, in high school, would go backcountry skiing. We'd skip school and go to the same valley over and over again; Alpental Valley, which is known as a dangerous place. We'd go up there in all conditions. It was dangerous, but we knew the valley well enough.

You spent two nights out on Burgundy Spires during a winter ascent. What sort of bivy equipment did you have?

Down gear, half bag and parka, Gore-Tex tent, three of us crammed inside it. On that trip we dragged Kevin Joiner out. He was a good friend who had been climbing since high school, too, but only got out about once a year, at most. He didn't want to lead anything. Before the climb Kit Lewis went to the liquor store; it was sort of a Christmas trip. He just went hog wild. We got up there, set up the tent on the glacier, sort of passed around a couple fifths of rum. This was the first time we'd been helicoptered in. We got left off and said, "Hey, let's celebrate."

Do you find yourself getting caught up, taking sides, in the ethical battles concerning rock climbing that have gotten a lot of print in climbing magazines?

Well, we make up our own rules. That's one of the things that attracts us to mountaineering. I enjoy reading all that stuff. It's pretty funny. We're not hung up on style, or whatever you call it. We just climb. Safety is really what I look at. Bolts, for example. I don't hesitate to use bolts. I'd feel bad if I started going out and putting them "everywhere," but I try to use them for belays.

To me it's important that, as a climber,

you're honest. There are climbers who are calling free what I would call aid climbing. Remember when Todd Skinner was out at Index, working on City Park? He was out there for a month. We'd go out on the weekends and watch him climb. We watched him on the day he did it free; right, yeah. He'd clip the rope up there, above him, hanging on aid, put a piece in, pull the rope up, clip it through. Okay, belayer's ready, and he hooks his fingers in the crack, and goes, "Pull me up." And he gets up there, and then he yells, "Ah, I'm on aid." He puts another piece in, pulls the rope up . . . when he actually did the route, he had to hang on the rope several times, half a dozen. He actually got it worked out to the point where he pretty much climbed it free, pretty much. But he said he climbed it free. Come on!

You seem to take middle ground in this argument, but there don't seem to be many of you out there.

I think there are more than you think out there. The vast majority, if you hang out down at the Vertical Club, you'd find that the climbing community looks at it more like I do.

Sort of a silent climbing majority.

Yeah, that stuff sells magazines. I read it. I laugh at it. I don't take it too seriously. I got worked up about talking about Todd Skinner, because he degrades what these really good free climbers do, people like Ron Kauk; there are dozens of them. I mean Skinner free-climbed the Salathe Wall, and he'll admit, if you get down to the details and ask, "Did you hang on the rope?", "Yeah, we had to hang on the rope. We did all the moves free, but hung on the rope going up the pitch." To me that's aid. They get this award from the American Alpine Club, The Climbers of the Year, for making this great climb, which to me is degrading to all the achievements of the other really good free climbers.

So you would stand more on the side of the purity of the climb, but if you're doing something else, that's fine. Just call it what it is.

Yeah, just call it what it is. These guys lied, distorted the truth. I suppose it will come out in the end. I don't know who to blame it on, the media? It was really hyped by North Face. Maybe it was commercialism. They promoted this climb. They had to come through because it was such a landmark climb, which it is, in the history of Yosemite and North American rock climbing.

That's great that they're up there trying to do it.

Cliff Leight: With some of the older climbers we've spoken to, they've almost all commented on the fact that climbing equipment was really limited, especially choices. They contrasted that with the variety of gear offered today. It's become a huge industry.

Jim: Gore-Tex is one of the biggest beefs I have. You've got a company that represents its product in advertisements as guaranteed waterproof. I go out with clients who have top-of-the-line $300 Gore-Tex suits. They get wet. And I'm wearing a $50 wind shell that I've Scotch-guarded that keeps me dry longer than their stuff. Eventually we both get wet and mine dries out like that. Theirs stays wet. And for anybody coming into the sport of climbing, Gore-Tex is a ten essential. It's not like, someone comes in and says, "I'm going to splurge and buy this nice Gore-Tex jacket." It's, "I have to have this or I'm going to die."

I've been out in connection with Gore-Tex, so I've had it over the years, and I've finally decided that the other stuff (a thin nylon rain shirt, of which I've had about three—I spray them with Scotch-guard—is as good. As I use the other stuff more and more in harsh conditions, like on Mount McKinley, Mount Foraker, the Cascades in the winter, I've decided it's every bit as good as Gore-Tex.

I know this guy, wants to start a company. He's got some great ideas, and he totally agrees with me about Gore-Tex, but he's making the stuff out of Gore-Tex. He says, "There's no way I can sell it unless I make it out of Gore-Tex." Gore spends millions of dollars on advertising. That's the other thing. The public is a problem. Every year, if the public wants what's new, whether it's simply a color or whatever, the companies are trying to outdo each other.

What do you tell people about Gore-Tex?

I don't try and tell them anything. If they want it, no problem.

I t is midmorning when I drop by to talk to Dan Cauthorn at the Vertical Club, so there are few climbers. Cauthorn, one of the owners, stands behind the counter. Dressed in loose, black sweat pants and a T-shirt, he is ready, when time allows, to get in some bouldering.

The Vertical Club, the first indoor climbing club in America, bears little resemblance to the slick athletic clubs spawned during the Yuppie '80s. Located next to the railroad tracks along Western Avenue in downtown Seattle, the former warehouse now contains artificial slabs, faces, and overhangs, almost all 15-20 feet high. At the bottom of each slab is a pile of gravel for soft landings. Some of the walls are cleft by narrow cracks, all are pockmarked with removable ceramic holds and stained with climber's chalk. The dominant color of the spartan climbing gym is black with a smattering of day-glo colors.

Unlike a growing number of Vertical Club members, Cauthorn does not consider himself purely a rock climber. He says, "I still look at rock climbing in terms of climbing mountains. I like to go face climbing, clipping bolts at Smith Rocks. But still I would like to practice on cracks, because that's what mountains have. You have to be good at doing that if you want to climb mountains."

Cauthorn and partner, Rich Johnston, were two steps ahead of the indoor climbing club boom. "When we started planning the Vertical Club, there was nothing at all except rumors of clubs in Europe. I think Rich was kind of tired of being a paralegal and I was guiding, selling skis and washing windows and there was nothing to lose. It was a good idea, but who'd ever have guessed what would happen in those next few years."

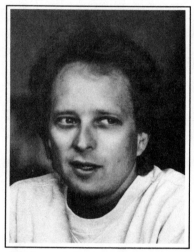

« *I talk to so many people in the general media and they think what we are doing here is the latest fad like hula hoops. They don't see that there is any history behind it or future to it. They just suddenly think, "Indoor rock climbing, I never even thought of such a thing, people climbing rocks. What fun is hanging by your fingertips?" »*
— Dan Cauthorn

▲

The Northwest just hasn't produced any rock climbing superstars.

Well, up until a year or two ago, there just hasn't been that kind of rock climbing to be done around here. Index is changing rapidly. I'm sure someone is putting bolts up there right now, as we speak, creating sport climbs at the 5.12-13 level.

Jim Nelson epitomizes this Northwest attitude. He is repelled by Twight. Mark Twight was a local climber and just decided he was going to be a professional and did it. You've probably gathered about the climbing community around here that it is in some ways insular. There's almost become a tradition of not making a big deal about climbing. You know, there's never been any magazines that have originated from this area. They're all from Colorado.

Jim and I grew up in the same neighborhood and began climbing together in Issaquah. He is three or four years older than me. Right off the bat he was really good, really bold. He used to lead the hard pitches. Plus he had a car. We did a bunch of stuff in the Cascades when we were teenagers. He started hanging out with different guys and went to Gasherbrum IV early on in 1980 with a bunch of guys from around here. It was a pretty bold attempt and they got pretty far up the mountain. But Jim got a bowel obstruction that just about killed him.

He didn't even mention that in the conversation I had with him.

Well, he's too low-key for his own good. His dedication to mountaineering and some of the things he's done is such, that he won't tell anyone about it. Then he gets all bent out of shape when other people get all the attention.

He was very matter-of-fact about his fall on Slesse.

I was right behind him. We were unroped. He tried to self arrest and his ice axe just stuck in the hard snow and he blew off of it and the axe just stayed there. He fell almost seventy feet, tumbling down this steep, slabby rock, and landed on these ice blocks. I walked around to this horizontal snow tongue. I thought, "He's probably dead."

He was just sitting there when I walked up to him and he said, "I really screwed up." He knew he was hurt, but he was just sitting there, and when I got there he went into shock, a natural response. He had broken a small bone in his leg, had obviously broken a rib or two and was really scraped up. He went into shock really bad and he started urinating blood so he had some internal injuries.

It was five or six at night so I stayed there that night and at first light hiked out. At that time they were still logging around there so there was a truck on the road and it had a radio. He was in a hospital less than twenty-four hours after the accident happened. He ruptured his spleen, had to have it removed, which is common procedure, and as a result the scar tissue from that operation blocked his intestines in Pakistan in 1980.

He was at base camp on the South Gasherbrum glacier at 18-19,000 feet and had this intestinal blockage. He went to base camp and it kept getting worse and worse. Finally he ended up on his back, and everyone realized that he had to get of out there immediately. They had a doctor who was doing what he could. Matt Kearns hiked out to Skardu in three days and got a helicopter and picked him up and they operated on him in Islamabad. Then he was flown to the States where he was hospitalized for a long time.

Shortly after he and Kit Lewis climbed Slesse, it flared up again, probably as a result of the Islamabad operation. Then he got it taken care of at the University of Washington Hospital. He feels pretty confident now that it is behind him. It hasn't inhibited his climbing to any degree except that he sure hasn't expressed any desire to go back to the Himalayas. But he did climb Mount Foraker which is pretty darn remote. Jim had a girl friend, Eve Dearborn, who was killed on Index, and that was devastating, but it hasn't fazed his will.

When did the Vertical Club start?

I think it was September of 1987 that Rich and I finally signed a lease on this place and that's what really started it. It's a lot of talk 'til you get a space. Then myself and a bunch of climbing buddies built it, and we opened in November about half done, and it's just kept growing since then.

Was there anything like it at the time?

The closest thing we patterned it to was the University of Washington climbing rock. When we first started there was nothing at all, except rumors of clubs in Europe. We just kept building here figuring out as we went what to do. Then a friend of mine from college, a guy named Brook, who works at Metolius in Bend, Oregon, came back from Europe with all these climbing holds and tiles and was all psyched about what he saw indoors. That kind of helped us, enforced what we were doing. Then all of a sudden here's this competition at Snowbird that next summer and it all snowballed.

It is interesting that, given the lack of real "climbing scene" in Seattle, that the first rock climbing club would start in Seattle.

Well, intuitively it just makes a lot of sense. There are a lot of climbers here and the weather's so bad. But you know what really made me feel that—and I still feel—this is going to be a lasting part of the scene here, is the rock at the University of Washington on a nice spring evening would just be packed, always.

Not only is it bouldering with this good landing, with opportunities to make up climbing problems, but people just really like to do it. It's real social, good practice.

Do you find that you are attracting people whose experience is limited pretty much to the Vertical Club?

That's happening now. Initially we attracted the climbers who lived here. There's so many of them and that was easy enough. Now people are coming in curious about rock climbing. They've been in other health clubs and done this, done that, wanted to always try it, but didn't know how or where to start. There are lots of people coming here after work just to work out, and a lot of them maybe don't even go rock climbing. Or maybe they just go scrambling in the mountains. It's like a different sport. The transfer to real rock is not as simple as you may think.

Are there an infinite number of routes that can be created here?

Especially with the modular holds. People like having the fixed walls where routes will never change. It's important to have routes wired and to be able to go through the same routine, but on the other hand everyone likes to have something new to do as well. The modular holds get changed nightly.

Are there times during the day when this place is packed?

Yeah, during the winter, a couple of nights after work, we'll be jamming, thirty to forty people. But climbers, being social animals, tend to do more talking than climbing when it's that crowded. Two people will be climbing and everyone else will be jammed in the middle near the weights . . . "Yeah, I was going to go up this weekend, blah, blah, blah." It's half the success of this place.

A typical night here, there will be a couple of people here who just want to learn how to climb, but most of the members have climbed a long time, all over the world. They're in their thirties and forties. So with that kind of membership you know that it isn't just a passing fad. These men and women are going to keep climbing whether the Vertical Club is here or not.

To a lot of us, it would seem, "Well, sure, it makes a lot of sense," but I talk to so many people in the media and they think what we are doing here is the latest fad like hula hoops. They don't see that there is any history behind it or future to it. They just suddenly think, "Indoor rock climbing, I never even thought of such a thing, people climbing rocks. What fun is hanging by your fingertips?"

Haven't you noticed that, in general, the media, especially television, has never been able to get a good handle on what climbing or mountaineering is about?

I think that has been part of the attraction of the sport to a lot of people, that it is esoteric and people don't understand and it is just as well that they stay away. That sort of attitude.

And the media has always seemed to search out a certain type of climber, one who is more media friendly, but not always someone who is necessarily respected within the climbing community.

Admittedly, Fred Beckey has kind of represented that one edge of the spectrum. I read an article in *The Weekly* that described him as "Wild Man Climber" Fred Beckey. And what Fred really represents in this whole wild man idea, is not what he actually does with his climbing, but that he has totally forged a different lifestyle, especially coming from the generation he came from. He said in essence, no wife, no nine-to-five job, not just climbing on weekends. He was saying that he had enough confidence that he didn't have to drop into that role. He knew that he could do what he wanted to do and that's what he did. I think that's what people find both inspiring and threatening about Fred, is that he really challenges the status quo.

I've worked with people who'll say, "God, I don't want to work here all the time. I want to go climbing." And somebody will say, "Well, the only person capable of that has been Fred Beckey, and you don't want to turn out like that."

A lot of the older climbers I interviewed still seem to see Fred in that light.

And I bet deep inside, many of them think, "Ah, I bet I could have done that." I've noticed a lot of climbers in their 50s who twenty years ago were on the cutting edge, but today are climbing better than ever. I bet Fred is climbing at a higher standard than ever. He probably pulled off 5.10 moves fifty years ago but nobody called them 5.10.

It seems as if the Vertical Club came into being at a propitious time, not only with rock climbing coming into vogue but larger companies like REI moving away from climbing gear. Has it opened the door for places like the Swallow's Nest and the Vertical Club?

The Swallow's Nest is getting out of it, too. You don't make money on climbing gear. You're dreaming if you think you're going to make your little, ideal shop and sell webbing and the like. It never works and never will. It's difficult for this gym on its own to show a profit or climbing classes alone. But combined, that's how I think we're going to make it. Even at that it's just teetering on the edge. Let's face it, there's just not a lot of money in it.

But then, for most climbers, it would be nice to be comfortable, but that doesn't always supersede climbing.

I kind of get a kick when I go rock climbing and look around and see all these guys doing all these real hard climbs. They're really into it, train here night after night and every weekend go climbing. You look at them and think, "how many of them have a wife? None. How many have a girl friend? None. How many have a real job? Maybe half and many of those have these totally obsessive jobs, lawyers, anesthesiologists. It takes a certain type of drive.

One characteristic of climbers—at least as I remember—who were on the cutting edge, was an almost poverty-level lifestyle. Is that population still around?

Certainly. We don't interact with them at the Vertical Club much, because they're not going to buy memberships. But if you go to Yosemite today, there will be like Pat Timson, Tom Hargis, and they'll be living out of their cars like they did twenty years ago. A guy came in here a couple of weeks and really started getting into it, "God, you know I think about climbing all the time. My wife's always getting on me, because that's all I'm thinking about. But I don't think she knows how much I think about it." It's that obsession. They're the sort of people who are talking to their bosses and thinking in the back of their mind, "I wonder where I'm gonna go climbing this weekend?"

DARRELL KRAMER AND GREG OLSON

*I*t is a fairly quiet evening at the Vertical Club except for Lou Reed's dolorous voice booming from the speakers. As Reed decries the sorry state of America, a few climbers attack the artificial climbing walls. One climber is following a familiar sequence of moves as a warmup to more serious climbing. Another, his legs splayed out on two tiny modular edges, sweats the next move. Another, Darrell Kramer, dusts the chalk off his hands, comes over to Cliff and me and shakes hands. Behind the counter, Greg Olson introduces himself. Darrell and Greg are climbing partners and among the new breed transforming rock climbing in Washington. They are rock climbers, not alpinists. They spend a great deal of time searching for new routes in the Index/Town Wall area, along the Icicle River near Leavenworth and on the basalt cliffs of eastern Washington.

Darrell, an accountant, dominates the conversation. According to Dan Cauthorn, owner of the Vertical Club, Darrell loves to argue climbing ethics, loves to take the position of devil's advocate just to stir the pot. A Californian, Kramer says he almost cried when he first ventured to Leavenworth to climb. "I drove out to Castle Rock on a Tuesday, and there was absolutely no one there. In California you can go out to a cliff and meet somebody. It wasn't at all what I had been expecting."

Greg, who works at the Vertical Club part-time, is soft-spoken and content to let Darrell do most of the talking. Neither looks the part of modern rock jock. Perhaps it is because they are out of uniform—the day-glo lycra tights, tie-dye shirts and multi-colored chalk bags. But their conversation is peppered with the almost arcane climbing jargon that sets rock climbers apart from the rest of the mountaineering community: terms like beta, dyno, redpoint, hang-dogging are dropped casually into the conversation, and not for effect.

❝When I first started climbing, I thought if I could climb 5.9 I'd be a damn good climber. Now people start climbing and you hear them talking at the Vertical Club and they're depressed, or bummed out, because they're not climbing 5.11.❞

— Darrell Kramer (right)

I have always been curious about the seeming lack of good lowland rock climbing areas in this state. Where are the good areas nowadays?

Darrell Kramer: I don't know. There are millions. Everybody seems to have their own cliff, their own secret cliff—sort of, "We're working on routes, but we won't tell you where." Index, Washington Pass, have all grown. Index now has big walls. Pete Doorish has put big wall routes on the Norwegian Buttress. At Town Wall there were probably more new routes put up last year than two years before that.

That proliferation must stem to a certain extent from the quality of climbing today.

Darrell: Yeah, but that's not always necessarily true, because, a long time ago, Pat Timson was a darn good rock climber down in Yosemite, and he certainly could have done all those routes at Index, don't you think?

Greg Olson: Oh, certainly.

Darrell: It was sort of a psychology. No one climbed anywhere but Leavenworth, and no one tried real hard things. How many years has Timson been climbing? He could have done all the classic lines at Index.

That's interesting, when you look at Washington mountaineering. Climbers have covered the Cascades, but the same can't be said of the lowland rock routes.

Darrell: It seems kind of crazy to drive twenty-four hours when you've got climbing around here.

So the quality of rock routes around here is better than one might think?

Darrell: At Index it's phenomenal. There are cracks at Index that are just as good . . . don't you think? But then again I'm an Index supporter. There are cliffs there that if they were in Yosemite they'd be just as popular as some of the big name routes. Japanese Gardens, that's a great pitch. There's just a lot of work to do them. It's mossy at first.

Do you remember your first rock climb?

Darrell: Yeah. My first lead was at Tuolumne Meadows, this climb called Great White Book. We really didn't know what we were doing, just sort of ran out the whole thing wearing old mountaineering boots. We thought that was what you used. We went for a week, did that climb, were terrified, and went home the next day.

You had seen people climbing and thought it would be fun?

Darrell: We just bought Robbin's *Basic Rockcraft* and kind of went for it. We made our own equipment, our own pitons, and just started climbing.

Greg, what was your first climb?

Greg: It was in the Peshastin Pinnacles. I didn't really know what I was doing either. I just had a pair of tennis shoes and a friend who kind of knew what he was doing, so he gave me the rack of stoppers and I just sort of went for it, on Martian Diagonal. But I really didn't know what to do with the stuff and ended up running out from the belay with no idea where to go.

So how did you learn?

Greg: I kind of got taken under the wing of a friend who was safety conscious, fortunately. I served sort of an apprenticeship following him around Castle Rock.

Darrell: I climbed for about a year-and-a-half and then said I'd take a course to see if I knew what I was doing. And actually I did.

From that point what was the progression, once you figured out you really liked it? Did you have a sense that you were good at rock climbing?

Darrell: Not really. I'll tell you that if I had been in California I probably wouldn't have enjoyed it as much. Up here it was just first ascents all over the place. Do your own thing. You could go out to Index on a beautiful, sunny day with nobody there. You'd hike around and find new cliffs. You could go up to Leavenworth to Midnight Rock—although it's probably harder now with more people, and do your own thing—and have fun.

In California it was a matter of too many people or a different attitude?

Darrell: I think here you could do pretty much what you wanted. I mean there's a different approach to climbing in that a lot of the climbs have moss and are dirty, so if you rappel down with a scrub brush and spend a day scrubbing the rock, the old ethics become kind of pointless. You can do what you want without fear of some people saying anything. In fact this guy (points to Greg) was one of the first guys to start putting up the new routes at Index with well-placed bolts. (looks at Greg) Oh-oh. That's what everyone does now because you've got to go down and scrub 'em; with Terminal Preppy and Toxic Reducer. Those are probably some of the most popular climbs there now. Or least Terminal Preppy was.

You went oh-oh?

Greg: Oh, it was kind of controversial at the time. Now it's standard practice, but people were offended at first. We really didn't know what we were doing. I mean we had no idea. We'd never seen anyone work on a new route before. We saw a nice looking slab and thought, "Well, gee, let's put a route there." That seemed like a logical way of going about it with the brush and all.

And what was the complaint?

Greg: Oh well, on ethical grounds. It wasn't from the ground up, not the traditional adventure ethic.

Darrell: But that's pretty much what's responsible for good routes in Washington now. Even on Icicle people brush out routes.

Do you think the different areas determine different ethical standards. Can there be ethical standards across the board for all climbing areas in the country?

Darrell: I don't know. It seems like whatever you do is fine as long as you're not . . . I mean some things are just in bad taste. Squeezing lines in too tight is bad taste no matter what style you do it in, whether from the ground up or rappel. That seems to be a problem now at Index, because now everyone has placed rappel points and bolts everywhere.

The climbing magazines are crowded with articles and letters dealing with various ethical issues. Do you have a purist or more pragmatic approach to your climbing? What constitutes bad form to you two?

Darrell: I guess drilling holds. That's happened before, but people pretty much look down on that. What happens more than anything is people clean routes of loose rock, and sometimes its hard to tell if a flake is really loose, or that if you hit it a little harder you'll make a bigger hold; creative cleaning.

Cliff Leight: Hang-dogging?

Darrell: No, in fact everything is . . . Washington seems, and this is pretty funny too, to have had hang-dogging and rappel bolting long before all this stuff was written about in the magazines. And no one seemed to care. And no one really cares now. If you hang-dog something no one really

cares one way or the other. And no one poaches lines either. If you tell people you're working on something they won't do it. In some cases people leave ropes up for months and nobody touches them.

Do you find that going from area to area that there is a big difference in the ratings?

Greg: Well, Washington has a no-risk tradition, so that sort of skews things. Routes have been so generously protected with bolts, whereas in California there is a whole different realm of psychological difficulty, that you don't find so much here.

You both started climbing in high school. Were there lots of kids in your high school climbing?

Darrell: No. I'd wait outside of school in my car and grab friends and say, "You're going to belay me."

Are you guys climbing all the time?

Darrell: I used to, but I hurt myself. I fell through a piece of glass and cut some tendons, so I haven't gotten out as much lately. It happened about two years ago. I've been doing slab routes, but I've been working out for about two months really hard. When I fell I also hurt my wrist and it's taken me a while to come back.

Are you guys afraid to fall?

Greg: I am, always. I'm terrified. But you fall so much nowadays and the protection is so good, so that after a while . . .

Darrell: And that's something different. Do you notice—I think I can speak for you, too, Greg—when I first started climbing, I thought if I could climb 5.9 I'd be a damn good climber. Now people start climbing and you hear them talking at the Vertical Club and they're depressed, or bummed out, because they're not climbing 5.11.

Tell me about it!

Darrell: It's really amazing. People go out now and they can boulder up 5.12 bolt routes, but they couldn't lead a 5.6 climb placing pieces. They can climb bolt routes, and they're not scared of falling at all. I don't know why that is. I'm still scared of falling.

Do you guys consider yourselves pretty bold climbers?

Darrell: I'm not.

Greg: I'm definitely not.

Darrell: I don't think anyone here in Washington is very bold. If you're putting up a route and you've scrubbed it off, you already know where all the holds are. So it's kind of cheesy to be bold, because if you know where all the holds are, being bold is a lot different than it is if you start from the bottom.

Do you do much mountain climbing or are you focused on rock?

Greg: Well, I kind of had a series of epics in the mountains. That's what probably led me to become a crag climber. I was really inexperienced and had a friend who was less experienced than I and we left to do the Coleman Headwall on Baker, and we got caught in a big storm and had to bivy on the summit. It was distinctly unpleasant. I swore not to repeat the experience.

What sort of goals do you set for yourself as climbers?

Darrell: To discover the most popular route in the state, at 5.9. That's a serious goal to find the perfect 5.9 route.

Cliff: Find the Outer Space look-a-like. (A classic route on Snow Creek Wall)

Darrell: Exactly. But I'm having trouble with that goal.

How would you characterize yourselves as climbers?

Greg: I'd say I'm a little rash, not as sensitive to the rock as I should be. I have great deal of perseverance. I've spent many hours scrubbing faces and trying routes, perhaps long after I should have quit trying.

Darrell: I'm a chicken but enthusiastic and I like to keep trying things. I like to do a whole lot of climbing rather than necessarily being good at just one thing.

CHAPTER
34
SUSAN PRICE

S usan Price grew up in Virginia and liked to consider herself an outdoorsperson but admits, "I hiked some in the Blue Ridge Mountains, although I hesitate to call it backpacking. But I had this idea that I would come out to the Northwest and do a lot of hiking and backpacking." Price decided to come to Washington after seeing slides of the Olympic Mountains. At the time she was looking for a place to do a few years of medical research. After the slide show her friends asked her where she wanted to go. She said Seattle. "It just happened that there was a program here and I really lucked out."

Although she originally planned to stay a few years and return to the east, those plans were most likely cast aside after her first glimpse of Mount Rainier. "I had been in Seattle a week, when Mount Rainier first came out of the clouds and I almost drove off the road. I decided that I wanted to climb Mount Rainier and I didn't want to use the guide service. I ended up taking the Mountaineers basic climbing course with the specific idea of climbing Rainier. The following summer I climbed the mountain.

"There were pretty high winds that day. Most of the people came back, including I think, the guide service. But the three of us decided to push on. I got blown off my feet several times; holding on to my ice axe as my feet were being blown off to the side. I probably wouldn't go up there again under similar circumstances, but I wanted the summit very badly."

It was shortly thereafter that Price discovered rock climbing. On a weekend climb at Leavenworth a friend lent her a pair of rock shoes. She says, "Up until that time I had been climbing in mountain boots. That was on Saturday, and by Monday I owned my first pair of rock shoes. It's been downhill ever since."

Her first foray into competitive climbing—The North American Open held in Seattle—came more or less as the result of a dare. Although Price failed to make the finals, she knew she

«I took a week off this spring and went climbing at Smith, and I really didn't want to come back. It would really be nice to take off and climb, maybe not forever, but for a few months. But there are other times when I'm really involved with my work and I begin to realize that, while climbing is a lot of fun, it's hard to justify as a life's work.»

— *Susan Price*

wanted to try again. She has had to work her training and competition around a rather demanding job—She is an anesthesiologist at Overlake Hospital—but she has managed to do so with rather impressive results. In the summer of 1990 she placed 17th at the World Cup in Berkeley, 8th at the competition in Snowbird and 3rd at the Canadian Nationals. "On the one hand I am very happy with the results when I remember that I have a full-time professional career and am older than most of the other competitive climbers," she says. "On the other hand I'd like to do even better."

Note: This past year Price took a year's leave of absence from Overlake, sold her house, and took off for a year of climbing.

▲

Was it at that point that you started thinking about competition?

I didn't think about competitive climbing until the summer of 1989. I joined the Vertical Club and went down there occasionally, but most of what was down there seemed too hard, so I got bored very quickly and didn't go down there. That summer I went up to Squamish and after that decided that the only way I was going to get better was if I got stronger. So in the fall of '88 I started going to the Vertical Club regularly. I started going to Index and Smith Rocks last year, but still never considered going into competition other than local competition at the Vertical Club.

At a certain point you must have broken through that barrier that separates most climbers from that upper level.

I think it must have been in the Spring of 1989. I had gotten much stronger by that point and started going down to Smith and trying harder climbs that I had never considered before.

When was your first competition?

At the last minute that summer, some vacation plans fell through, and I ended up driving down to Snowbird just to watch the World Cup competition. I had started reading about them and thought it would be intriguing to see people climb who were in this totally other league. I was really inspired after watching but realized that I liked to eat too much to ever be a world-class competitor. They all looked anorectic. But I was inspired enough to lose five pounds.

I guess it was in October of 1989 that the North American Open was held in Seattle. I thought it was just going to be a little regional contest, so at the last minute I decided to enter. It was a lark. I had no expectation. At that point I had flashed a couple of 10d's and led a couple of 11a's but not without falling. I knew I wasn't in the league with the competitors at Snowbird or actually the league that turned out to be compet-

ing at this competition in Seattle. But I didn't know that until I got there.

There was a climber's meeting the night before and they were calling out names for the order of competition the next day, and I started hearing some names I recognized from magazines. At that point I knew I was in big trouble. I was ready to drop out, but there were some guys from Seattle who were entered, and we all went out for a couple of beers and they convinced me that I should still show up the next day. My only hope was that I would at least get off the ground and not totally humiliate myself by not being able to do the first move.

What was it like?

It was fun. One of the most fun things was that you spent several hours in isolation waiting for your turn, so I had a chance to meet a lot of women climbers. There aren't that many other women out there trying to push their limits. It was really inspiring to sit around and talk and realize that there really were women out there climbing hard and succeeding.

Had you ever been involved in any athletic competition before?

Not really. I had been in the one bouldering contest at the Vertical Club. I had been in a couple of real small-scale fun runs. But I didn't have any expectations of doing well. I just didn't want to humiliate myself. I had even decided it would be okay if I were dead last as long as I got off the ground. Actually, as soon as I got a few moves up the climb, I relaxed and realized it was going to be fun.

Was it less difficult than you had imagined?

It was designed so that it got progressively harder. It was a little easier than I expected in that I was able to get a lot higher than I thought I could. That was the semi-final and then they took six people for the finals. There was also a speed climbing competition that I didn't take at all seriously and didn't do particularly well in, but it was fun; just one more chance to get up on the wall.

Was there an audience?

Well, the semi-final was held in the morning, so there weren't a lot of people there although some of the local media was there. Fortunately, I didn't notice that until after the speed climbing.

So how did you do?

I didn't make it into the finals, but I would have been the next person, which was seventh overall. Just to have gotten as high as I did was great.

What were your thoughts after the competition?

Mostly I was just happy to have done it and really excited about the prospects of trying to climb harder things. I thought that if I could fit myself into the same mental framework that I had in competition, then I could climb a lot better and a lot harder. Normally when I'm leading I'm just thinking about falling. In competition, it never crossed my mind, even though I knew I would fall because I knew I wasn't going to make it to the top of the wall. It wasn't a factor.

There was one other woman from Seattle who entered who fared a little better than I did. I had met her but had never climbed with her before. It turned out that we were climbing at about the same level. We agreed to go to Smith Rocks that winter and we decided we would just jump on things much harder than anything we'd tried to climb before. We were just going to do it. Furthermore we talked about the next competition in Colorado in December. We sort of came to this pact that, "If you go, I'll go." Her name is Laura Lonowski. That was really a turning point, entering that competition, because it set me on a course to climb harder and focus more on rock climbing.

How did the next competition go?

I did a little better. I got into the finals this time, finished sixth. And I was just that much more psyched to keep doing it. I've stopped setting limited goals. If I could just climb at X level I would be happy. At one time I thought I'd be happy if I could climb at 5.8 that would be enough. I'm not setting those goals anymore. It's more just seeing how good I can get. I don't have any delusions of grandeur that I'll ever be a superstar on the competition circuit. Maybe if I were ten years younger I might take it more seriously.

What do you think you have to do to compete at the highest level? Where are you now?

I'm pretty comfortable at 5.11 and starting to try to redpoint some 12a's. I've been climbing at Smith a lot, and there are not a lot of climbs that are in the 5.11+ category. You kind of have to make a jump from 11d to 12a, and I've been trying to make that jump.

What do you think it's going to take to make that next step up? Will it be more physical or mental?

It's both. I think there's a mental state of mind that you have to adapt to in taking up sport climbing, of being willing to take falls. Some days I can be bold and get up there and climb above the bolt and not worry about it. Other days I just can't do it. I get up there and it just feels too hard and I'll just back down. There are some people who are climbing at a very high standard who are not doing it in a sport climbing way, but it takes longer to push your limits through traditional climbing. It's easier and faster in sport climbing. I still love traditional climbing, even though I'm putting most of my efforts into sport climbing right now. The best part of it is adapting to the sport climbing mentality.

How do you balance your work with your avocation, passion or whatever you call climbing?

It gets pretty schizophrenic sometimes. Fortunately being in anesthesia, as opposed to a lot of other branches of medicine, my schedule is fairly rigidly defined. Usually when I'm off I'm off. When I'm not working I can leave town and go to Smith and not feel I'm leaving something undone. It's always difficult to balance because you always want to have more time to put into each one. I took a week off this spring and went climbing at Smith, and I really didn't want to come back. It would really be nice to take off and climb, maybe not forever but for a few months. But there are other times when I'm really involved with my work and I begin to realize that, while climbing is a lot of fun, it's hard to justify as a life's work.

Do you see what you do as a climber working for you as an anesthesiologist?

It is in the sense that it provides a relief from the stress. I think it's important to get away from your work, forget about it sometimes. When I'm climbing work doesn't exist.

CHAPTER

35

STEVE JONES, SUSAN KINNE, JAY HAAVIK

Around the dinner table in Susan Kinne's home in West Seattle the conversation is not about first ascents, harrowing expeditions or flashing 5.12s at Smith Rocks. There is plenty of talk about leaky tents, goofy bushwhacks, bonehead climbs and being scared.

At one end of the table sits Susan Kinne, a staff scientist at the Fred Hutchinson Clinic, a board member of the Pacific Crest Outward Bound School and former OB instructor. Across from her is Steve Jones, a veterinarian and passionate bushwhacker. He claims to have no desire to do hard mountaineering. He loves the solitude of the mountains and has even begun to take extended trips in the isolated Brooks Range in Alaska. He still retains his Arkansas twang. Next to Steve is Jay Haavik, a wood carver, who came into climbing rather late. He was almost 40, but he has become a good rock climber. Jay is most willing to admit that he harbors dreams of attempting ambitious climbs.

Over soup, salad, and several glasses of wine, we recount misadventure after mountain misadventure in great, often hilarious, detail. It is almost as if we have suffered silently through too many macho climbing bull sessions where death, near-death, daring and lunacy are celebrated. Our stories fit nicely into the gullies and thick forests of the small Cascade Peaks, the easy routes. And we laugh until we ache.

« I have this theory, that a lot of people who go into the mountains have an initial reaction to not like the experience, the scale, the remoteness, the scariness. But I also think that they go into the mountains because they want to master their fear . . . the pleasure may come later on, but there's always that sense of fear and anxiety that attracts you into the mountains. »

— Jay Haavik

*Pictured,
left to right:
Steve Jones,
Susan Kinne,
Jay Haavik*

▲

When did you first become interested in the Pickets?

Steve Jones: Since the first time I read *Routes and Rocks.*

Cliff Leight: You're probably the only other person I've ever met who's done the Mineral Mountain High Route.

Steve: What an ass-drag. Chilliwack Pass,

172

isn't that a marvelous place? I'd never been in such a hellhole. This was in '79 and we spent two nights camped here (points to topo) and climbed Ruth. That was my third climb of Ruth. All my climbs are just little scrambles. I've never done anything technical. I've followed up, probably, a low fifth class. But most of my stuff has been mostly mountaineering trips into the high country. My love is just route finding, and brush. I love brush. If it doesn't have a bushwhack, it's not worth doing.

Cliff: Maybe we should get together.

Steve: We almost had a dry camp, just below that point. We were down in the woods and I got a fix on the Copper Mountain Lookout to figure out just how much farther we had to go, and we were able to get up to some water.

Cliff: The funny part of the route is that you reach a certain point and you look down and there's the Chilliwack Trail. You've been beating the bushes for hours and hours, miles and miles, and there's this highway down there. You think, "Why don't we hike down to the trail."

Steve: My first trip into the Pickets was the Luna Cirque traverse in 1971; my first cross-country trip.

When you came out here from Arkansas did you join the Mountaineers?

Steve: It was the first thing I did. Joined the Mountaineers, went on a snowshoe trip. It was the first mountain trip, up to Cayuse Pass back when they kept the road open. I couldn't get over standing on eight feet of snow. The most snow I'd ever seen was eight inches. Then I hooked up with a fellow I'd met through Zero Population Growth, Hans Sauder, a Mountaineer, who liked to put together his own trips with other Mountaineers and not sign up for group trips. At the most we'd go with six people. We went up Big Beaver Creek, and then up to Luna Arm.

Then you do like bushwhacking.

Steve: They broke me in right. Our high camp was at Luna Pass, which is just south of Luna Peak. The worst day I've ever had bushwhacking was dropping down out of there into the Luna Cirque. It was late enough in the day that we didn't take the prescribed route below the glaciers. That stuff was cracking off of the glaciers. So we bushwhacked a short distance down Luna Creek, and Hans said, "That is not an escape route, because it took Beckey three days bushwhacking

out of Luna Creek."

For it to take Beckey three days to bushwhack out of something, it's got to be godawful. Then we bushwhacked back up to Challenger Arm and up to the camp marked on the topo. So we dropped from 7,200 feet to 3,600 feet and back up to whatever that is with full packs. I cried on that. They put me out on front on that bushwhack up Challenger Arm, and I got up about a hundred feet and said, "Somebody else is going to have to lead." It was slide alder. I've never seen anything like it.

Now, you weren't ever in Luna Cirque?
Steve: Yeah, yeah, we were.

But you didn't want to stay in it?
Steve: What we wanted to do is avoid getting high on that wall under the glaciers which were cracking off lots of ice. By the time we got down in the bottom of Luna Cirque, it was late enough in the day that there was a lot of icefall.

So rather than waiting and relaxing . . .
Steve: That's right

You decided . . .
Steve: To bushwhack.

Got it. (much laughter) So you dropped from Luna Cirque, at 7,200 feet to 3,600 feet and back up to Challenger arm in one day. That night did you still want to be a mountaineer?
Steve: Well, by the time we got through the cocktail hour I was fine. We always take along about sixteen ounces of gin, olives and onions, because you've got to have those in your martini or it's not a martini, or a Gibson, depending what your flavor is.

Did you climb Challenger?
Steve: No.

Did you climb anything?
Steve: No. There was one fellow on the trip who would have loved to climb everything in there. He was an accomplished climber, but he would have been by himself. Hans was the leader and he's not a climber, but a mountaineer. The leader sets the rules. I've been on trips with him and he gets nervous when I want to go out and climb something.

I would venture to say that your traverse was a first, and a last. To work that hard to get into the Pickets, and not climb any peaks, in fact drop 3,600 feet into a jungle to avoid them, and then climb back up and just leave. What was your feeling after that trip?

Steve: I kept going back for more. I've got my footprints all over this place. But there was the isolation, the severe topography, just the exhilaration of where it was. It was as isolated as I've ever been. And I've been more isolated since. I've taken a number of trips to the Brooks Range in the '80s.

Jay, when did you start climbing?
Steve: He's a late bloomer.

How were you introduced?
Jay Haavik: My son—he was fourteen at the time—and he happened to be over at the University of Washington one day and got really interested in the climbing wall over there, and he wanted to take some rock climbing classes. He needed transportation to get to some of these places, so I said I'd go along. That's how I got into it. We took some classes from Tom Hargis and Linda Givler. He and I spent most of our weekends his senior year in high school on climbs. We climbed a lot around Index, a lot of major peaks. Since that time I've had the bug.

It seems that young children have very little fear of rock, that the fear is instilled in them as they get older.

Jay: David is not that way. I'm probably more reckless, or rather, I take more chances. I seemed to be the one who was more willing to push it. David's fairly cautious. His climbing buddies seem to want to take more chances.

I wonder what he felt like when you would lead a pitch?

Jay: The roles would become reversed. He would become the father and I'd become the son. He'd tell me, "Dad, don't do that." He'd get mad at me. One time we were doing one of the real classic 5.9-10 routes at Index, and I led the first pitch. I set up the protection all wrong, so when he was following, if he had slipped he would have pendulummed. He was really pissed. He was cussing and swearing at me. "Dad, you did this all wrong." And that was very typical of how it would be when we climbed. He knew he knew more than I did. I was stronger than him, and I would take more chances. But technically he was much better.

Susan, you're from Wisconsin? How were you introduced to mountaineering?

Susan Kinne: I took a mountaineering class my freshman year at Reed College. I thought it would be a cool idea. I hated it. I didn't like walking uphill. I didn't like sleeping on the ground,

all that ridiculousness. It wasn't fun.
Steve: What happened?
Susan: I made friends with some of the other people in the class. I really liked them and wanted to do what they did, and the next thing I knew I was stumbling up the old Mount St. Helens in the slime in November. I'd never carried a frame pack before, and they gave me this expedition-sized Kelty and a pair of snowshoes. And these were people who ran everywhere. They seriously believed that you were supposed to run, literally run, the last mile of the trail out.
Steve: With their packs and everything?
Susan: We went into Kennedy Hot Springs like a rocket, and up to Boulder Basin. Some friends and I went back in to climb Glacier Peak this summer, and it's an indication of how hard I was being worked, that I had no memory of any of that. I didn't remember Kennedy Hot Springs.
Steve: Well, you were in a blind stupor then.
Susan: They were just driving my ass up. Pulling yourself up by trees to get up into Boulder Basin. No memory of that.
Steve: And it really is that steep.

My dad backed down that trail one year, after climbing Glacier, to save his knees. That's probably a first, the only one he'll ever have. Maybe he was thinking in terms of that.

Jay: I have this theory, that a lot of people who go into the mountains have an initial reaction to not like the experience, the scale, the remoteness, the scariness. But I also think that they go into the mountains because they want to master their fear. They go back in again and again, but they never completely master that. There's always that edge of fear. The pleasure may come later on, but there's always that sense of fear and anxiety that attracts you into the mountains.
Susan: That's what Dick Emerson said, or wrote, that one of the things he was working on on the American Everest Expedition, was climbing as this delicate, sort of titrating your danger. And that you changed the rules every time it got too easy. That each person is engaged in this continual process of exactly that; trying to up the risk to just enough so that the risk is manageable.
Steve: So Susan, if you didn't like it why did you continue?
Susan: By the time I got through the course, I was sufficiently fond of the people that I wanted to do what they did. They basically knew what was

going on and I didn't feel unsafe. The first technical climb was on Three Fingered Jack and sure enough I froze on this crawl. It was a fixed rope and I had to get walked across it. A friend had to talk me into jumping down a couloir coming off the east side of Mount Jefferson. You just have to do it. You stand there until it becomes obvious you have to do it.

When did you become an Outward Bound instructor?

Susan: I dropped out of school for a year and traveled in Europe. When I came back, Outward Bound needed instructors. They needed women instructors, women who could hold ice axes. That was about the standard at that time. I didn't know a thing about Outward Bound, but a girl friend from Reed had worked there and said, "Go down and talk to them." They hired me, and I was an assistant in the Three Sisters for one course, which scared the shit out of me in some ways. I mean, taking high school students up Broken Top with no rope. The instructor said, "Well, heck, if you rope them together and anybody falls, they're all going to die anyway."

Steve: So if they're not roped up only one dies.

Susan: I'm thinking, "Oh, is this how they do it?" The next month they gave me a patrol and sent me out. There I was on Mount Washington trying to find a route. I'd only climbed it once before. I got up there with an entire patrol of 16-year-old girls, got off route on the east face. You know that stuff is just horrible rock. I'm standing, looking down between my toes at 3,000 feet of rotten lava, thinking, "I'm sure the route doesn't go this way." I got out part-way to a chimney with a sling in it. I'd run out of rope. My assistant was saying, "That's the route." I'm thinking, "I can't bring anyone up here. I can't put them anywhere." I had to back off and down, sit my patrol down and explain the difference between objective and subjective hazard. "We know this is a safe route. We know another patrol climbed this yesterday. I, however, am not capable of leading you up this route now, so we are going to go back down."

I think, for me, Outward Bound was the medium through which I came to really love the outdoors, because it stopped being the "out for two days and being on the run the whole time." You had the luxury of being out for that long, like

your trips in the Pickets or Brooks Range. You're just out there for twenty-six days. And those were the days when women didn't climb on their own. They climbed with their boy friends, because there weren't that many women climbing. And so to get out there and just have to do it for yourself is profoundly frightening, but it is **so** neat.

I still find that the Three Sisters is just magic country. It is not the most interesting mountain terrain in many ways. It's a lovely course area, but it's peopled with so many happy ghosts. It really is memory lane. After nearly twenty years, there are so many associations. I think now, for me, that's a lot of why I enjoy going into the mountains in general.

Jay: Even if you're a place you've never been before?

Susan: I think it's an atmospheric factor. There are places in the Glacier Peak area and the North Cascades now, that increasingly, have memories and associations as well. But it's just sort of a predictable miracle. You go out and you're going to feel better, even if the weather is weird, even if the party is less than perfect, or the route turns out to be strange and you get lost. There's some kind of trustworthy recharging taking place, that reconnects you with all those past climbs.

I think, increasingly, just the chance to get out becomes real important.

Susan: It doesn't have to be an epic about which you can boast, like yesterday, getting out and skiing and performing the ritual number of headplants into the powder, doing intensive snowpack analysis. I fell down so hard I broke my glasses, right under Chair Five. A real crowd pleaser.

Steve: A group of us went into the Bear and Redoubt area, did the Indian Creek bushwhack up into Bear and didn't climb anything. We went over to the base of Redoubt, and I wanted to climb it in the worst way. I thought, "When is the next time I'm going to be in here; probably never." But Hans said, "No, we're not going to climb it."

It really is being there that is important. Many rock climbers are perfectly happy to drive to the base of the climb, hop out of their cars and immediately start rock climbing. That's not what it's about for me. If I can scramble up it, I'll take some little dicey moves to get up something, because I like the idea of having a goal and getting to the top. I like saying I climbed so many peaks, but when it comes right down to it, it's getting there, experiencing the whole scene. I got into alpine flora in a big way. I take macro pictures of alpine flora. That's my thing now.

There's probably a lot of that down in Luna Creek.

Steve: Yeah, there is. But I'm not going back there to look for it. But that's always been the major thrust of my climbing.

Susan: Coming down out of Thunder Basin into the White River, just south of Glacier Peak, is definitely one that should be in your future. It is one of the bottom ten bushwhacks I can remember; probably nothing to someone like you with your vast fund of comparisons. But just in terms of short, cliff sections with blackberries and other vines, slippery climbing boots over the rock, and then overlaid with good-sized avalanched trees with lots of pine needles on them. And it's ninety degrees and the flies are biting.

Steve: It was OK until you got to the flies.

Cliff and I remember the worst flies we ever had were on the trail to Hannegan Pass. I've never cried in the mountains. I cried, and that was right out of the car. All I can remember were tears of rage, and I was an adult. I recited this mantra all day, "Goddammm, Sonofabitch" for however many miles it took to get rid of them.

Steve: I'll tell you the fastest trip I ever made was climbing Shuksan on the south side. The black flies drove Larry and I out of the car and right up to our base camp, and I hardly remember it. You could not stop. You stopped and the damn things would carry you off. You had to keep moving. The only thing you could do was get your boots on in the car, put your pack on and get the hell out of there. Just a swarm of them and every one wanted a piece of your meat.

Steve, I get the feeling that your aspiration was never to be a great climber. What about you Susan?

Susan: I hated rock climbing. I never liked it, and it took me fifteen years to admit that I didn't like rock climbing. You were supposed to like rock climbing. In that era, working for Outward Bound in particular, you had to be an ax-wielding feminist because it was a bit of an oppressive environment. You certainly couldn't admit you didn't like rock climbing.

That was one thing I always appreciated about you, was your willingness to admit that you didn't like rock climbing. It must have been difficult, because there was, perhaps not overtly, a macho atmosphere surrounding Outward Bound.

Susan: But that was where the quality was, the ability to climb hard rock. At that time we were all a lot younger—these were people in their early to mid-twenties when your testosterone is your neuro-transmitter. That was where the action was. There weren't that many people I knew who appreciated wandering around in the mountains. It was always, "try a harder route, try a harder peak." We were supposed to spend all our weekends and free time between OB courses climbing rock. I like climbing easy rock. It's really quite fun, and it was a delight to rediscover that sometime later.

Steve: But that's different—climbing Glacier, Adams, Rainier, Sloan—from trying a new route on Liberty Bell. They are equatable things as far as I'm concerned.

Jay, you went from beginner to climbing 5.10 in a relatively short period of time. Did you wish that you had started climbing sooner?

Jay: I really do. I've often thought about that. I wish I had started twenty or thirty years ago. I have aspirations to do some things, and I don't know whether I'll ever have the chance to do them. I was in Ecuador last January climbing and really had a great time. I'd like to go back and do some of that. I'd like to go to the Himalayas. I seem to do well at high altitude.

What's the worst night you've ever spent in the mountains?

Steve: Up on top of Hannegan Peak with Karin, my wife. This was her first camping trip. We were up there for three days in early September, and I picked what I thought would be a good spot, and it was, until it rained. It was in a slight depression which filled up with rain rapidly. I had an old REI A-frame tent, and the wind, on the second night, came up and the poles buckled. I had a climbing rope along. I don't know why, probably just to prop my feet off the bottom of the tent. But Karin was sleeping right on the bottom of the tent. She was awash and couldn't figure out how I could sleep through all this. She was drowning.

I didn't have a watch or flashlight. So we didn't know what time it was, it was raining like crazy and she was sure we were going to drown up there, and even if the sun came up in the morning and she wasn't sure that was going to happen—that we'd never find our way back down the trail because it would be washed out. And if we were to find our way down the trail, we'd never get the car turned around. I had to calm her down all night.

Jay: Was that the last time she ever went climbing with you?

Steve: We got up just as it was getting light, and the wind must have been gusting to sixty miles per hour, and the best you could do was just lay on the tent and roll it up. We packed up our wet gear and hiked out. She was convinced we were going to die up there.

Jay: I've never had a bad night.

(Everyone else: "Never?")

Jay: Maybe I forgot about it. I've been tent-bound for days, but I guess I see that as being part of the experience.

What about having to share a tent with someone who farts a lot.

Steve: That's me. So that's no problem.

Susan: There are a bunch of us who have nom d'ski. Our mutual friend, Tom Thompson, is the king of midair. His sons who ski really well are known as the chairman of the board and the Sultan of Steep. His wife is Turbo Woman. His name is the King of Foul Air.

Steve: There's either a bad joke on one end or a bad fart on another.

What's the dumbest thing you've ever done in the mountains?

Jay: It was with my son. We were climbing Rainier. The first time we were going to do this, just the two of us. As often is when you climb the standard route, you run into lots of other people. And so we were kind of on a rope. There were a bunch of other ropes around us. As we got up to around 14,000 feet, a lenticular cap came up, and it got really windy, roaring really hard. I had really wanted to climb it. And my son wanted to go back.

I said to David, "Other people are going to go back, why don't you hook up with them, and I'll go on ahead." I was so intent on wanting to get to the top, that I wasn't keying in on what he was all about and where he was. He was only fifteen. He said he didn't want to go back down. He wanted to stay with me. I wasn't picking up his signals. I said, "Look if you don't want to go on, why don't you go back. I want to go on to the top." Finally he had to break down and tell me that he didn't want to go on, and he didn't want to be left alone, go back with strangers. I was pissed. I let him know that I was pissed. I didn't want to turn back, because we were really close to the top.

We laugh about it now, he and I. And I describe that as my worst climb in the mountains, because I was so intent on getting to the top that I forgot about him. And he was scared. We had never been in that situation before, and he didn't want to be left alone with strangers. Later on when I got back down, I realized I had acted in an irresponsible way. I've often thought about that. It was a bad time.

Cliff: There's nothing worse than being on a trip where you get ahead of someone and you wait for them. As soon as they drag up to you, you take off. And they get pissed and you don't know why.

Susan: Reasonable grounds for murder, or at least assault.

Steve: Were you on the receiving end or giving?

Cliff: The giving end. On the Mineral Mountain High Route, I remember going with a friend who had never bushwhacked and he was carrying a heavy pack. We got to Mineral Mountain, and there were four mountain goats. One must have been ill, because the three would all walk ahead and then look back at this one straggler who'd just catch up and then they'd take off. My friend said, "You see that last goat? That's me." That really drove the point home.

It's a good thing he didn't hit you.

Cliff: He couldn't. He was too tired.

▲

CHAPTER

36

LOWELL SKOOG

*L*owell Skoog shares a strong bond with climbers of other generations, people like Joe Firey and the Ptarmigans, who explored the Cascades, often without the aid of guidebooks or detailed maps. With the proliferation of access roads, guidebooks and sheer numbers of mountaineering enthusiasts, the opportunities to experience "The mystery of the unknown" in the Cascade wilderness has been lost to present-day climbers and future generations.

Skoog's solution would be what he calls a White Wilderness, a mountain area devoid of guidebooks where climbers have the opportunity for "not just physical recreation, but for spiritual rejuvenation . . . where the goal of bagging a peak is less important than the experience gained trying . . . and every effort is made to ensure that one person's impact is not felt by the next person."

The White Wilderness proposal appeared in two issues of the *Mountaineer* and the response, "It's a great idea, but . . ." was not unexpected. Skoog has no illusions about the idea ever becoming reality, but it is an idea that has informed his climbing for over a decade.

Lowell Skoog has sought out what new adventures are left in the Cascades, not necessarily covering new ground, but seeing familiar territory in unique fashion: on skis. He made the first ski traverse of the Picket Range, The Isolation Traverse from Backbone Ridge to El Dorado, and the Ptarmigan Traverse in a day. He has often been accompanied by brothers, Carl and Gordy.

Although he has climbed in the Canadian Rockies, the British Columbia Coast Range, Alaska and South America, Skoog still finds his greatest satisfaction in the Cascades. He has not run out of new ways to travel among old friends. In the fall of 1990 he cached food and supplies in two locations in the Cascades in hopes of completing the following spring a 100-mile, two-week ski traverse along the crest of the Cascades, a traverse he calls "The American Alps Traverse." During the late spring, Skoog, a software engineer, tries to be ready to go at a moment's notice if the often difficult Northwest weather presents a window of opportunity.

《The routes that people do are really an expression of their personalities. I know that with my

ski trips, I have looked for routes that somehow resonated with my own personalities. 》
— Lowell Skoog

The interview is conducted in Skoog's home in north Seattle. Tall, thin, boyish, he brings a refreshing, almost naive enthusiasm to the conversation.

▲

Lowell Skoog: I'm from Bellevue. There are six kids in our family. Three of us are real active in skiing and climbing, although my older brother, Gordy, has two kids now and doesn't get out as much as he used to. My younger brother, Carl, is sort of my favorite ski partner. We go on a lot of these traverses together. He's usually the one I grab and say, "Lets go."

My dad died a few years back, but he was a real avid skier. It's interesting when you think of the evolution of Northwest outdoor activities. He was sort of the old-style Scandahoovian ski jumper. Nobody does nordic ski jumping anymore, but he was a member of the Konigsburger ski club, and they used to go and do jumps. I remember going to watch my dad and my uncle. They weren't great jumpers, but they were fun to watch. Because every time they went off the jump it was like hands swinging in the air and then they'd land and go, "Ah nuts."

Did you ever have a yen to jump?

No, my other brother did, but I never did. My folks weren't into climbing. We just got into it, my brothers and I, through friends. I started climbing after high school in 1974. It was kind of funny. My first climbing experience was pretty strange for someone from the Northwest. It was in the Picket Range. What a place to start.

I started climbing with Gary Brill, and Gary has always been pretty ambitious. Back in those days we had what we called Brill hikes, which was any hike that Gary planned, which often turned out to be an epic. We didn't know anything, about belays, anything. We didn't know what a prusik sling was. I think it might have been the first time I ever wore crampons. His plan was to traverse the Northern and Southern Pickets.

All we had were tube tents, and instead of a climbing rope, we had a polypropylene rope that they used to rope off avalanche areas at Alpental. My boots were a pair of fifteen dollar boots I bought at Valu Mart. I was so embarrassed with them, that when I went to REI to rent my crampons, I went downstairs and fit a pair of crampons on then went upstairs and told them the size I wanted so I wouldn't have to give them my boots.

We climbed Whatcom Peak, were scared to death on Challenger and didn't summit. We were intimidated as anything by the Luna Cirque. It looked like the moon. I'd never seen anything like it. When we got up to Luna Lake, we went up the false summit of Luna Peak, and then we had a marine push come in where it was marine clouds and fingers coming over the peak. We just got psyched out and hightailed it out the Luna High Route. We didn't complete the traverse, but did actually traverse through the Northern Pickets, through some pretty rugged country.

After that trip, I realized how little we knew; well actually I didn't realize how little we knew. I had this theory, still do, that if you're self-taught, if you survive the first couple of years maybe everything will be okay. It's those first two years when you don't know what you're doing.

When did you start doing the ski traverses?

That was a little later in the early '80s after I got some ski mountaineering gear. I was a poor student up until that time, and started doing a few trips like Silver Star, the south side of Baker, going up to Boston Basin. Even then the impetus for going on these ski traverses wasn't the skiing part of it. The first traverse we did was the Ptarmigan in '82, and none of us had ever done the Ptarmigan before and had always wanted to. We thought, well, let's ski it. We had heard that Steve Barnett wanted to do that route, and he did it some years later. It had been done in 1981. So in '82, Gary, Cary Ritland, Mark Hudson and myself skied the Ptarmigan, and something clicked.

Traditionally you'll do the Ptarmigan in about a week in the summertime. We went through there in three days and climbed four peaks along the way. You packed it all into one quick trip.

The year after that we did the traverse from Snowfield to El Dorado, and after that, Brian Sullivan at the end of that trip, said, "Now all we need to do is the Pickets." I had never even thought about that. We had been back to the Northern Pickets in 1980 and sort of redeemed ourselves. I started thinking about the Pickets. I decided that it was a little bit nutty, but if you pulled it off, it would be a trip you would always

— Photo courtesy Lowell Skoog

(1) Lowell Skoog skiing off the east
summit of Fury, May 19, 1985.
(2) Cliff Leight on the Lithuanian Lip
on the second pitch of Liberty Crack.

2

— Dan Waters Photo

— Dan Cauthorn Photo

2

(1) Jim Nelson on Dragon Tail above Colchuck Lake. (2) Susan Price climbing "Pig Pen," a route at American Fork, Utah. (3) Susan Price competing at the World Cup in Berkeley, California, 1990.

3

— Dan Waters Photo

(1) Eric Dilski on Mount Rainier's Liberty Ridge, Willis Wall in distance. (2) Lowell Skoog on southeast face of Fury, May 1985. (3) Jens Kulgurgis ascending the Thunder Glacier, May 1987.

2

3

remember. I could kind of think of a route that would link up and allow us to ski it. At that time I was becoming more sensitive to the fact that you perceive the terrain a little differently when you're on skis. There is this feeling of flow where you kind of conform to the terrain.

It was a neat trip and it seemed that the conditions conspired to make it even neater. It wouldn't have really meant that much to me if we'd gone in there and it had been cloudy. I would have felt that we had to go back. On the fourth day of the trip, we had clouds come in, and we thought we were stuck, because we were right in the middle of the Pickets on Mount Fury. This was early season, and I knew that if we had to bail out, we'd either go down into Goodell Creek, which was a real jungle, or we'd go down McMillen Creek and that would put us down on Big Beaver Creek. In May we knew the water would be really high.

We thought we were stuck, and the amazing thing was that we went up Mount Fury in the afternoon after sitting around feeling sorry for ourselves and we popped out of the clouds and were on this undercast marine flow. It gave you this real feeling of isolation to be up there, really cut off from the world. And of course in early season there was nobody else up there. The really lucky thing was on the two succeeding days the clouds didn't go away, but they fell. So each day they'd fall just enough so that we could continue the trip.

There had been some method to our madness in planning this trip. One of the things we thought about was getting off the south slopes of the eastern cirques as early in the morning as possible and in the heat of the day be on the north slopes. I sort of feel that I've got spring snow conditions figured out, although anytime someone tells you they have avalanches figured out, that's the time to watch out. But most of the hazard is from stuff coming off rocks or from you starting a slide, and normally in that case the snow that will go is the snow from you on down. You make sure not to ski above each other.

It seems that you have become not only a student of snow conditions but a student of weather as well.

Yeah I'm kind of a weather hog, although I mostly listen to the weather radio and watch the TV weather map a lot. I'm not a meteorologist or anything.

Does your job allow you the flexibility to take advantage of good ski weather in the spring?

I'm really lucky that way. I'm an engineer. I got my degree in electrical engineering, electronics design. But I'm mostly doing programming, software engineering. Because my work is somewhat project oriented, I don't have a customer waiting. So I can kind of tell my boss, "Well, sometime in the next couple of weeks I might disappear for a couple of days." And they've all put up with it.

What were the logistics of doing the Ptarmigan Traverse in a day?

I guess if there's one day that's a memory day, that's it. After having done the trip in the summertime, then the spring as a ski trip, some friends and I were saying, "I wonder how fast you could do that." We had done it in three days and they were thinking, how about two, and I was thinking forget the sleeping bag, let's do it as a one-day trip. I talked my younger brother Carl into it. You know, he's a sucker for these things.

That's one of the interesting things, finding partners who have the same interests as you do. I don't tend to like to go out by myself. I like to share the trip with somebody else. It's hard sometimes to find people who are crazy in the same way you are. Fortunately, my brother Carl and I are crazy in the same way.

There was a forecast of good weather, but by the time we got to the trailhead, about 10 p.m., it was socked in completely. We slept for a little while. You know you don't sleep very well when you're thinking about this trip. Sometime before 2 a.m. we got up and headed up the trail to Cascade Pass. We originally thought of going straight up the valley and up the snow fields, but it was too foggy. It was in the middle of the night and cold and the beams of our headlights were illuminating this patch of snow. It had been a week before anyone had been there, so tracks were pretty well melted out. Here you are on one of the biggest trails in the North Cascades and we're losing the trail, getting lost. We were trying to figure out how we were going to do this trip if we couldn't even find Cascade Pass before dawn.

We were thinking that this was going to be a long, hard day and we didn't want to get too tired. It was an unknown. Sure we know the route, but how tired are we going to be and is it going to be any fun or is it going to be brutal? As we were leaving the pass, we were still in the fog and we were just remembering the route, kicking steps into the void. The wind was blowing. Even with the headlight beams you couldn't see anything. As we were climbing up along Mixup Arm to the Cache Glacier, we reached the edge of these clouds and they suddenly just withdrew and there were stars and snow.

The snow turned really hard and we had to put on our crampons. There was this cloud that was rolling over the pass, like fingers, from the west and the east was all clear. We cramponed up to Cache Col. It was firm enough that we actually didn't ski until we got to Spider-Formidable Col. We were on this northwest aspect slope and it's not getting any sun even though the sun came up right around Cache Col. It was very firm, so to ski it would have been pretty dangerous. We weren't interested in killing ourselves.

It was neat as we were cramponing to Kool-aid Lake, there was a party of NOLS students. One guy had gotten up to watch the sunrise and he was out taking pictures and here these two guys at 5:30 in the morning come tromping across with their crampons on. We got to Spider-Formidable Col and out from the shade and suddenly you could put skis on. It was this contour glide, zip right across to Yang Yang Lakes and then from there it was climbing with skins and then zipping across. An experience of being really free.

Most people take seven to nine days to do the Ptarmigan.

I remembered the last time I was at the lakes. It took a long time to get there and we were really tired. But here we were fresh. We got to Yang Yang Lakes at breakfast and that was day two when I'd done it in the summer. We got to White Rock Lakes at lunch, that was day three. We got up to the head of the Dana Glacier in early afternoon and then headed down and started to hit reality as we got down into Bachelor Creek. It was overgrown and it was getting late. The fatigue started to come over us. I remember I fell into a creek, fell off this greasy log and into a creek. I had wet tennis shoes and clothes. And then we got to the end of the road at 11 p.m. and our car isn't even there. We'd parked five miles down the road. We just laid down on the picnic table and crashed.

I don't make any claim that it was any kind of superhuman feat of human endurance, and we weren't really racing. But it was just another way

to experience the mountains; going someplace you'd been and just going light. It was amazing to see what you can pack into a day. What you get a feel for is the entirety of the trip. You start to feel the whole set of terrain and how it all relates. I still like those times when you're out for a long time. Just getting away for a long time gives me something: watching a sunset, just sitting outside the tent and cooking dinner.

Where haven't you been?

There are a couple of more trips in the Cascades. I have sort of this secret planning map of trips. I've studied the map and found that there aren't that many major crest lines anymore that I want to do. There are a few odds and ends. But my dream trip in the Cascades is to link up some of these routes. I have a route which I call the American Alps Traverse. It would be about a hundred-mile trip from Diablo Lake to Glacier Peak, and it would probably take the better part of two weeks, probably require two caches along the way. To me it would just be an experience that I haven't had, being out there long enough that you really start to break your connections with town.

I remember reading an article, an interview with John Clark, the guy who's been exploring up in the Coast Range. He says it takes him ten days before all of the city drops off. To me that would be pretty neat to actually do a trip that long in the Cascades. It's still fun to try and do these trips close to home.

I've been to Peru, to Nepal, trekking and some climbing, and I'm still kind of inspired by the fact that you don't have to go that far. There's really neat things to do around here. It's cheaper, doesn't take as much time, prevents you from being an ugly American and trashing up foreign mountainsides.

The Coast Range is luring me. Last summer I climbed Mount Waddington. There are a few things I want to do in the Cascades, and then I think I'm going to move up there. We flew into Waddington in a helicopter, and I have mixed feelings about that. It's the way everyone goes now, but I remember being at a wilderness conference in Seattle where there were a bunch of the oldtimers, and Harvey Manning was giving a talk. I'm sensitive to the values that they had. There was a real value towards the wilderness and the uniqueness.

At this wilderness conference I didn't know

any of the other climbers there, the local hotshots. And I was wondering whether the younger climbers really care as much about the wilderness values as the older ones and what might that mean. I do think that there is a sense among our climbing community that there is more to the experience than just the technical climb.

I'd be lying if I didn't admit that a big motivation in some of these traverses is, geez, nobody's ever done this before. But there's also the motivation that there is this element of unknown, that you have got to solve these problems. That's something that wilderness mountains give you. A mountain range that is completely known doesn't.

I wonder a little bit about what it's going to be like as most of the mysteries disappear. How will people find the kind of satisfactions that the oldtimers had exploring and that I've had a feel for with my ski trips?

One of my heroes is Joe Firey who's been going up to the Coast Mountains for years and years. I sort of feel like maybe that's the way I want to eventually go is sort of make that my haunt if I feel I've been everywhere in the Cascades. It's got the things that attract me too: the glacial landscape, the wild, unknown country.

Having read the Munday's book on Waddington, it would be interesting to approach the interior as they did.

One of the things I mention in my slide show when I talk about our single-day ski traverse of the Ptarmigan is that when we did that, in 1988, it was the fiftieth anniversary of the original traverse by the Ptarmigans. And that was kind of going through my head, thinking about those original Ptarmigans. What they did really impressed me, to go and completely find the route and do all these new climbs. Joe Firey has really been a pioneer, seeking out the obscure places of the Cascades. Many of these high routes he and his family first did; some of the ones in the Pickets, Snowfield to Eldorado, along Ragged Ridge, along the headwaters of Bacon Creek.

Joe is very low-key about his accomplishments. More often than not he might say merely, "It was a good trip."

He's really laid back. Not knowing their family dynamics, I guess one of the things that impressed me about the Fireys was that despite all these climbs, Joe seemed to have a balance in his life. That's one of the things I try to get in myself. Sometimes I am tempted to quit it all and go out and be a wild man, a mountain nut. I like seeing people like Joe who seem like they've done it both; been really active in the mountains and yet raised a family. My wife and I still wonder do we really ever want to have kids. We just don't know. We don't know how active we could stay, how to do it. I know I've asked Carla Firey, "How did your folks do it." She said something like, "They'd hire a sitter for two weeks and take off."

Listening to you, it seems that the mountains are a spiritual place for you.

I'm not really a religious person, but it's almost like a religion. What I think of as religion's purpose is to connect you to the world, and to me that's what mountaineering is for. It kind of sets you right. I don't know if that might be one of the things that draws people. It wouldn't be worship for me but rather meditation, getting up in the mountains.

You look at a bunch of mountains, but when you conceive of a route through those mountains you don't look at it in the same way anymore. Now you see the route. The route is more than topography. I suppose a religious person could say the same force of creation that goes into creating the mountains themselves is active in you when you create this route.

The routes that people do are really an expression of their personalities. I know that with my ski trips, I have looked for routes that somehow resonated with my own personalities. I'm interested in all the mountains, not necessarily little features or just big features.

Stan Kostka looking west from
summit of Isolation Peak,
Mount Baker in the distance.

— Clff Leight Photo

❝ *I would say that I became noted as one of the leading "third-rate climbers" in the Northwest. I can hear my friends yelling, "Fourth rate.* **❞**

— *Harvey Manning*

❝ *I took a bad fall on Foggy Peak. My leg turned black all the way down to the foot. That Monday at the hospital where I was a resident, my colleagues took one look at me and said, "Kramar, we don't care what you do on weekends, but on Monday you're here, no excuses.* **❞**

— *Piro Kramar*

❝ *I joined the Mountaineers in 1929. I immediately became one of these peak baggers and was determined to get my Mountaineer pins.* **❞**

— *Jane MacGowan*

Pencil sketch of Cascade Crest by Jim Hays, showing Glacier Peak at far right, Dome and Spire at center, including route of the Ptarmigan Traverse. From a photograph by Tom Miller taken from Formidable Peak.